SOCIAL THEORY AND THE STUDY OF ISRAELITE RELIGION

SBL
Society of Biblical Literature

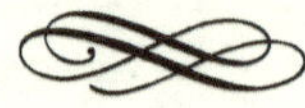

Resources for Biblical Study

Susan Ackerman
Hebrew Bible/Old Testament Editor

Number 71

SOCIAL THEORY AND THE STUDY OF ISRAELITE RELIGION

Essays in Retrospect and Prospect

SOCIAL THEORY AND THE STUDY OF ISRAELITE RELIGION

ESSAYS IN RETROSPECT AND PROSPECT

Edited by
Saul M. Olyan

Society of Biblical Literature
Atlanta

SOCIAL THEORY AND THE STUDY OF ISRAELITE RELIGION
Essays in Retrospect and Prospect

Library of Congress Cataloging-in-Publication Data

Social theory and the study of Israelite religion : essays in retrospect and prospect / Saul M. Olyan, editor.
p. cm. — (Society of Biblical Literature resources for biblical study ; no. 71)
Includes bibliographical references.
ISBN 978-1-58983-688-4 (paper binding : alk. paper) — ISBN 978-1-58983-689-1 (electronic format)
1. Judaism—History—To 70 A.D. 2. Bible. O.T.—Criticism, interpretation, etc. 3. Social sciences—Philosophy. I. Olyan, Saul M.
BM165.S63 2012b
296.09'01—dc23 2012017968

Printed on acid-free, recycled paper conforming to
ANSI/NISO Z39.48-1992 (R1997) and ISO 9706:1994
standards for paper permanence.

Contents

Abbreviations

AASOR	Annual of the American Schools of Oriental Research
AB	Anchor Bible
ABD	*Anchor Bible Dictionary.* Edited by David Noel Freedman. 6 vols. New York: Doubleday, 1992.
ABRL	Anchor Bible Reference Library
AfOB	Archiv für Orientforschung: Beiheft
AJSR	*Association for Jewish Studies Review*
AnBib	Analecta biblica
AnOr	Analecta orientalia
AOAT	Alter Orient und Altes Testament
AOS	American Oriental Society
ASA	Association of Social Anthropologists
ASOR	American Schools of Oriental Research
BA	*Biblical Archaeologist*
BARev	*Biblical Archaeology Review*
BASOR	*Bulletin of the American Schools of Oriental Research*
BBRSup	Bulletin for Biblical Research Supplement
BDB	Brown, F. S., S. R. Driver, and C. A. Briggs. *A Hebrew and English Lexicon of the Old Testament.* Oxford: Clarendon, 1907.
BETL	Bibliotheca ephemeridum theologicarum lovaniensium
BibInt	*Biblical Interpretation*
BibOr	Biblica et orientalia
BJS	Brown Judaic Studies
BZAW	Beihefte zur Zeitschrift für die alttestamentliche Wissenschaft
CAD	*The Assyrian Dictionary of the Oriental Institute of the University of Chicago.* Edited by Ignace J. Gelb et al. Chicago: Oriental Institute, 1956–.
CBC	Cambridge Bible Commentary

CBET	Contributions to Biblical Exegesis and Theology
CBQ	*Catholic Biblical Quarterly*
CC	Continental Commentaries
ConBOT	Coniectanea biblica: Old Testament Series
CTH	*Catalogues des textes hittites*
FAT	Forschungen zum Alten Testament
GBSOT	Guides to Biblical Scholarship, Old Testament Series
HAT	Handbuch zum Alten Testament
HKAT	Handkommentar zum Alten Testament
HSM	Harvard Semitic Monographs
ICC	International Critical Commentary
Int	*Interpretation*
JAAR	*Journal of the American Academy of Religion*
JANER	*Journal of Ancient Near Eastern Religions*
JAOS	*Journal of the American Oriental Society*
JBL	*Journal of Biblical Literature*
JCS	*Journal of Cuneiform Studies*
JESHO	*Journal of the Economic and Social History of the Orient*
JJS	*Journal of Jewish Studies*
JNES	*Journal of Near Eastern Studies*
JQR	*Jewish Quarterly Review*
JSJSup	Journal for the Study of Judaism Supplements
JSOT	*Journal for the Study of the Old Testament*
JSOTSup	Journal for the Study of the Old Testament Supplement Series
JSS	*Journal of Semitic Studies*
KAT	Kommentar zum Alten Testament
LHBOTS	Library of Hebrew Bible/Old Testament Studies
NAB	New American Bible
NCBC	New Cambridge Bible Commentary
NET	New English Translation
NICOT	New International Commentary on the Old Testament
NIV	New International Version
NJB	New Jerusalem Bible
NJPS	New Jewish Publication Society Version
NLT	New Living Translation
NRSV	New Revised Standard Version
OBO	Orbis biblicus et orientalis
OBT	Overtures to Biblical Theology

OEANE	*Oxford Encyclopedia of the Ancient Near East.* Edited by Eric M. Meyers. 5 vols. New York: Oxford University Press, 1997.
OIP	Oriental Institute Publications
OTL	Old Testament Library
PEQ	*Palestine Exploration Quarterly*
RB	*Revue biblique*
RBL	*Review of Biblical Literature*
SAA	State Archives of Assyria
SAACT	State Archives of Assyria Cuneiform Texts
SAALT	State Archives of Assyria Literary Texts
SBLABS	Society of Biblical Literature Archaeology and Biblical Studies
SBLAIL	Society of Biblical Literature Ancient Israel and Its Literature
SBLDS	Society of Biblical Literature Dissertation Series
SBLMS	Society of Biblical Literature Monograph Series
SBLRBS	Society of Biblical Literature Resources for Biblical Study
SBLSBS	Society of Biblical Literature Sources for Biblical Study
SBLStBL	Society of Biblical Literature Studies in Biblical Literature
SBLSymS	Society of Biblical Literature Symposium Series
SBLWAW	Society of Biblical Literature Writings from the Ancient World
SHR	Studies in the History of Religions
SJLA	Studies in Judaism in Late Antiquity
SJOT	*Scandinavian Journal of the Old Testament*
ST	*Studia theologica*
SWBA	Social World of Biblical Antiquity
TCL	Textes cunéiformes du Louvre
TDOT	*Theological Dictionary of the Old Testament.* Edited by G. Johannes Botterweck and Helmer Ringgren. Translated by John T. Willis, Geoffrey W. Bromiley, and David E. Green. Grand Rapids: Eerdmans, 1974–.
TLOT	*Theological Lexicon of the Old Testament.* Edited by Ernst Jenni and Claus Westermann. Translated by Mark E. Biddle. 3 vols. Peabody, Mass.: Hendrickson, 1997.
TSAJ	Texte und Studien zum antiken Judentum
UF	*Ugarit-Forschungen*
VT	*Vetus Testamentum*

VTSup	Vetus Testamentum Supplements
WBC	Word Biblical Commentary
WMANT	Wissenschaftliche Monographien zum Alten und Neuen Testament
WUNT	Wissenschaftliche Untersuchungen zum Neuen Testament
ZAW	*Zeitschrift für die alttestamentliche Wissenschaft*

Introduction

Saul M. Olyan

Social theory and the study of Israelite religion have had a long and fruitful relationship. Classics such as Paul D. Hanson's *Dawn of Apocalyptic* (1979), Norman K. Gottwald's *Tribes of Yahweh* (1979), Robert R. Wilson's *Prophecy and Society in Ancient Israel* (1980), and Carol Meyers's *Discovering Eve* (1988) utilized social theory extensively, setting the stage for more recent work making use of classical and contemporary theory.[1] This volume, which grows out of a symposium at Brown University during the winter of 2010, is intended both to assess past, theoretically engaged work on Israelite religion, and to provide a forum for the presentation of new approaches to particular problems and to larger, interpretive and methodological, questions. The volume gathers together previously unpublished research by senior and mid-career scholars well known for their contributions in this area of study, and by junior scholars whose writing is just beginning to have a serious impact on the field. It begins with an essay by Robert Wilson that assesses some of the contributions made by theoretically engaged biblical scholars to the study of Israelite religion during the

1. Paul D. Hanson, *The Dawn of Apocalyptic: The Historical and Sociological Roots of Jewish Apocalyptic Eschatology* (rev. ed.; Philadelphia: Fortress, 1979); Norman K. Gottwald, *The Tribes of Yahweh: A Sociology of the Religion of Liberated Israel, 1250–1050 B.C.E.* (Maryknoll, N.Y.: Orbis, 1979); Robert R. Wilson, *Prophecy and Society in Ancient Israel* (Philadelphia: Fortress, 1980); Carol Meyers, *Discovering Eve: Ancient Israelite Women in Context* (New York: Oxford University Press, 1988). As Robert Wilson points out in his essay in this volume, the modern relationship between social theory and the study of Israelite religion goes back to the nineteenth century. Thus the classics I mention here are all of relatively recent vintage, part of what scholars often refer to as the "second wave" of biblical scholarship engaging the social sciences ("Social Theory and the Study of Israelite Religion: A Retrospective on the Past Forty Years of Research").

past half century, points to continuities and disjunctures in their engagement with social theory, and identifies areas in need of further development (e.g., more critical reflection on how theory is chosen). Nine other studies follow, each of which engages social theory critically as it explores particular problems or themes.

Susan Ackerman examines cult centralization and its sociopolitical implications through the lenses of kinship and gender, assessing the theories of Max Weber and the work of several contemporary scholars who have elaborated upon Weber's ideas (Baruch Halpern and Joseph Blenkinsopp). By showing that women's participation in the annual clan sacrifice to the ancestors was in the main unaffected by centralization—since the role of women in such a sacrifice was very likely minimal to begin with—she complicates arguments that centralization necessarily eroded all aspects of local, kin-based cult, including the practices of women.

Stephen L. Cook evaluates Gerhard Lenski's theoretical insights into social change and the tensions it produces as he reconsiders the shifting role of the Levites in Israelite cult and society, who struggle to respond to their marginalization by forces of the increasingly centralized state through their promulgation of Deuteronomy.

Ronald Hendel considers the prophetic critique of cultic rites in light of Pierre Bourdieu's notion of *doxa* and Mary Douglas's ideas about the social and conceptual characteristics of antiritualists, who respond negatively to the "implicit meanings" or "self-evident truths" (*doxa*) embraced by the majority. In contrast, they find support in their own set of *doxa* and the social relationships that undergird these assumptions and practices.

T. M. Lemos identifies postcolonial theories of empire, migration, and gender that she finds useful for understanding the Judean diaspora, while criticizing both the less than salutary use of theory and ethnographic data by some biblical scholars and the wholesale dismissal of them as a resource by others. Her paper includes some very apt observations on what she believes to be appropriate method for biblical scholars who seek to make use of social theory or ethnography.

Eschewing theoretical models that posit an oral/written dichotomy, Nathaniel B. Levtow explores the ritual and sociopolitical dimensions of the production and destruction of texts in ancient Israel in a novel way, bringing into relief their destabilizing and potentially transformative potential, and thereby challenging the notion that the process of textualization is necessarily a conservative phenomenon intended to preserve tradition.

Carol Meyers critically engages recent research in ethnography and anthropological archaeology in order to consider the social/socioeconomic and political/politico-economic functions of Israelite seasonal festivals.

I assess the potential cross-disciplinary utility of recent theoretical work on violence in social anthropology through a study of the role of violence in biblical mourning contexts.

Rüdiger Schmitt considers witchcraft accusations in the Hebrew Bible in light of several theories of witchcraft (from social anthropology and medieval and early modern European history), subjecting such theories to critical assessment and finding that they have potential for insight into ancient West Asian materials, though this is limited by contextual differences.

Rounding out the volume, David P. Wright explores in some depth the challenges inherent in applying theoretical models and social-scientific methods to ritual texts with the Priestly-Holiness complex as his major focus, suggesting ways in which theory might nonetheless be helpful to the biblical scholar.

Though the contributors to this volume explore a wide range of topics, their essays suggest an interest in common themes. Issues of gender are central to the studies of Ackerman, Lemos, and Schmitt; social change is a major focus of the papers of Ackerman and Cook; an interest in the relationship of text and ritual characterizes the investigations of Levtow and Wright; the dynamics of shame and honor are treated by Lemos, Levtow, and Olyan; and the contributions by Ackerman, Hendel, and Meyers have festival life as a focus.

The papers in this volume also share common characteristics. Some focus on the work of a single theorist such as Lenski or Weber (Cook, Ackerman), or a pair of theorists such as Douglas and Bourdieu (Hendel), and evaluate, either explicitly or implicitly, the utility of the work for understanding biblical materials. Others consider a range of theoretical work on a particular topic (Lemos, Levtow, Meyers, Olyan, Schmitt). The theory may come from social or cultural anthropology (Hendel, Lemos, Meyers, Olyan, Schmitt), sociology (Ackerman, Cook), postcolonial studies (Lemos; Wright briefly), ritual studies (Levtow, Wright), or it may represent some combination of theoretical models of varying provenance (Levtow, Schmitt, Wright).

Several of the contributors to the volume conclude that the theoretical model(s) they consider, or some aspect(s) of it (them), can be confirmed or upheld on the basis of the biblical data as these scholars interpret it

(Cook, Hendel, Olyan, Schmitt, Wright). Some challenge theory on the same basis, bringing into relief its limitations (Ackerman, Cook, Lemos, Levtow, Olyan, Schmitt, Wright) and suggesting ways in which it might be modified or adapted in order to increase its utility for biblical studies (Ackerman, Olyan, Wright). Yet all conclude, either explicitly or implicitly, that engagement with theory can enrich our understanding of Israelite religion, and often does so.

None of the contributors to this volume allows theory to predetermine or overly influence conclusions regarding the data set in question, a tendency witnessed all too frequently among biblical scholars who have worked with social theory in the past. Privileging of theory vis-à-vis the ancient primary data has resulted in work that has been subjected to serious and justified criticism. One example of such criticism is Theodore Lewis's critique of Brian Schmidt's use of sub-Saharan African and Native American ethnography on the feeding of the dead and conclusions derived from it—that the dead are necessarily weak if they receive food—to understand ancient West Asian (including Israelite) provisioning of ancestors.[2] The many critical reactions to Norman Gottwald's use of the peasant revolt model to explain Israel's origins is another important example.[3] In each case, the contributors to this collection engage theory critically, carefully considering its utility for understanding the materials of interest in light of the materials themselves and what they communicate. In a word, they tend as a group to do what Robert Wilson and T. M. Lemos call for in their essays in this volume: they select their theoretical material carefully and self-consciously and assess critically its value as they engage it. Even if the

2. Theodore J. Lewis, "How Far Can Texts Take Us? Evaluating Textual Sources for Reconstructing Ancient Israelite Beliefs about the Dead," in *Sacred Time, Sacred Place: Archaeology and the Religion of Israel* (ed. Barry M. Gittlen; Winona Lake, Ind.: Eisenbrauns, 2002), 189–202; Brian B. Schmidt, *Israel's Beneficent Dead: Ancestor Cult and Necromancy in Ancient Israelite Religion and Tradition* (Winona Lake, Ind.: Eisenbrauns, 1996).

3. See, e.g., Wilson's characterization of Gottwald's work as a "classic Marxist scenario" in his essay in this volume and the comments of J. F. Priest, "Sociology and Hebrew Bible Studies," in *Methods of Biblical Interpretation* (excerpted from the *Dictionary of Biblical Interpretation*; Nashville: Abingdon, 2004), 283: "It has … been sharply criticized as being a pure construct with no biblical evidence to support it." For other reactions to Gottwald's book, some negative, some positive, see, e.g., Roland Boer, ed., *Tracking "The Tribes of Yahweh": On the Trail of a Classic* (JSOTSup 351; Sheffield: Sheffield Academic Press, 2002).

theory in question is found to be helpful in its received form, it has nonetheless been subjected to critical evaluation and not simply embraced and "applied" uncritically and unself-consciously to the data.

Similarly, contributors who utilize modern ethnographic materials have assessed them for their appropriateness and understand them to be at most suggestive rather than determinative (see, for example, Meyers's comments on the appropriateness of using ethnography from agricultural societies when studying Israelite life and on the likelihood of gender inclusivity in Israelite festival participation). Theory might suggest new topics for exploration, or possible connections that might not otherwise occur to the researcher; it might raise new, potentially fruitful questions.[4] But its utility must be evaluated on the basis of the scholar's reading of the relevant primary data, and theory can (and should) be reworked on that basis to increase its utility, or rejected if it cannot be usefully reformulated.

An important example of this process of evaluation and—in this particular case—rejection is Stephen L. Cook's *Prophecy and Apocalypticism* (1995). In this study, the author not only critiques Paul Hanson's use of deprivation theory from sociology (e.g., that of Karl Mannheim and Max Weber) to reconstruct the *Sitz im Leben* of apocalyptic literature, but concludes that deprivation theory itself is inadequate to the task of explaining both the biblical data and later ethnographic data from some millennial groups.[5] As Cook's study demonstrates, there are rather unsalutary consequences to privileging theory at the expense of the ancient data, though happily these can be avoided with a more balanced approach to both theory and primary evidence.

Theorizing is increasingly becoming an interdisciplinary project, and one to which we biblical scholars can contribute on the basis of our own data sets. We and others who study the ancient world cannot observe, interview, or interrogate living and breathing subjects, and we are not in a position to contribute to the theoretical projects of anthropologists or sociologists, not being anthropologists and sociologists ourselves (see similarly the remarks of Lemos and Schmitt in this volume). We do, however, have access to texts and material data from which we can assess the larger

---

4. See similarly Priest, "Sociology and Hebrew Bible Studies," 283, 284.

5. Stephen L. Cook, *Prophecy and Apocalypticism: The Postexilic Social Setting* (Minneapolis: Fortress, 1995); Hanson, *Dawn of Apocalyptic*. The work of Otto Plöger (*Theokratie und Eschatologie* [Neukirchen-Vluyn: Neukirchener, 1968]), which influenced Hanson, is also assessed by Cook.

utility of theoretical formulations from other disciplines, thereby contributing to interdisciplinary theorizing of topics such as ritual, gender, race, disability, foodways, and violence. Of course, we can also opt to theorize exclusively for our own discipline should our goals be less ambitious. We can engage theory fruitfully even if our data is textual in nature as long as we acknowledge the goals of the texts (e.g., to innovate), the limits of what we can learn from them, and how they might differ in nature from the data upon which theorizing in the social sciences is often based (Wright). As the example of Cook's challenge to deprivation theory and the essays in this volume demonstrate, biblical scholars can contribute decisively to theorizing, including the assessment of theory, its reformulation, and, if necessary, its rejection.

On a final note, it is my pleasure to acknowledge the sponsors of the gathering out of which this volume has emerged, the 2010 Ruth and Joseph Moskow Symposium. The Program in Judaic Studies at Brown University, which hosts the yearly Moskow Symposium, was the event's primary sponsor. The conference received additional support and cosponsorship from the Department of Egyptology and Ancient West Asian Studies, the Program in Ancient Studies, and the Department of Religious Studies. I am deeply grateful to each of these units and their chairs, David Jacobson, James Allen, John Bodel, and Susan Harvey, for providing the financial backing that made the gathering possible. I would also like to acknowledge Jill Blockson for her hard work on the logistics during the final months before the symposium, and Thea Levy for her generosity in establishing the Moskow fund to honor the memory of her parents. Finally, I offer my thanks to each of the contributors to the volume.

Social Theory and the Study of Israelite Religion: A Retrospective on the Past Forty Years of Research

Robert R. Wilson

In a volume devoted to the topic of social theory and the study of ancient Israelite religion, it is appropriate to sketch briefly how the use of social theory in biblical studies has changed over the last forty years or so, roughly the length of time I have been engaged in the study of the Hebrew Bible and its social world. During that time much has happened in the sociological study of Israel's religion, and although I have followed scholarly trends closely, I cannot claim to have looked at everything that has been published. Even if I had, the field has become so complex that I certainly could not summarize it in a brief paper. Therefore, in what follows I will indicate generally how social theory was used by biblical scholars between 1965 and 1980, at the beginning of what has been called "the second wave" of sociological approaches to the religion of ancient Israel.[1] Then I will suggest that although the use of social theory has changed in recent years, those changes have not been radical ones. Finally, I will indicate the work that still needs to be done. My remarks will necessarily be very general, and I am well aware that I will overlook individual scholars and individual studies that do not illustrate the broad trends that I will sketch. I will also

1. The phrase "second wave" serves to distinguish the sociological approaches that began to be used around 1965 and continue into the present from the "first wave" of sociological approaches that began in the late nineteenth century and then gradually died out about the beginning of World War II. The designation "second wave" seems to have been first employed in print by Frank S. Frick in "Norman Gottwald's *The Tribes of Yahweh* in the Context of 'Second-Wave' Social-Scientific Biblical Criticism," in *Tracking 'The Tribes of Yahweh': On the Trail of a Classic* (ed. Roland Boer; JSOTSup 351; London: Continuum, 2002), 17–34.

confine my remarks to the ways in which biblical scholars have used social theory, and I will not venture into the broader topic of how the modern discussion of "high theory" in general has or has not influenced the study of ancient Israel.[2]

Social theory, of course, is not a modern phenomenon but goes back at least as far as the Greek philosophers. Similarly, Jewish and Christian commentators of the Middle Ages were already aware of the importance of understanding Israelite society as a way of better understanding the biblical text.[3] However, the real influence of social theory on the study of Israelite religion is normally thought to have begun with the rise of the social sciences in the nineteenth century. By that time, historians of ancient Israel had become increasingly aware of the sociological problems associated with the study of an ancient culture. Philosophers of history had already called attention to the way in which historians were influenced by their own social settings, and students of ancient Israel were keenly aware of the foreignness of the biblical social world. In the nineteenth-century setting, the newly emerging social sciences offered promising resources to help biblical scholars address the sociological problems raised by their subject matter and by the methods with which they studied it.[4]

Because the scholars involved in the second wave used primarily the theoretical tools that they had inherited from the nineteenth and early twentieth centuries, it is worth reviewing briefly the work of the most influential social scientists from that period, at least as far as their importance to biblical scholarship is concerned. In retrospect, it is clear that

---

2. For a discussion of the impact of "high theory" on biblical studies in recent years, see Stephen D. Moore and Yvonne Sherwood, "Biblical Studies 'after' Theory: Onwards Towards the Past, Part One: After 'after Theory,' and Other Apocalyptic Conceits," *BibInt* 18 (2010): 1–27; idem, "Biblical Studies 'after' Theory: Onwards Towards the Past, Part Two: The Secret Vices of the Biblical God," *BibInt* 18 (2010): 87–113; and idem, "Biblical Studies 'after' Theory: Onwards Towards the Past, Part Three: Theory in the First and Second Waves," *BibInt* 18 (2010): 191–225.

3. For examples of this sort of interpretation, see Robert R. Wilson, *Sociological Approaches to the Old Testament* (GBSOT 9; Philadelphia: Fortress, 1984), 1–3, and the literature cited there.

4. For a discussion of these nineteenth-century developments, see Wilson, *Sociological Approaches*, 3–12; and idem, "Reflections on Social-Scientific Criticism," in *Method Matters: Essays on the Interpretation of the Hebrew Bible in Honor of David L. Petersen* (ed. Joel M. LeMon and Kent Harold Richards; SBLRBS 56; Atlanta: Society of Biblical Literature, 2009), 505–8.

among the emerging social sciences, sociology and anthropology were to exercise the greatest influence on the study of ancient Israel's religion. Although sociology and anthropology share some common elements so that the lines between the two are not always sharp, they normally differ in their starting points and goals. Sociology is traditionally thought to be concerned with "the regularities in social conduct that are due neither to the psychological traits of individuals nor to their rational economic decisions but that are produced by the social conditions in which they find themselves."[5] These social conditions involve the complex relationships that normally exist among individuals in society as well as the beliefs and values that people hold about themselves and about other individuals. A characteristic feature of sociology, then, in the minds of the discipline's founders, is an emphasis on the *regularities* of human conduct and on the *overall patterns* of social change. This emphasis is reflected in the way that sociologists tend to work. Following the methods of the natural sciences, sociologists tend to begin their work by examining contemporary or historical societies in order to formulate theories or hypotheses to account for personal behavior or social change. These general theories are then tested against historical data or, more commonly, against contemporary data gathered for this purpose through interviews and statistical surveys. The results of the tests then lead to acceptance, rejection, or modification of the theories, but the emphasis remains on the theories. For this reason sociologists tend to have difficulty with unique or rare social phenomena that do not fit into general patterns. Sociology tends to be a generalizing science, a fact strongly emphasized by one of its most influential practitioners, Max Weber.[6] Sociology, then, begins with general social theories that can be applied to numerous societies, and as a discipline it often operates at a high level of abstraction.[7]

In contrast to sociology, anthropology tends to focus on particular aspects of individual cultures and deals with questions of human origins,

5. Bert F. Hoselitz, ed., *A Reader's Guide to the Social Sciences* (rev. ed.; New York: Free Press, 1970), 1.

6. Max Weber, *The Methodology of the Social Sciences* (ed. and trans. E. A. Shils and H. A. Finch; New York: Free Press, 1949).

7. For an example of the way in which sociologists formulate a thesis and then test it in a specific social situation, see the classic study of Leon Festinger, Henry W. Riecken, and Stanley Schachter, *When Prophecy Fails* (1964; repr., Mansfield Centre, Conn.: Martino, 2009).

social organization, customs, folklore, and beliefs. At least in the twentieth century, anthropologists have tended to avoid the general theories of the sort that sociologists stress and instead have concentrated on the analysis of particular societies and cultural phenomena. When anthropologists have generated theories or described broad cultural patterns, they have tended to do so by gathering and comparing numerous examples of individual cultural phenomena. In short, theory, if it appears at all in the work of anthropologists, tends to appear at the end of a typical anthropological study, and not at the beginning, as in the case of sociology. This, of course, is not to say that classic anthropologists were innocent of theory. They clearly began their work with preconceived notions of what was important in a given culture, and too often these notions were based on their own cultural biases and norms. No one escapes theory in this sense. But anthropology has classically not been a generalizing social science.

By the time that second-wave social world studies began in the mid-1960s, the classic work of several sociologists and anthropologists was available to supply both theories and methods for biblical scholars. Among sociologists, the work of Herbert Spencer (1820–1903) was still in evidence, although most social scientists had already rejected or at least severely modified his major theory. Strongly influenced by the work of Charles Darwin in the natural sciences, Spencer proposed a theory of social Darwinism, which held that societies undergo an inevitable evolutionary development. As small homogeneous societies increase in size, there is more competition for goods and services, a situation that leads to social unrest, which is eventually resolved by increased specialization and enforced cooperation. If military force plays a role in this process, small groups must combine into larger ones for mutual protection, and the differentiation process continues. Eventually industrialized societies can arise, but these too have their own evolutionary patterns.[8] Although Spencer's work was influential as a social theory in its day, it was eventually rejected as an adequate explanation for social development. However, the evolutionary theories on which it was based strongly influenced contemporary ideas of the development of religion, literature, and culture. In this form it influenced the work of biblical scholars such as Wellhausen and Gunkel, who saw in Israel's religion and literature evolutionary tendencies. Such ideas were still in the

8. For a discussion of Spencer's work, see Wilson, *Sociological Approaches*, 13, and the literature cited there.

air in the 1960s, although by that time few scholars any longer associated them directly with Spencer.

More influential than Spencer was the work of Karl Marx (1818–1883). Marx wrote widely on a variety of topics, but today he is remembered primarily for his argument that the forces underlying historical change are economic and social rather than ideological. Marx saw history as a series of interactions among different social groups, each having particular economic interests. Social systems containing such divergent groups are basically unstable, and this instability is increased as technology develops. A society's technological resources are at the disposal of the ruling class, which is therefore able to control the society's means of production and to exploit the working classes (the proletariat). The ruling class seeks to perpetuate this situation and actively opposes social change, often by using increasingly harsh means of repression. In contrast, the working classes, once they recognize their exploitation, seek to reverse their oppression and eventually revolt.[9] Although many aspects of Marx's complex system have been criticized and rejected, his basic ideas flourished into the 1960s and found a new life in neo-Marxist thought and in certain types of theological thought. His basic premise, that historical forces are essentially social and economic rather than ideological, echoes in the work of some modern biblical scholars, including some more recent ones who analyze Israelite religion in terms of its power dynamics rather than in terms of religious beliefs, practices, and commitments.[10]

The classic antithesis to Marx's work on social forces is found in the work of Max Weber, who argued that history is shaped not by economics but by a society's commonly held value orientations. This makes room for religion in sociological analyses and suggests that religion must be studied as part of the complex of forces that shape the social world. Although

9. Wilson, *Sociological Approaches*, 13–14, and the literature cited there.

10. Among scholars of the second wave, Marxist categories are particularly prominent in Norman K. Gottwald, *The Tribes of Yahweh* (Maryknoll, N.Y.: Orbis, 1979), although many other influences are visible in his work as well. Marx's notion that a society's technological resources are at the disposal of the ruling class lies behind recent claims that scribal activity in ancient Israel was designed to support the interests of the government or the temple, although modern proponents of this position do not set it in a Marxist framework. See, for example, Philip R. Davies, *Scribes and Schools: The Canonization of Hebrew Scriptures* (Louisville: Westminster John Knox, 1998); and William M. Schniedewind, *How the Bible Became a Book* (Cambridge: Cambridge University Press, 2004).

Weber's general claim about the importance of values in society has not had much influence on the study of ancient Israelite religion, his book *Ancient Judaism* has been enormously influential, and biblical scholars still use his ideas on this subject.[11] Particularly important were his suggestion, taken over from Wellhausen, that covenant was the basis of early Israelite social unity and his idea of charisma as a prominent feature of Israelite prophecy. The former concept was elaborated in a major way by George Mendenhall on the basis of ancient Near Eastern parallels, while the latter idea continues to be a feature of discussions of ancient Israelite leadership.[12]

However, the students of Israelite religion who were part of the second wave of social world studies were not only able to draw on the theoretical work of the classic sociologists. They also had at their disposal the work of anthropologists, who in the years after World War I had gradually refined earlier work in the field and corrected some of the methodological weaknesses of nineteenth-century anthropological research. By the 1960s anthropological research had progressed in a number of areas that attracted the interest of biblical scholars.

The first area of interest was the development of the discipline of social anthropology, which tended to focus on social organization rather than on social customs and which can therefore be considered a sort of comparative sociology. Taking a cue from sociologist Emile Durkheim's stress on the ways in which the components of a culture were interrelated, early social anthropologists such as Bronislaw Malinowski (1884–1943) and A. R. Radcliffe-Brown (1881–1955) argued that societies are best understood by conceiving them in biological terms. Just as a biological organism consists of interacting parts that together form an integrated whole, so a society is composed of individuals and groups tied together by social relations. As a result, individual aspects of a society cannot be studied in isolation, but rather each social component must be considered as it relates to every other component. Each component thus has particular functions within the whole, and for this reason the label "functionalism" is sometimes

---

11. Max Weber, *Ancient Judaism* (trans. and ed. Hans H. Gerth and Don Martindale; Glencoe, Ill.: Free Press, 1952).

12. George E. Mendenhall, "Ancient Oriental and Biblical Law," *BA* 17 (1954): 26–46; idem, "Covenant Forms in Israelite Tradition," *BA* 17 (1954): 50–76; David L. Petersen, "Max Weber and the Sociological Study of Ancient Israel," *Sociological Inquiry* 49 (1979): 117–49; Rodney R. Hutton, *Charisma and Authority in Israelite Society* (Minneapolis: Fortress, 1994).

applied to this sort of social anthropology. Against the background of this theory of society, Radcliffe-Brown and his followers stressed that individual societies had to be studied intensely in order to understand how their complex social interactions took place. The drawback of this approach was that individual social anthropologists tended to focus on a single society and to neglect comparison with other societies. As a result, common social patterns were slow to emerge. In addition, social anthropologists tended to focus on societies at a single moment in time. The question of historical social development was often neglected.[13]

However, one of the great contributions of functionalism was that it generated a large number of detailed studies of individual cultures and thus encouraged the development of a second area of anthropological research, the field of ethnography. In the period after World War II ethnographers collected an enormous amount of information about particular societies, many of them relatively small, non-Western, and preindustrial. This collection of data, much of it uninterpreted, became an attractive source of comparative material for biblical scholars seeking analogies to the society of ancient Israel.

Finally, after World War I major developments began to take place in archaeology, that branch of anthropology that deals with ancient and nonliving societies. By the 1960s a new sort of archaeology began to develop that was influenced by broader trends in the study of history generally. Historians had begun to drift away from concentrating solely on writing political history, and scholars developed a new interest in social history. This shift of interest is often connected with the French *Annales* tradition of history writing, which stressed the long-term relationships of people to their environments, the relationships of people to their social contexts, and the ways in which people related to particular events. This new sort of social history served as a stimulus for second-wave biblical scholars to explore the sociological dimension of Israelite history. Among archaeologists concentrating on Israel in the biblical period, the new emphasis in history writing led to scholars asking more sociologically oriented questions of their data and employing more interpretive models from the social

---

13. Wilson, *Sociological Approaches*, 19–20; A. R. Radcliffe-Brown, "On the Concept of Function in Social Science," in *Structure and Function in Primitive Society* (New York: Free Press, 1965), 178–87; E. E. Evans-Pritchard, "Social Anthropology," in *Social Anthropology and Other Essays* (New York: Free Press, 1964), 1–134; Robert K. Merton, *On Theoretical Sociology* (New York: Free Press, 1967), 78–138.

sciences. In turn, the new perspective on archaeological data provided raw material for second-wave scholars interested in reconstructing the social dimensions of Israelite religion.[14]

By the middle of the 1960s, then, scholars active in the second wave of social world studies had a number of new theoretical tools at their disposal, as well as much new data from archaeological excavations and from newly developing perspectives on ancient Near Eastern history in general. However, it is important to remember that the scholars who are associated with the second wave did not constitute a movement, and in fact for a number of years they had very little communication with one another. They were basically individuals who were dissatisfied, for various reasons, with current approaches to the study of Israelite religion and were for personal reasons, probably no longer recoverable, attracted to a social-scientific approach. They did not always begin their research with a particular social theory in mind, and when they did refer to theory they were often eclectic in their theoretical choices. Theories were often applied inconsistently, and contradictory theories were sometimes employed at the same time. The same is true of their use of method. Although virtually all of the second-wave scholars still adhered to the historical-critical method and saw themselves as writing a sort of social history, they were generally comparative in focus and eclectic in method. Nowhere is this eclecticism clearer than in the mammoth study of Norman Gottwald, *The Tribes of Yahweh*. Unlike many scholars in the second wave, he was clearly strongly influenced by a single social theorist, Karl Marx.[15] Marxist terminology appears throughout the book, and Gottwald's reconstruction of the formation of early Israel is a classic Marxist scenario. In terms of method, Gottwald advocates a stress on the economic and social dimensions of

14. For a discussion of how the *Annales* approach influenced archaeologists, see Thomas E. Levy and Augustin F. C. Holl, "Social Change and the Archaeology of the Holy Land," in *The Archaeology of Society in the Holy Land* (ed. Thomas E. Levy; London: Leicester University Press, 1998), 2–8. For a treatment of the influences of the "new" archaeology on biblical studies, see Hans M. Barstad, "The History of Ancient Israel: What Directions Should We Take?" in *Understanding the History of Ancient Israel* (ed. H. G. M. Williamson; Proceedings of the British Academy 143; Oxford: Oxford University Press, 2007), 25–29.

15. For thorough discussions of Gottwald's use of Marx, see Charles E. Carter, "Powerful Ideologies, Challenging Models and Lasting Changes: Continuing the Journey of *Tribes*," in Boer, *Tracking 'The Tribes of Yahweh*,' 46–58; and Roland Boer, "Marx, Method and Gottwald," in Boer, *Tracking 'The Tribes of Yahweh*,' 98–156.

ancient Israel rather than on the theological dimensions that had dominated earlier scholarship. Yet in his treatment of early Israel, religion plays a crucial role as a binding force in society, and in this sense Gottwald sounds more like Weber than Marx, even though these two theorists cannot easily be reconciled. Gottwald uses other theories as well, including structuralism, functionalism, and the macrosociology of Gerhard and Jean Lenski. Nevertheless, in terms of method Gottwald seems to be more firmly in the sociological camp than most of the other scholars of the second wave. He seems to begin with theory and then to move to individual bits of data.[16]

In contrast to Gottwald's preference for theory, the scholars of the second wave who worked on prophecy seem to have followed a more anthropological approach. Although still historical-critical in method, they preferred to focus on prophetic phenomena in individual societies and then tried to make generalizations on the basis of a number of individual cases. In terms of comparative method, they tended to use anthropological studies in the same way that they used ancient Near Eastern texts and archaeological data. Individual cases were used to form a model, which was then tested and refined in various ways when the model was applied to the biblical material. This is clearly the method followed by Thomas Overholt in his use of Native American prophetic movements, and I was quite explicit about the use of comparative material in my own work on prophecy.[17] In neither case was theory appealed to explicitly, although theories of various kinds were clearly in operation.

Since the advent of second-wave studies, the field of the sociological study of Israelite religion has become immensely more complex. It is impossible to mention all of the developments that have occurred, but

---

16. In emphasizing the eclectic use of theory and method by Gottwald and other scholars of the second wave, I do not intend to imply that eclecticism is necessarily bad. The complex historical and interpretive problems that face the historian of ancient Israelite religion may be so serious that the application of many theories and methods is required in order for any progress to be made at all.

17. Thomas W. Overholt, "The Ghost Dance of 1890 and the Nature of the Prophetic Process," *Ethnohistory* 21 (1974): 37–63; idem, "Prophecy: The Problem of Cross-Cultural Comparison," *Semeia* 21 (1982): 55–78; idem, *Prophecy in Cross-Cultural Perspective: A Sourcebook for Biblical Researchers* (SBLSBS 17; Atlanta: Scholars Press, 1986); idem, *Channels of Prophecy: The Social Dynamics of Prophetic Activity* (Minneapolis: Fortress, 1989); Robert R. Wilson, "Early Israelite Prophecy," *Int* 32 (1978): 3–16; idem, "Prophecy and Ecstasy: A Reexamination," *JBL* 98 (1979): 321–37; idem, *Prophecy and Society in Ancient Israel* (Philadelphia: Fortress, 1980).

some generalizations can still be made. On the sociological side, explicit appeals to classic social theorists have reemerged, and particularly in Germany the work of Weber is again attracting interest.[18] Here the investigation of ancient Israel begins with a theory, which is then applied directly to the Israelite sources. In a different direction, there has been a great deal of work on ritual, and this field has worked with its own theories as well as employing more anthropological approaches.[19] In the anthropological line, the work of second-wave scholars has been developed and expanded, as is the case, for example, in Lester Grabbe's study of religious officials in Israel, Richard Horsley's exploration of religion and politics in the Second Temple period, and Wilda Gafney's treatment of women prophets in Israel.[20] We are beginning to get our first attempts at a sociological synthesis in the form of comprehensive social histories of Israel, thanks to recent books by Victor Matthews, Don Benjamin, and Rainer Kessler.[21] Moving in still another direction, the past few years have seen a large number of studies focusing on specific aspects of Israelite religion. Particularly important have been studies of the roles of women and gender in Israel, a topic first treated in detail by Carol Meyers and taken up later by other scholars, such as Phyllis Bird, Naomi Steinberg, and Nancy Jay.[22]

---

18. For a discussion of current sociological approaches to Israelite religion in Germany, see Rainer Albertz, "Social History of Ancient Israel," in Williamson, *Understanding the History of Ancient Israel*, 347–54; and Rainer Kessler, *The Social History of Ancient Israel: An Introduction* (Minneapolis: Fortress, 2008), 5–12.

19. See, for example, Saul M. Olyan, *Rites and Rank: Hierarchy in Biblical Representations of Cult* (Princeton: Princeton University Press, 2000); idem, *Biblical Mourning: Ritual and Social Dimensions* (New York: Oxford University Press, 2004).

20. Lester L. Grabbe, *Priests, Prophets, Diviners, Sages: A Socio-historical Study of Religious Specialists in Ancient Israel* (Valley Forge, Pa.: Trinity Press International, 1995); Richard A. Horsley, *Scribes, Visionaries, and the Politics of Second Temple Judea* (Louisville: Westminster John Knox, 2007); Wilda C. Gafney, *Daughters of Miriam: Women Prophets in Ancient Israel* (Minneapolis: Fortress, 2008).

21. Victor Matthews and Don C. Benjamin, *Social World of Ancient Israel: 1250–587 B.C.* (Peabody, Mass.: Hendrickson, 1993); Kessler, *Social History*.

22. Carol Meyers, *Discovering Eve: Ancient Israelite Women in Context* (New York: Oxford University Press, 1988); Phyllis A. Bird, *Missing Persons and Mistaken Identities: Women and Gender in Ancient Israel* (Minneapolis: Fortress, 1997); Naomi Steinberg, *Kinship and Marriage in Genesis: A Household Economics Approach* (Minneapolis: Fortress, 1993); and Nancy Jay, *Throughout Your Generations Forever: Sacrifice, Religion, and Paternity* (Chicago: University of Chicago Press, 1992).

With all of this activity, it should come as no surprise that the field remains diffuse, and in my opinion many of the generalizations that I made about scholarly work at the beginning of the second wave still apply. Scholars working on the sociology of Israelite religion remain more or less isolated from each other, although groups of like-minded scholars are beginning to emerge, and there is more collegial conversation than there was in the past. However, it seems to me that scholars are still eclectic in their use of theory, and they are still eclectic in method. This situation may be both inevitable and necessary, but even so there is still room for new work on the question of how theories and methods are selected and applied. Scholars would benefit from becoming more conscious in their choice of theories and need to be more aware of the strengths and limits of the theories they choose. The key word here is *conscious*, since in the past we have often applied theories without thinking carefully about what we are doing. The same is true of method. In this area too there has been an explosion of discussion suggesting new methods to try and arguing for the limits of older, more traditional ones. It is not clear to me that all of the new methods will work in the study of Israelite religion, particularly if the goal of the study is the writing of some sort of social history. Indeed, the past twenty years have seen the development of "high theories" of meaning and literature that would call into question any attempt to use ancient texts and artifacts to write history at all, let alone social history. In some ways the emergence of "high theory" is the ghost that lurks in the corner whenever we study Israelite religion. It is an annoying ghost, but it is a very large ghost, and sooner or later we will have to come to terms with it.

Cult Centralization, the Erosion of Kin-Based Communities, and the Implications for Women's Religious Practices

Susan Ackerman

It was one of the greatest among social theory's *'ĕlōhîm*—the sociologist Max Weber—who in his now classic study *Ancient Judaism* originally posited a causal relationship between the first two issues that I evoke in this essay's title: one, the program of cult centralization mandated in the book of Deuteronomy; and, two, the erosion of kin-based communities. In particular, Weber focused on the erosion of kin-based *religious* communities that, in his view, Deuteronomy's program of cult centralization brought about and that it even sought to effect. To be sure, Weber acknowledged that centralization was to some extent a de facto condition in the rump state of Judah in the late seventh century B.C.E. (the place and the period to which Weber, following the standard biblical scholarship of his day and, indeed, of ours, ascribed Deuteronomy's "core" chapters of Deut 12–26).[1] Nevertheless, Weber argued that the cultic component of this de facto centralization should be analyzed less as a result of the Assyrians' incursions into Judah in 701 B.C.E. (as many scholars have otherwise proposed),[2] but rather as a process that was primarily domestically inspired. More specifi-

---

1. In Weber's words (Max Weber, *Ancient Judaism* [trans. and ed. Hans H. Gerth and Don Martindale; Glencoe, Ill.: Free Press, 1952], 65–66), "the realm of [late-seventh-century] Judah was in fact almost identical with the polis of Jerusalem with its small satellite towns and villages."

2. Most recently Diana Edelman, "Hezekiah's Alleged Cult Centralization," *JSOT* 32 (2008): 400; and Elizabeth Bloch-Smith, "Assyrians Abet Israelite Cultic Reforms: Sennacherib and the Centralization of the Israelite Cult," in *Exploring the Longue Durée: Essays in Honor of Lawrence E. Stager* (ed. J. David Schloen; Winona Lake, Ind.: Eisenbrauns, 2009), 35–44.

cally, Weber wrote that cult centralization as mandated in Deuteronomy was an effort to "weaken … the old patriarchal position of the house-father and … the old cohesiveness and joint liability of the sib,"[3] and especially the sib's (or clan's)[4] religious cohesion.

This weakening was accomplished, in Weber's view, first, through cult centralization's attempts to discourage sib- or clan-based rituals and feasts having to do with an ancestor cult, rituals and feasts that, as Weber saw it, would otherwise have been a major source of clan solidarity and clan-centered cultic allegiances.[5] Second, Weber proposed that the sibs' or clans' religious cohesion was eroded through what Weber described as "the profanation of all private meals" in Deuteronomy, a result of the Deuteronomic "monopolization of the cult in Jerusalem."[6] (Weber is thinking here of texts such as Deut 12:15–16, 20–25, which maintain that animal sacrifice can be conducted only at the Jerusalem temple, rather than in localized settings.) As a result, Weber argued, "cultic meals under the control of the sib head were henceforth impossible," leading Weber to write in sum: "The profanation of all private meals was, after the rejection of the cult of the dead, the last blow which Yahwism dealt to a possibly sacred significance of the sib."[7]

Weber's essays on ancient Judaism originally appeared almost one hundred years ago, in the 1917–1919 issues of the *Archiv für Sozialwissenschaft und Sozialforschung*, and with a disclaimer, for as Weber admitted there, he was a relative amateur in the fields of biblical and ancient Near Eastern studies.[8] We could hardly expect, therefore, that all of Weber's ideas about cult centralization in relation to Israel's kin-based social organization would have compelled the audience of his day, especially the audience of biblical scholars, or would continue to compel biblical scholars today. Indeed, in contemporary discussions of ancient Israelite

3. Weber, *Ancient Judaism*, 66.

4. "Sib" is how Weber's translators render his German term *Sippe*, rather than use (as I will predominantly in this discussion) the somewhat more common Scots-Irish word "clan" (Gaelic *clann*; Old Irish *cland*), which Weber is said to have rejected "as 'ambiguous' "; see "Glossary and Index, 1. Subjects," in Weber, *Ancient Judaism*, 475, s.v. sib.

5. Ibid., 146.

6. Ibid., 186.

7. Ibid., 186.

8. Hans Gerth and Don Martindale, "Preface," in ibid., ix.

cult centralization, Weber's work is only infrequently cited.[9] Nevertheless, among modern scholars, two—Baruch Halpern and Joseph Blenkinsopp—have returned productively to Weber's notion that "a centralized state cult which claimed the exclusive allegiance of those living within the confines of the state"[10] must by definition position itself in opposition to kin-based religious communities in general and, in particular, to the ancestor cult as these kin-based religious communities' most crucial component. Halpern and Blenkinsopp have also elaborated upon Weber's original insights by considering more thoroughly why the clans' religious significance might have motivated a centralization agenda within the text of Deuteronomy, as well as having motivated the Judahite kings Hezekiah and Josiah with whom centralization is, according to the biblical text, most closely identified.

My purpose in this essay, as suggested by the third issue I evoke in its title, is to build upon Halpern's and Blenkinsopp's work to attempt a further elaboration still: to ask about women's role in ancient Israel's kin-

9. An important exception is Naomi Steinberg, who, in her article "The Deuteronomic Law Code and the Politics of State Centralization" (in *The Bible and the Politics of Exegesis: Essays in Honor of Norman K. Gottwald on His Sixty-Fifth Birthday* [ed. David Jobling, Peggy L. Day, and Gerald T. Sheppard; Cleveland: Pilgrim, 1991], 161–70), cites Weber, as well as a cross-cultural study by Yehudi A. Cohen, "Ends and Means in Political Control: State Organization and the Punishment of Adultery, Incest and the Violation of Celibacy," *American Anthropologist* 71 (1969): 658–87, in order to argue that it was in the interest of the Israelite state, as it attempted to secure power for itself, to "redirect … individual loyalties in a way that [would] not conflict with allegiances to the political organization." "In a social system where lineage has previously been of primary importance," she goes on to say, the means for accomplishing this redirection were that "the local kinship relationship must be subverted" (Steinberg, "Deuteronomic Law Code," 167). However, Steinberg's discussion of how this subverting of "local kinship relationship" is effected concerns not so much the undermining of the ancestor cult and the elimination of clan-based sacrificial meals—the two characteristics of cult centralization on which Weber, as we have seen, focused—but rather the reconceptualization (as her article title implies) of family laws in Deuteronomy. In these laws (Deut 19:1–25:19), Steinberg argues, "the marital bond is strengthened at the expense of the kinship bond," which is to say that as the nuclear family, based on the core unit of husband and wife, is built up, the extended family, or the community organized around a clan paterfamilias and his patrilineal descendants, is undermined (Steinberg, "Deuteronomic Law Code," 167).

10. Joseph Blenkinsopp, "Deuteronomy and the Politics of Post-Mortem Existence," *VT* 45 (1995): 1.

based religious communities and thus to consider the effects that the centralization program of the book of Deuteronomy, and of Kings Hezekiah and Josiah, had on Israelite women's religious lives. I begin, though, by reviewing Halpern's and Blenkinsopp's analyses so that the framework they provide for my own arguments is clear.

Halpern and Blenkinsopp

Of Halpern's and Blenkinsopp's analyses, Halpern's, found in articles published in 1991 and (in abbreviated form) in 1996,[11] is the earlier and the more intricate. Yet it is also (and in part because of Halpern's intricacies) less fully consonant with Weber's thesis than is the account put forward in Blenkinsopp's 1995 and 1997 essays.[12] For example, while Halpern agrees with Weber that it is the seventh (and also, according to Halpern, the late eighth) century on which discussions of centralization must focus,[13] Halpern accords more significance than Weber suggests to the Assyrians' presence in late-eighth- and seventh-century B.C.E. Judah and the effect of this Assyrian presence on at least King Hezekiah's centralization program. In fact, Halpern describes centralization as beginning with Hezekiah's "abandoning the countryside to the [Assyrian] aggressor" in order that Judah's armies "huddle behind city walls" in Jerusalem and other fortified bastions, in the hope that they would be delivered from the Assyrians'

11. Baruch Halpern, "Jerusalem and the Lineages in the Seventh Century BCE: Kinship and the Rise of Individual Moral Liability," in *Law and Ideology in Monarchic Israel* (ed. Baruch Halpern and Deborah W. Hobson; JSOTSup 124; Sheffield: Sheffield Academic Press, 1991), 11–107; idem, "Sybil, or the Two Nations? Archaism, Alienation, and the Elite Redefinition of Traditional Culture in Judah in the 8th–7th Centuries B.C.E.," in *The Study of the Ancient Near East in the Twenty-First Century: The William Foxwell Albright Centennial Conference* (ed. Jerrold S. Cooper and Glenn M. Schwartz; Winona Lake, Ind.: Eisenbrauns, 1996), 291–338.

12. Blenkinsopp, "Deuteronomy and Politics," 1–16; idem, "The Family in First Temple Israel," in *Families in Ancient Israel* (Family, Religion, and Culture; Louisville: Westminster John Knox, 1997), 48–103, esp. 78–82, 88–92.

13. This as opposed to scholars such as Steinberg ("Deuteronomic Law Code," 168–70), who would see a centralizing agenda as part of Israelite politics from the time of the united monarchy. For a refutation of what he calls this "devolutionary" model that sees kingship and clans in opposition from the beginning of Israel's monarchical period, see David S. Vanderhooft, "The Israelite *mišpāḥâ*, the Priestly Writings, and Changing Valences in Israel's Kinship Terminology," in Schloen, *Exploring the Longue Durée*, 486–88.

onslaught through Egyptian intervention.[14] Halpern furthermore argues that as part of this "hedgehog defense,"[15] Hezekiah would have moved the residents of Judah's countryside into Judah's fortress cities. However, this was not, as one might want to think, because of Hezekiah's humanitarian concerns on behalf of this vulnerable community, but rather, according to Halpern, "to preserve it [the rural population] as an economic resource, so far as possible, against Assyrian depredations."[16]

Still, this "centralized urbanization of the rural population" for economic reasons, Halpern goes on to suggest, posed a religious problem for Hezekiah: "abandoning the countryside" meant abandoning land that was sanctified in character, both because the countryside comprised the bulk of "the land promised by Yhwh to Israel" and because the countryside was preeminently "the land of the ancestors."[17] In making this second point, Halpern refers to the ancient Israelite understanding that the countryside's lands were composed of the many *nĕḥālôt*, or patrimonial estates,[18] to which Israel's various lineages laid claim. These claims stemmed, first, from the lineages' assertion that the *nĕḥālôt* had been passed down through the generations from each lineage's fathers to its sons. But more important was the lineages' conviction that the *nĕḥālôt* were safeguarded into

14. Halpern, "Jerusalem and Lineages," 18–19; idem, "Sybil," 313.

15. Halpern, "Jerusalem and Lineages," 18–19, using a term he describes himself as borrowing from the British military theorist B. H. Liddell Hart.

16. Ibid., 26.

17. Ibid., 26–27.

18. As is well known, the meaning of the term *naḥălâ* is more multivalent and complex than the translation "patrimonial estate" or the more commonly found renderings of "heritage" or "inheritance" would suggest. Indeed, so multivalent and complex is the term *naḥălâ* and the concepts associated with it that no one definition can adequately gloss its every occurrence in the Bible, much less the use of the cognates of *naḥălâ* found elsewhere in ancient Near Eastern literature. Still, it is clear that in several instances in the Bible *naḥălâ* does refer to the land each Israelite family claimed perpetually to hold as an inalienable patrimonial estate, passed down through the generations from father to son. In addition to the standard lexica, dictionaries, and encyclopedias, I have found especially helpful the discussions of Gillis Gerleman, "Nutzrecht und Wohnrecht: Zur Bedeutung von *ʾḥzh* und *nḥlh*," *ZAW* 89 (1977): 313–25; Norman C. Habel, *The Land Is Mine: Six Biblical Land Ideologies* (OBT; Minneapolis: Fortress, 1995), passim, but esp. 33–35; Paul D. Hanson, *The People Called: The Growth of Community in the Bible* (San Francisco: Harper & Row, 1986), 63–65; and Theodore J. Lewis, "The Ancestral Estate (*naḥălat ʾĕlōhîm*) in 2 Samuel 14:16," *JBL* 110 (1991): 598–99, 605–7, with extensive references.

the perpetual future for a lineage's sons and their descendants through the ritual devotions that these sons and descendants directed to the spirits (*'ĕlōhîm*) of their deceased ancestors.[19] These devotions included the proper burial of a deceased ancestor's corpse in the family tomb, the periodic provisioning of the deceased's ghost with food and drink offerings, and the commemoration and regular invocation of the deceased through the pronouncing of his name.[20]

In order for Hezekiah to be able to abandon a countryside thus consecrated, it thereby follows (according to Halpern's argument) that the king needed to desacralize it, "by dismantling the rural cult."[21] More specifically, as Halpern writes, it was, "for Hezekiah's purposes," "essential to amputate the ancestors, those responsible for the bestowal of rural property on their descendants," from their families' *nĕḥālôt*. Otherwise, because "they, and they alone, consecrated possession of land," these ancestors would stand "between Hezekiah and a population herded into fortresses."[22] Hezekiah's cult centralization program that closed countryside shrines (2 Kgs 18:4, 22) was thus undertaken, as Halpern would have it, because it "desacralized the land sanctified by the 'high places' and ancestral shrines" and so "justified ideologically prising the peasantry into forts" by "severing the old ancestral and customary ties."[23]

In short, even as Halpern (as opposed to Weber) speaks of centralization generally as a component of Judahite foreign policy, or at least Judahite foreign policy in the era of Hezekiah's reign, he nevertheless con-

---

19. On *'ĕlōhîm* with the meaning "deceased spirits," see 1 Sam 28:13; Isa 8:19; Num 25:2, as quoted in Ps 106:28; and probably Exod 21:6. More specifically, on Exod 21:6 see Karel van der Toorn and Theodore J. Lewis, "*tĕrāpîm*," *TDOT* 15:783; and, as cited there, Friedrich Schwally, *Das Leben nach dem Tode nach den Vorstellungen des alten Israel und des Judentums einschliesslich des Volksglaubens im Zeitalter Christi* (Giessen: Ricker, 1892), 37–39; Herbert Niehr, "Ein unerkannter Text zur Nekromantie in Israel," *UF* 23 (1991): 301–6; and Alan Cooper and Bernard F. Goldstein, "The Cult of the Dead and the Theme of Entry into the Land," *BibInt* 1 (1994): 285–303, esp. 294 and n. 23 on that page. On Num 25:2 as quoted in Ps 106:26, see Theodore J. Lewis, *Cults of the Dead in Ancient Israel and Ugarit* (HSM 39; Atlanta: Scholars Press, 1989), 167; idem, "Ancestral Estate," 602.

20. Lewis, *Cults of the Dead*, 53, citing Miranda Bayliss, "The Cult of Dead Kin in Assyria and Babylon," *Iraq* 35 (1973): 116.

21. Halpern, "Jerusalem and Lineages," 27.

22. Ibid., 74.

23. Ibid., 27.

cludes, just as Weber had argued, that centralization in its cultic manifestation ultimately had an outcome that was domestic in its impact: the "weakening … of the old cohesiveness and joint liability of the sib,"[24] and in particular the weakening of the religious cohesion of sib or clan groups through the dismantling of the countryside shrines and sanctuaries where clan cohesion, especially by means of the rituals of the ancestor cult, had been fostered. Halpern, moreover, and more so than Weber, focuses on the "other side of the coin," so to speak, that the erosion of clans' solidarity and clans' religious significance implies: the strengthening of royal authority. As Halpern writes, through the decoupling of the clans from their countryside shrines and sanctuaries and from their claims to the *nĕḥālôt* that the rituals performed at these shrines and sanctuaries had guaranteed, "the relation of the individual or the family to the central authority, instead of to the land," is secured.[25] In other words, due to centralization's "effective disenfranchisement of the countryside," the monarchy was empowered.[26] More simply put: "Hezekiah's policies disenfranchised the clans, advantaging court parties."[27] Or, more simply still: the clan system's loss, in terms of power, was the monarchy's gain.

Nevertheless, as Halpern would have it, this situation did not fully persist after Hezekiah's death. To be sure, the monarchy's centralized authority necessarily remained in place in certain respects under Hezekiah's successor, his son Manasseh, in order that Manasseh could fulfill his tribute obligations to Judah's Assyrian overlords. Yet to be able to fulfill these tribute obligations, Manasseh found himself needing to exploit the economic potential of the Judean countryside. Thus he needed to send the countryside's previous inhabitants out from the one Judahite city that remained among those to which they had been relocated, Jerusalem, in order that they resume working the land.[28] Still, even though "resettl[ing] the land under central direction meant fracturing large lineages," which helped sustain Hezekiah's earlier efforts at clan destabilization, this "rural reclamation resacralized the land."[29] As a result, at least to some degree, the clans were reenfranchised. Under Josiah, however, Hezekiah's program of

24. Weber, *Ancient Judaism*, 66.

25. Halpern, "Jerusalem and Lineages," 27.

26. Ibid., 19.

27. Halpern, "Sybil," 321; see similarly idem, "Jerusalem and Lineages," 59.

28. Halpern, "Jerusalem and Lineages," 64.

29. Halpern, "Sybil," 324.

desacralization was revived and, in Halpern's words, "with a vengeance,"[30] now deployed explicitly with the aim of promulgating royal authority at the clans' expense. Consequently, all shrines other than the Jerusalem temple—including other shrines in Jerusalem (see 2 Sam 15:30–32; 1 Kgs 11:1–3; and cf. 2 Kgs 23:13) and, plausibly, state-sponsored sanctuaries elsewhere in Judah (Arad?)[31]—were eradicated and, with them, the last vestiges of cult sites that might sustain clan structures, clan-based systems of social organization, and (most important) clan groups' ability to manifest power. As Halpern writes, "alienation abounded: from land, gods, kin, ancestors, tradition," as "village folk culture was discarded in favor of cen-

---

30. Ibid., 328.

31. Halpern, "Jerusalem and Lineages," 66; idem, "Sybil," 317. The date of the dismantling of Arad's fortress temple is debated. One major school of thought would suggest that the temple's sacrificial altar was abandoned toward the end of the eighth century B.C.E. (Stratum VIII), as part of the cult centralization efforts of Hezekiah, and that use of the temple itself was discontinued in the late seventh century B.C.E. (Stratum VII), as part of the subsequent cult centralization efforts of King Josiah; see originally Yohanan Aharoni, "Arad: Its Inscriptions and Temple," *BA* 31 (1968): 26–27; and subsequently Ze'ev Herzog, Miriam Aharoni, Anson F. Rainey, and Samuel Moshkovitz, "The Israelite Fortress at Arad," *BASOR* 254 (1984): 19–22 (on Stratum VIII), 22–26 (on Stratum VII); Ze'ev Herzog, Miriam Aharoni, and Anson F. Rainey, "Arad—an Ancient Israelite Fortress with a Temple to Yahweh," *BARev* 13/2 (1987): 35; also William G. Dever, "Were There Temples in Ancient Israel? The Archaeological Evidence," in *Text, Artifact, and Image: Revealing Ancient Israelite Religion* (ed. Gary M. Beckman and Theodore J. Lewis; BJS 346; Providence, R.I.: Brown Judaic Studies, 2006), 313–15; Dale W. Manor and Gary A. Herion, "Arad," *ABD* 1:334a–b, 335b; Amihai Mazar and Ehud Netzer, "On the Israelite Fortress at Arad: The Casemate Wall of Stratum VI," *BASOR* 263 (1986): 89; and Yigael Shiloh, "Iron Age Sanctuaries and Cult Elements in Palestine," in *Symposia Celebrating the Seventy-Fifth Anniversary of the Founding of the American Schools of Oriental Research (1900–1975)* (ed. Frank Moore Cross; Zion Research Foundation Occasional Publications 1-2; Cambridge, Mass.: American Schools of Oriental Research, 1979), 155. But cf. Ze'ev Herzog, "Arad: Iron Age Period," *OEANE*, 1:175b: "The abolition of the temple is attributed to the cultic reform carried out by King Hezekiah in 715 BCE (2 Kgs. 18:22)"; similarly, idem, "The Date of the Temple at Arad: Reassessment of the Stratigraphy and the Implications for the History of Religion in Judah," in *Studies in the Archaeology of the Iron Age in Israel and Jordan* (ed. Amihai Mazar; JSOTSup 331; Sheffield: Sheffield Academic Press, 2001), 156–78; idem, "The Fortress Mound at Arad: An Interim Report," *Tel Aviv* 29 (2002): 35, 40, 69–72.

tralized … authority."[32] As a result of Josiah's centralization program, that is, the monarchy's place as Judah's sole locus of power was cemented.

Like Halpern, Blenkinsopp, first in an essay published in 1995 and then (although less substantively and not necessarily as consistently)[33] in his contribution to the 1997 volume *Families in Ancient Israel*, argues that the program of cult centralization promoted in Judah in the seventh century B.C.E. must be understood less in relation to foreign policy issues engendered by Judah's Assyrian suzerains (indeed, Blenkinsopp makes no mention at all of the Assyrians in his analysis), and more in relation to domestic issues concerning the clans, clan-based religious ideologies, and especially the clan-based ancestor cult.[34] Blenkinsopp defines this ancestor cult, consonant with Halpern's analysis, as the belief that "the dead, including dead ancestors, lived on in some capacity [and] that the living could, given certain conditions, interact with them." He then goes on to note that this interaction (again, consonant with Halpern's analysis) "took the form of cultic acts offered to them [the dead] or on their behalf":[35] as above, the proper burial of a deceased ancestor's corpse in the family tomb; the periodic provisioning of the deceased's ghost with food and drink offerings; and the commemoration and regular invocation of the deceased through the pronouncing of his name.[36]

Moreover, and more important for our purposes here, Blenkinsopp describes the interactions in which the living engage with the dead as "constitut[ing] an important integrative element of the social, religious, and emotional bond of kinship."[37] It thereby follows that for Blenkinsopp,

---

32. Halpern, "Sybil," 336.

33. See the concerns raised in this regard by Vanderhooft, "Israelite *mišpāḥâ*," 486.

34. Cf., though, Mary Douglas: "One God, No Ancestors, in a World Renewed," in *Jacob's Tears: The Priestly Work of Reconciliation* (Oxford: Oxford University Press, 2004), 183–84, who first summarizes Blenkinsopp's position and then attempts (mistakenly, in my opinion) to counter it, by arguing (on p. 184) that Blenkinsopp's "unspoken assumption that the cult [of the ancestors] would not disappear without being attacked is … dubious," as "it is not at all certain that the society of Israel was ever organized into strong lineages." "We may seriously doubt," Douglas continues (citing comparative anthropological data that question "whether many so-called patrilineal societies are indeed 'patrilineal' in any important sense"), "whether the people of biblical Israel were patrilineal enough for the cult of their ancestors to be worth attacking."

35. Blenkinsopp, "Deuteronomy and Politics," 3.

36. See above, n. 20.

37. Blenkinsopp, "Deuteronomy and Politics," 3.

just as for Halpern, the state, in aiming "to transfer allegiance from the kinship network to itself,"[38] could not tolerate the ancestor cult that was so constitutive of clan-based identities and loyalties. In Blenkinsopp's words, "Since ancestor cult was an essential integrative element of a social system based on lineage, it was opposed in the name of a centralized state cult which claimed the exclusive allegiance of those living within the confines of the state."[39] Unlike Halpern, however, Blenkinsopp focuses not on Hezekiah's and Josiah's dismantling of the sanctuary sites where the ancestor cult would have been promulgated as the means by which the state attempted to claim its residents' exclusive allegiance, but on this dismantling program's ideological complement: the text of Deuteronomy as the manifesto of a centralization agenda. More specifically, Blenkinsopp proposes that Deuteronomy be "read as an official state document"[40] that "aimed at undermining the ethos and practices of the lineage system and the veneration of ancestors which formed the core of that system."[41]

Still, even as Blenkinsopp focuses on different evidence than does Halpern regarding the promulgation of a centralization agenda, his conclusions, like Halpern's, are highly reminiscent of Weber's. Indeed, in order to buttress his analysis, Blenkinsopp cites extensively Weber's general arguments about centralization and the ways in which "the gradual consolidation of a civil and religious bureaucracy, accompanied by the concentration of power and wealth in cities and the growth of international trade, inevitably combine to diminish the social significance of a descent system and undermine its ethos."[42]

Moreover, in rearticulating Weber's older arguments about the negative effects of centralization on clan-based rituals and feasts having to do with ancestor worship, Blenkinsopp furthers Weber's analysis by bringing together the two effects of centralization on kin groups that Weber saw as historically sequential (recall in this regard Weber's quote stating that "the profanation of all private meals was, *after* the rejection of the cult of the dead, the *last* blow which Yahwism dealt to a possibly sacred significance of the sib" [emphases mine]).[43] Blenkinsopp argues, conversely, that

38. Ibid., 1.
39. Ibid.
40. Ibid.
41. Ibid., 15.
42. Ibid., 3–4.
43. Weber, *Ancient Judaism*, 186.

there is a close link between the requirement articulated in Deuteronomy that mandates that the Israelites sacrifice only at a central sanctuary and the Deut 26:14 requirement forbidding the Israelites to give sacrificial portions to the dead. (According to this text, the Israelite is required to confess, "I have not given any of it [the firstfruit offerings sanctified to God] to a dead person.") More specifically, in Blenkinsopp's interpretation, Deuteronomy juxtaposes, at the beginning and end of Deuteronomy's core code of legal material (Deut 12–26), a description of the "right" kind of cultic meals as Deuteronomy sees it—those celebrated in Yhwh's company after sacrifices are offered at the central sanctuary in Jerusalem (12:2–28, and esp. 12:5–7, 11–12, 14, 17–18, 25–27)—with a condemnation in 26:14 of these Jerusalem meals' "wrong" counterpart, namely, mortuary meals, which would be eaten in the company of one's deceased ancestors at a family shrine.[44] From this, Blenkinsopp concludes that "it is arguable that the Deuteronomic requirement … is aimed directly at the annual clan sacrificial meal."[45]

Blenkinsopp identifies three texts, all in 1 Samuel, moreover, that might describe this annual clan meal: (1) 1:1–2:10, 18–21, the story of the annual journey that Elkanah makes, together with his family members, including his wives Hannah and Peninnah, to sacrifice at Shiloh; (2) 9:1–26, the story of Saul's coming to a shrine where Samuel is to bless a sacrifice, perhaps on behalf of Samuel's kin group at Samuel's hometown of Ramah; and (3) 20:1–21:1 (in most of the Bible's English versions, 20:1–42), the story of how David, during the period when he served as a courtier to King Saul, absented himself from the celebration of the New Moon festival at Saul's royal court in order to participate in his family's "yearly sacrifice" at Bethlehem. "In none of these instances," Blenkinsopp admits, "is there any mention of dead members of the kin group as participants, of cult being offerent [*sic*] to them, or of their being given food and drink."[46] Nevertheless, he argues that "given what we know of familial and tribal cults and the kind of thinking which informed them, we would conclude that the ancestors of the kinship group, those who had already been 'gathered to their people,' were also thought to participate."[47] Regarding these meals' participants, Blenkinsopp also writes: "as an important affirmation

44. Blenkinsopp, "Deuteronomy and Politics," 15.
45. Ibid., 7.
46. Ibid., 8.
47. Ibid., 7.

of solidarity among living and dead members of the clan (*mišpāḥâ*), presence at this event [the annual clan sacrifice and meal] was mandatory, *at least for adult males*" (emphasis mine).[48] With these words, however, Blenkinsopp brings to the fore the question that will be my concern in the rest of this essay: Were the women of a kinship group—the dead women, but equally the living—thought to participate in their clan's annual sacrificial meal?

Women's Participation in Clan Sacrificial Meals

To answer, let me begin by examining somewhat more carefully the three biblical texts that Blenkinsopp cites as possible accounts of clan sacrificial meals: 1 Sam 1:1–2:10, 18–21; 9:1–26; and 20:1–21:1 (Eng. 20:1–42)—and let me begin more specifically by considering 20:1–21:1, which, as I will explain, is the only one of the three that I would take to pertain to the ritual of an annual clan sacrifice. In this text, as part of his scheme to determine the depth of Saul's antipathy toward him, David asks his ally, Saul's son Jonathan, to tell the king, when Saul inquires after David's absence at the royal court's New Moon feast, that Jonathan has given David permission to miss the festal meal with Saul and others of the king's household. The alleged reason is so that David can return to his hometown of Bethlehem to participate in a sacrifice and subsequent meal that his clan is convening there (*zebaḥ mišpāḥâ*). Unlike the royal court's New Moon celebration, however, this clan sacrifice, according to 20:6 (the other mention of this sacrifice, in 20:29, is less clear), is said to take place only yearly (*zebaḥ hayyāmîm*)[49]—perhaps always in conjunction with a day of the new moon.[50] Or perhaps the conjunction with the New Moon feast that is posited in the 20:1–21:1 (Eng. 20:1–42) story is only coincidental.[51] We can be more definitive, though, in suggesting that David's claim that his

48. Blenkinsopp, "Family in First Temple Israel," 79.

49. On the meaning "*yearly* sacrifice" for the phrase *zebaḥ hayyāmîm* (which literally means "the sacrifice of days"), see P. Kyle McCarter, *I Samuel: A New Translation with Introduction and Commentary* (AB 8; Garden City, N.Y.: Doubleday, 1980), 53, note on 1 Sam 1:3, and 62, note on 1 Sam 1:21.

50. Roland de Vaux, *Ancient Israel: Its Life and Institutions* (trans. John McHugh; New York: McGraw-Hill, 1961), 470.

51. This is what Menahem Haran, *Temples and Temple-Service in Ancient Israel: An Inquiry into the Character of Cult Phenomena and the Historical Setting of the Priestly School* (Oxford: Clarendon, 1978), 306, 307, seems to imply.

brother has commanded him to join his family for this occasion indicates that a family's yearly sacrifices were presided over by the male clan head (presuming here that we are to understand that by this point in the story David's father, Jesse, who is said already in 17:12 to be elderly, has died [but cf. 22:3–4]).[52]

The venue of such clan sacrifices was presumably some family shrine or sanctuary[53]—perhaps the sort of family shrine that seems indicated in the biblical record in the account of Micah's *bêt 'ĕlōhîm* in Judg 17–18. Perhaps too, in the case of 1 Sam 20:1–21:1 (Eng. 20:1–42), the reference is to the same shrine or sanctuary at which Samuel offered sacrifice in the company of Jesse and David's brothers when he came to Bethlehem in 1 Sam 16:5 to anoint David as Israel's future king.[54] Some scholars, including Blenkinsopp, as I have already intimated, have similarly taken the setting of the story of a sacrifice over which Samuel presided in 9:11–14 to be the family shrine of Samuel's clan at Ramah (a shrine that is perhaps alluded to in 7:17)[55] and thus have argued that the subsequent ritual meal held in the

52. Alternatively, one could follow the Greek tradition to read in 1 Sam 20:29 that David's "brethren" commanded him to attend their clan's yearly sacrifice.

53. Patrick D. Miller, *The Religion of Ancient Israel* (Library of Ancient Israel; Louisville: Westminster John Knox, 2000), 69.

54. Haran, *Temples and Temple-Service*, 34 (on the proposition that sites a Davidic family temple in Bethlehem), and 307, 308.

55. First Samuel 7:17 describes Samuel as erecting an altar in Ramah, which that text takes to be Samuel's hometown (but cf. 1:1). Scholars who assume that the 7:17 Ramah altar is to be equated with the shrine where Samuel presides in 1 Sam 9 include Peter R. Ackroyd, *The First Book of Samuel* (CBC; Cambridge: Cambridge University Press, 1971), 77; Yairah Amit, "Literature in the Service of Politics: Studies in Judges 19–21," in *Politics and Theopolitics in the Bible and Postbiblical Literature* (ed. Henning Graf Reventlow, Yair Hoffman, and Benjamin Uffenheimer; JSOTSup 171; Sheffield: JSOT Press, 1994), 32; Haran, *Temples and Temple-Service*, 309, 311; Ralph W. Klein, *1 Samuel* (WBC 10; Waco: Word, 1983), 70, 87; David Toshio Tsumura, *The First Book of Samuel* (NICOT; Grand Rapids: Eerdmans, 2007), 107; John T. Willis, "An Anti-Elide Narrative Tradition from a Prophetic Circle at the Ramah Sanctuary," *JBL* 90 (1971): 308; idem, "Cultic Elements in the Story of Samuel's Birth and Dedication," *ST* 26 (1972): 45. Cf., however, McCarter, *1 Samuel*, 163 and 175, note on 1 Sam 9:5, who, while he unequivocally locates the shrine mentioned in 7:17 in Benjaminite Ramah (see McCarter, *1 Samuel*, 148), understands the shrine in 1 Sam 9 to be located in Ephraimite Ramathaim, the town that McCarter takes one strand of the Samuel tradition (based on the text from 1:1 cited above) to identify as Samuel's hometown. See also Miller, *Religion of Ancient Israel*, 162. Hans Wilhelm Hertzberg, *I and II Samuel* (trans. J. S. Bowden; OTL; Philadelphia: Westminster, 1964), 79, somewhat similarly sees two

1 Sam 9 shrine (9:22–24) was Samuel's clan's yearly sacrificial feast.[56] The same suggestion, as again I have already intimated, has been made about 1:1–2:10, 18–21—that this text's setting is the yearly clan sacrifice in Shiloh that the Ephraimite Elkanah presides over on behalf of his family, including his two wives, Hannah and Peninnah.[57] This is because the same phrase used in 20:6 to describe David's family's clan sacrifice (*zebaḥ hayyāmîm*) is used to describe the sacrifices of Elkanah's family in 1:21 and 2:19. But, as I have discussed elsewhere,[58] I would take the setting of 1:1–2:10, 18–21, to be the annual fall festival of the Ingathering, or Sukkot, which makes better sense, I have argued, of another distinctive phrase that is used to describe the occasion of Elkanah's sacrifices, *mîyāmîm yāmîmâ* (1:3; 2:19).

That 9:1–26 describes a clan sacrifice is perhaps more plausible, but as Patrick D. Miller has pointed out, certain anomalous features in the text—for example, the presence at the sacrificial feast of invited guests from outside Samuel's patriline (Saul and his servant) and the seating of the outsider Saul as the feast's guest of honor—make it difficult to substantiate the claim that this sacrificial feast is a clan-based event. Rather, Miller follows Ralph W. Klein in suggesting that, "with its invited guests," the sacrificial meal of 9:1–26 is better interpreted as an "anticipatory coronation banquet," in this case anticipating Saul's being anointed as king in the next episode of the Samuel account (9:27–10:8).[59] This could well explain

---

strands of tradition in 1 Sam 9, one of which concerns (and originally stemmed from) Benjaminite Ramah and the other of which concerns (and originally stemmed from) the tradition that located Samuel's hometown in Ephraimite Ramathaim.

56. In addition to Blenkinsopp, "Deuteronomy and Politics," 8, see, e.g., Bernard R. Goldstein and Alan Cooper, "The Festivals of Israel and Judah and the Literary History of the Pentateuch," *JAOS* 110 (1990): 21; Menahem Haran, "Zebaḥ Hayyamîm," *VT* 19 (1969): 17–19; idem, *Temples and Temple-Service*, 309–11; and Karel van der Toorn, *Family Religion in Babylonia, Syria and Israel: Continuity and Change in the Forms of Religious Life* (Leiden: Brill, 1996), 215.

57. In addition to Blenkinsopp, "Deuteronomy and Politics," 8, see, e.g., Goldstein and Cooper, "Festivals of Israel and Judah," 21; Haran, "Zebaḥ Hayyamîm," 11–14; idem, *Temples and Temple-Service*, 304–5; and Henry Preserved Smith, *A Critical and Exegetical Commentary on the Books of Samuel* (ICC; Edinburgh: T&T Clark, 1899), 185. Goldstein and Cooper also see an allusion to the annual clan sacrifice in 1 Sam 13:11, the *môʿēd hayyāmîm*.

58. Susan Ackerman, *Warrior, Dancer, Seductress, Queen: Women in Judges and Biblical Israel* (ABRL 17; New York: Doubleday, 1998), 253–87.

59. Miller, *Religion of Ancient Israel*, 68, citing Klein, *1 Samuel*, 89–90 (see also p. 87). Klein in turn relies on Tryggve N. D. Mettinger, *King and Messiah: The Sacral and*

why Saul is given a special portion at the sacrificial meal that Samuel had specifically asked be set aside (9:23–24),[60] the "thigh" (*haššôq*) and the "fat tail" (reading here *hāʾalyâ* [*hʾlyh*] for the MT *heʿālêhā* [*hʿlyh*], "that which is upon it [i.e., the thigh]").[61] Because, moreover, politics in the ancient world was overwhelmingly men's business (as it is, more often than not, in our world as well), positing a royal context for 9:1–26 could well explain why only thirty or so *men* (*hēmmâ kišlōšîm ʾîš*) are said to be present at the festal meal.[62] Men are also the only guests present at the other "anticipatory coronation banquets" that Miller (following Klein) locates in biblical tradition:[63] 1 Sam 16:1–13 (where Samuel invites the elders [*male*] of Bethlehem, along with Jesse and his sons, to the sacrificial feast at which David is anointed as Israel's future king); 2 Sam 15:11–12 (where two hundred *men* of Jerusalem are invited to join Absalom at Hebron for the sacrificial feast at which he asserts himself as king); and 1 Kgs 1:9, 18–19, 41, 49 (where Adonijah invites all his *brothers*, the "king's sons," and also the various "royal officials" [*male*] of Judah to the sacrificial feast that he gave when he made his play for the throne as his father David lay dying).[64]

Civil Legitimization of Israelite Kings (ConBOT 8; Lund: Gleerup, 1976); and Ludwig Schmidt, *Menschlicher Erfolg und Jahwes Initiative* (WMANT 38; Neukirchen-Vluyn: Neukirchener, 1970).

60. Indeed, as McCarter points out (*1 Samuel*, 180, following, in part, Jacob Milgrom, "The *šwq htrwmh*," *Tarbiz* 42 [1973/74]: 1–11), this is the portion that in other biblical sources is said to be reserved for *priests* (Exod 29:27; Lev 7:34; 10:14, 15; Num 6:20), and the verb used in 1 Sam 9:23–24 to describe the meat served to Saul (*hārîm*) is also used elsewhere to describe the sacrificial portion "set apart, separated, reserved" as the priestly share.

61. Klein, *1 Samuel*, 83.

62. Phyllis Bird, "Women's Religion in Ancient Israel," in *Women's Earliest Records from Ancient Egypt and Western Asia: Proceedings of the Conference on Women in the Ancient Near East, Brown University, Providence, Rhode Island, November 5–7, 1987* (ed. Barbara S. Lesko; BJS 166; Atlanta: Scholars Press, 1989), 294, similarly notes that the feast's participants were only men, as does Tsumura, obliquely, in *First Book of Samuel*, 280, as well as van der Toorn (explicitly) in *Family Religion*, 215. Tsumura, moreover, understands the significance of the feast's all-male guest list in a way similar to what I have proposed here: "The thirty invited guests … are probably the nobles of the region; to eat with Saul at their head seat could mean their obedience and subjugation to him." Van der Toorn's overall interpretation of this passage, however, differs from the one I have offered.

63. Miller, *Religion of Ancient Israel*, 68.

64. On this last text, see also Gerald Klingbeil, "'Momentaufnahmen' of Israelite

Klein in addition mentions in his list of coronation banquets 1 Sam 11:15, the sacrificial feast at Gilgal that is held to renew Saul's kingship,[65] where we can also note that "the people" (*hāʿām*) that Samuel invites to this event turn out to be only the *men* of Israel (*ʾanšê yiśrāʾēl*). Perhaps we should include too in this catalogue Jesus' last supper just prior to his crucifixion as "king of the Jews," at which he was joined by only his *male* disciples.

But would women have been excluded from their clans' annual sacrificial gatherings and ritual meals in the same way they seem excluded from these "anticipatory coronation banquets"?[66] To some degree, we can certainly answer yes, in the sense that married women surely did not participate as a matter of course in the annual sacrifices of their natal clans; given the ideological force of ancient Israel's systems of *patri*local marriage and *patri*lineal descent, it would be unthinkable for the tradition to have women annually take leave of their husbands' households to return to the homes of their birth families in order to participate in a ritual that marked membership in their fathers'—as opposed to their marital—clans. Conversely, 1 Sam 20:29 takes it as a given that the *men* of a clan should be present for their family's annual sacrifice, to the extent that David, although not at the time resident in his hometown of Bethlehem, can claim to have been commanded (*ṣiwwâ*) by his brother to journey some 14 kilometers (8.5 miles) from Saul's royal fief in Gibeah to the Davidic clan's cult center in order to participate in the sacrificial ritual there.[67] Somewhat similarly, I would assume that when Blenkinsopp writes of the annual clan sacrifice that "it was … taken for granted that forebears or ancestors, those already 'gathered to their people,' participated,"[68] what we should more specifically take for granted is that male "forebears" and "ancestors" participated, but not necessarily a clan's deceased females. Note in this regard that (if

---

Religion: The Importance of the Communal Meal in Narrative Texts in I/II Regum and Their Ritual Dimension," *ZAW* 118 (2006): 38–39.

65. Klein, *1 Samuel*, 87.

66. Haran, *Temples and Temple-Service*, 306, argues it is clear women and children were included in their clans' annual sacrificial meals, based on his assumption that 1 Sam 1–2 is a narrative concerning the annual clan feast of Elkanah's family. As we will see, however, the matter is not so clear-cut if this text is excluded (as I have proposed) from our catalogue of "annual clan sacrifice" accounts.

67. But cf. above, n. 52, on the reading "brethren" in the Greek tradition for the MT "brother."

68. Blenkinsopp, "Family in First Temple Israel," 79; see similarly idem, "Deuteronomy and Politics," 7.

biblical genealogies are any guide) women are normally absent from the "genealogical accounts" that were "employed" on the occasions of clan sacrifices, according to Avraham Malamat, in order "to invoke the names of dead ancestors."[69]

Deceased women also seem to be excluded from fundamental rituals of the ancestor cult in other respects. Unlike men, for example, they need not be buried in their family's tomb (I think here of Rachel, who is buried in a roadside grave rather than being transported from the site of her demise to her family's burial cave in Machpelah).[70] Similarly, while I would in general agree with the assessment that has been argued, most recently and thoroughly, by Karel van der Toorn and Theodore J. Lewis that the *tĕrāpîm* figurines mentioned in some eight passages in the Bible are representations of a family's deceased ancestors,[71] I suspect that it was not the norm to make this sort of ancestor figurine to represent a woman

69. Avraham Malamat, "King Lists of the Old Babylonian Period and Biblical Genealogies," in *Essays in Memory of E. A. Speiser* (ed. William W. Hallo; AOS 53; New Haven: American Oriental Society, 1968), 173 n. 29; this quote brought to my attention by van der Toorn, *Family Religion*, 214.

70. Benjamin D. Cox and Susan Ackerman, "Rachel's Tomb," *JBL* 128 (2009): 135–48.

71. Van der Toorn and Lewis, *TDOT* 15:783, 787–88; see also Karel van der Toorn, "The Nature of the Biblical Teraphim in the Light of the Cuneiform Evidence," *CBQ* 52 (1990): 204 and 215–17; idem, *Family Religion*, 223–25; idem, "Israelite Figurines: A View from the Texts," in *Sacred Time, Sacred Place: Archaeology and the Religion of Israel* (ed. Barry M. Gittlin; Winona Lake, Ind.: Eisenbrauns, 2002), 54; idem, "Recent Trends in the Study of Israelite Religion," in *Modern Societies and the Science of Religion: Studies in Honor of Lammert Leertouwer* (ed. Gerard Wiegers in association with Jan Platvoet; SHR 95; Boston: Brill, 2002), 228–29; Lewis, *Cults of the Dead*, 178; idem, "Ancestral Estate," 603; idem, "Teraphim," *Dictionary of Deities and Demons in the Bible* (ed. Karel van der Toorn, Bob Becking, and Pieter W. van der Horst; rev. ed.; Leiden: Brill, 1999), 849–50; idem, "Divine Images and Aniconism in Ancient Israel" (review article of Tryggve Mettinger, *No Graven Image? Israelite Aniconism in Its Ancient Near Eastern Context* [ConBOT 42; Stockholm: Almqvist & Wiksell, 1995]), *JAOS* 118 (1998): 43; similarly, Rainer Albertz, *A History of Israelite Religion in the Old Testament Period*, vol. 1: *From the Beginnings to the End of the Monarchy* (trans. John Bowden; OTL; Louisville: Westminster John Knox, 1994), 38; Blenkinsopp, "Deuteronomy and Politics," 12; Meindert Dijkstra, "Women and Religion in the Old Testament," in Bob Becking et al., *Only One God? Monotheism in Ancient Israel and the Veneration of the Goddess Asherah* (Biblical Seminar 77; London: Sheffield Academic Press, 2001), 168; and Oswald Loretz, "Die Teraphim als 'Ahnen-Götter-Figur(in)en' im Lichte der Texte aus Nuzi, Emar und Ugarit," *UF* 24 (1992): 134–78, esp. 152–68.

after her death, although this does seem to be an expected part of male mortuary practice.

Indeed, as van der Toorn states, the ancestor cult in all its aspects "was addressed predominantly to male ancestors."[72] Van der Toorn supports this conclusion by a careful look at both Israelite and comparative evidence. With regard to the latter, he cites, for example, an Old Babylonian prayer to the moon god that "enumerates the names of the dead addressed by the living."[73] Women are included in this list, but "are mentioned only as 'wife of' one of the ancestors, or … as 'daughter' of an ancestor."[74] In fact, in both this prayer to the moon god and in similar incantations, women are often *only* the "wife of"; they are not even given a name.[75] Within Old Babylonian tradition, van der Toorn concludes, "women were apparently not regarded as ancestors themselves."[76]

In considering Israelite evidence that supports this same conclusion, van der Toorn again turn to names, more specifically, theophoric kinship names. Most typically, of course, these names' kinship terms have been taken to refer to the god that their bearer and/or the name's bestower were thought to have worshiped. For example, an Israelite such as Abiel, a name that means "My father (*ʾăbî*) is *ʾēl*," is understood to have worshiped as his divine *ʾāb* (father), Israel's *ʾēl* (god), Yhwh (or, according to some, an anonymous tribal *ʾēl* who was Yhwh's precursor).[77] Van der Toorn suggests, however, that these names' kinship terms be taken not as references to some metaphorical familiarity that the bearer claims with a deity, but as actual kinship terms that are used in their bearers' names to refer to deceased ancestors who have been deified upon their demise. Abiel thus refers to "my [ancestral] father" who is (or, more specifically, has become upon his death) a deified spirit known as an *ʾēl* or an *ʾĕlōhîm*.[78]

72. Van der Toorn, *Family Religion*, 229.

73. Karel van der Toorn, "Family Religion in Second Millennium West Asia (Mesopotamia, Emar, Nuzi)," in *Household and Family Religion in Antiquity* (ed. John Bodel and Saul M. Olyan; Oxford: Blackwell, 2008), 27.

74. Ibid., 28.

75. Ibid., 29.

76. Ibid., 28.

77. The history of scholarship concerning the so-called theophoric names and concerning the proponents of various interpretations of them has been well catalogued by van der Toorn, "Ancestors and Anthroponyms: Kinship Terms as Theophoric Elements in Hebrew Names," *ZAW* 108 (1996): 1–4.

78. For this meaning of *ʾēl*/*ʾĕlōhîm*, see above, n. 19.

As van der Toorn explains, his hypothesis—that "the gods referred to in these theophoric names are not gods in the usual sense of the term, but deified ancestors"[79]—would account well for the fact that the names in question can use kinship terms such as *ʾāḥ*, "brother," or *ʿam*, "paternal uncle," which otherwise are not epithets used of known divinities. This hypothesis also avoids some of the contested reconstructions of tribal religion that maintain that the kinship terms refer to an anonymous tribal god.[80] More important for our purposes, however, "the interpretation of the theophoric kinship names as evidence of an early ancestor cult" reveals that "the cult was addressed to male ancestors only."[81] This is because all the kinship terms used in the names in question refer to *male* clan members (such as the previously cited terms *ʾāb*, "father," *ʾāḥ*, "brother," and *ʿam*, "paternal uncle," and also terms such as *dôd*, "father's senior brother," and *lĕmû*, "clan"). Conversely, van der Toorn writes, "in Hebrew anthroponymics there is not one feminine kinship term used as a theophoric element."[82] Once more, van der Toorn concludes, "The ancestor cult was apparently concerned primarily with patrilineal ancestors."[83]

As with the dead, one is thus led to ask, so too with the living? That is, is the ancestor cult celebration enacted at a clan's annual sacrificial feast an event during which a clan's living women, like their dead counterparts, played little to no part? Note once more in this regard Blenkinsopp's comment that "presence at this event [the annual clan sacrifice and meal] was mandatory, *at least for adult males*" (emphasis again mine).[84] Note also van der Toorn, who is more definitive: "Women never participate. … they remain outsiders to the community of … the ancestors and the male adults. Or, to put it more mildly, they belong to that community by virtue of their ties, either by blood or marriage, to the men. They participate in the second degree, so to speak."[85] Alan M. Cooper and Bernard R. Goldstein articulate

---

79. Van der Toorn, "Ancestors and Anthroponyms," 6.

80. Ibid., 4.

81. Ibid., 6.

82. Ibid., 7.

83. Ibid.

84. Blenkinsopp, "Family in First Temple Israel," 79.

85. Karel van der Toorn, "Nine Months among the Peasants in the Palestinian Highlands: An Anthropological Perspective on Local Religion in the Early Iron Age," in *Symbiosis, Symbolism, and the Power of the Past: Canaan, Ancient Israel, and Their Neighbors from the Late Bronze Age through Roman Palaestina* (ed. William G. Dever and Seymour Gitin; Proceedings of the Centennial Symposium, W. F. Albright Insti-

basically the same conclusion, but from a woman's—more specifically, a married woman's—point of view: "In a marital relationship, the wife has a right to ask her husband to intervene with the clan deities, but her contact is with her husband, not with those deities."[86]

Telling finally in this regard is Gen 31:54, which, although it is not presented by its author(s) and/or redactor(s) as an annual clan celebration involving a "ritual communion [meal] with the ancestors,"[87] nevertheless shares some key features with these sorts of occasions. For example, the context of the text's festal meal is familial and the feast's sacrifice is presided over by Jacob, functioning as the clan's male head. After the sacrifice, those who join Jacob to eat are, in the words of the NRSV translation, "his kinsfolk," whom one might most logically take to be those who are traveling with Jacob as he journeys from his father-in-law's home in Paddan-aram to Canaan—his two wives Rachel and Leah, his eleven sons (Benjamin was not yet born), and his daughter Dinah—and also his father-in-law Laban, who has just entered into a covenant with Jacob and agreed to end his pursuit of him. But the Hebrew term translated as "his kins*folk*" by the NRSV is, in fact, *'eḥâw*, which means literally "his brothers," and, more figuratively, "his kins*men*." This might suggest that only men were invited to Jacob's family feast, as might also be suggested by two other occurrences of *'eḥâw* in Gen 31, in verses 23 and 25. There the term is used to describe the entourage with which Laban travels in his pursuit of Jacob. Given that this pursuit was antagonistic in nature ("It is in my power to do you harm," Laban tells Jacob in v. 29), it defies logic to think that Laban's posse included any of his women kin; Laban's *'aḥîm*, his "kinsmen," who travel with him according to 31:22 and 25 are literally that, kins*men*. So too, it follows, would the *'aḥîm* who eat of Jacob's sacrificial feast in 31:54 be literally his "kins*men*," meaning women were excluded from that family banquet—as they may similarly have been excluded, as we have seen above, from their clans' yearly sacrificial meals.

Indeed, one wonders whether an ancient Israelite audience would have grasped, when hearing the Gen 31 story, the subtlety that whatever the conceit of the text's sacrificial repast from Jacob's and Laban's point of view

---

tute of Archaeological Research and American Schools of Oriental Research, Jerusalem, May 29–May 31, 2000; Winona Lake, Ind.: Eisenbrauns, 2003), 403.

86. Alan M. Cooper and Bernard R. Goldstein, "At the Entrance to the Tent: More Cultic Resonances in Biblical Narrative," *JBL* 116 (1997): 214.

87. The quote comes from van der Toorn, *Family Religion*, 217.

(a meal cementing the agreement into which the two had entered in the previous verses),[88] the meal was in fact the same sort of "ritual communion with the ancestors" that many scholars understand David's family to have convened in 1 Sam 20:1–21:1 (Eng. 20:1–42). After all, present in Jacob's camp (although unbeknownst to him) were the *tĕrāpîm* that Rachel had stolen from her father Laban; and what are these *tĕrāpîm*, I have followed van der Toorn and Lewis in suggesting, but images of a clan's deceased male forebears, safeguarded by their descendants as a way of fostering their family's corporate identity through the generations? Upon closer inspection, therefore, Gen 31:54 looks more and more like the apparently all-male clan banquet of 1 Sam 20:1–21:1 (Eng. 20:1–42), a ritual occasion that binds the patriline's men, both living and dead, together in solidarity, while Rachel and Leah, who might claim membership in both their father's genealogy and their husband's, find themselves not fully integrated into either. Rather, they are kept at the periphery of the feast—traveling in Jacob's company, but excluded from the sacrificial rites that bind their husband's entourage and their father's together.

Concluding Reflections: Women and Cult

Ironically, therefore, although called in 1 Sam 20:29 a *zebaḥ mišpāḥâ*, the annual clan sacrificial meal may not really have been for the *mišpāḥâ* writ large, as a clan's women members are arguably pushed to its margins. But within the context of this paper, there is greater irony still. In an article published in 1987 entitled "Women's Studies and the Hebrew Bible," Jo Ann Hackett posited that "hierarchical and centrally-structured institutions have been less open to participation by women in most societies than have local and non-hierarchical institutions," which "means that an increase in the centralization of a society's institutions will often coincide with a decline in participation by women within those institutions."[89] Also in 1987, in her programmatic essay "The Place of Women in the Israelite

88. Alan W. Jenks, "Eating and Drinking in the Old Testament," *ABD* 2:253b.

89. Jo Ann Hackett, "Women's Studies and the Hebrew Bible," in *The Future of Biblical Studies: The Hebrew Scriptures* (ed. Richard Elliott Friedman and H. G. M. Williamson; Semeia Studies 16; Atlanta: Scholars Press, 1987), 147; see also idem, "In the Days of Jael: Reclaiming the History of Women in Ancient Israel," in *Immaculate and Powerful: The Female in Sacred Image and Social Reality* (ed. Clarissa W. Atkinson, Constance H. Buchanan, and Margaret R. Miles; Boston: Beacon, 1985), 17.

Cultus," Phyllis Bird argued this point more specifically regarding ancient Israel and more specifically still regarding ancient Israelite religion: "the degree of centralization," she writes, had "significant consequence for the nature and extent of women's participation" in the Israelite cult.[90] Yet while these are assessments of centralization with which I generally agree, it may be that with regard to their participation in the annual clan sacrificial meal, women experienced no particular difference in this aspect of their lives as cult centralization began to effect the erosion of Israel's kin-based religious communities. After all, as Halpern and Blenkinsopp have compellingly shown, cult centralization had as its goal the shifting of religious power from the clans to the state, and this meant primarily a shifting of power from the clans' patriarchs to the king in his role as paterfamilias of the nation. This was, in short, a men's game of "give and take," and women—as they had only the most marginal of roles in the ancestral cult to begin with—may have had nothing in terms of its observances that needed to be taken away.

90. Phyllis Bird, "The Place of Women in the Israelite Cultus," in *Ancient Israelite Religion: Essays in Honor of Frank Moore Cross* (ed. Patrick D. Miller, Paul D. Hanson, and S. Dean McBride; Philadelphia: Fortress, 1987), 403–4.

The Levites and Sociocultural Change in Ancient Judah: Insights from Gerhard Lenski's Social Theory

Stephen L. Cook

In recent decades, the works of the American sociologist Gerhard E. Lenski (b. 1924) have attracted the interest of biblical scholars, who have found them illuminating of the social dynamics of ancient Israelite history. As Robert R. Wilson states in his contribution to the present volume, Lenski's work has played a notable role in the "second wave" of biblical scholarship incorporating social-scientific theories and methods in the study of the Hebrew Scriptures.[1] From about 1980 on, Lenski's work has impacted this subfield within the biblical guild. Among its many possible applications in shedding light on the social world of ancient Israel, I find Lenski's social theory helpful in grappling with the changing place and role of the Levites in Israelite religion and society. Biblical scholars are now realizing how

1. I am grateful for the review of social-scientific research in Hebrew Bible studies provided by Robert R. Wilson, a seasoned researcher in this area. For additional elaboration on the "second wave" that Wilson discusses, see Ronald A. Simkins and Stephen L. Cook, "Introduction: Case Studies from the Second Wave of Research in the Social World of the Hebrew Bible," *Semeia* 87 (1999): 1–14; Charles E. Carter, "Chapter 3: Social Scientific Approaches," in *The Blackwell Companion to the Hebrew Bible* (ed. L. G. Perdue; Oxford: Blackwell, 2001), 36–57. Among contemporary biblical scholars drawing on Lenski's works, one might mention Carol Meyers, Charles Carter, Marvin L. Chaney, Keith W. Whitelam, Richard A. Horsley, Anthony J. Saldarini, and Patricia Dutcher-Walls, among many others. For an argument that ancient Israel departs in certain regards from Lenski's model, see Walter J. Houston, "Exit the Oppressed Peasant? Rethinking the Background of Social Criticism in the Prophets," in *Prophecy and Prophets in Ancient Israel: Proceedings of the Oxford Old Testament Seminar* (ed. John Day; LHBOTS 531; London: T&T Clark, 2010), 101–16.

much work remains to be done in understanding the Levites and their history, and I believe that Lenski's model can be of real assistance.[2]

Gerhard Lenski, now professor emeritus at the University of North Carolina at Chapel Hill, offers social theorists a general model of human societies and their distributive practices that incorporates sociocultural change over time and the imperfections of all human systems. This model understands that societies evolve over time and tend to develop a range of internal inequalities as they do so. These twin insights into human society—ongoing development and inevitable tensions—are crucial to grasp if one is to understand the social history of the Levitical lineage of priestly functionaries within Israel.[3]

In this present study of the Levites, I rely particularly on two of Lenski's books, now classics: *Power and Privilege* (1966) and *Human Societies* (1970). In these works Lenski devotes considerable attention to the dynamics of advanced agrarian societies, which were often neglected by social scientists until the years just prior to Lenski's research in the mid- to late 1960s, but which constitute precisely the social context in which the Levites subsisted in disenfranchisement for much of their history and in which emerged the biblical books associated closely with them, such as Deuteronomy and Jeremiah.[4]

---

2. One indication of the new scholarly energy around the Levites is the formation in 2009 of a new program unit focused on them within the Society of Biblical Literature, the "Levites and Priests in History and Tradition" consultation.

3. For Lenski's recognition that societies must be conceived of not as ideal systems but as fraught with tensions and imperfections, see his *Power and Privilege: A Theory of Social Stratification* (New York: McGraw-Hill, 1966), 34, 41, 239; and idem, *Human Societies: A Macrolevel Introduction to Sociology* (New York: McGraw-Hill, 1970), 68, 96, 257, 258.

4. For additional notes on how Judah closely fits this societal type during the period of Deuteronomy's first appearance and during Jeremiah's prophetic career, see Stephen L. Cook, *The Social Roots of Biblical Yahwism* (SBLStBL 8; Atlanta: Society of Biblical Literature, 2004), 46–47, 269–70; Patricia Dutcher-Walls, *Narrative Art, Political Rhetoric: The Case of Athaliah and Joash* (JSOTSup 209; Sheffield: Sheffield Academic Press, 1996), 150–55. For the provenance of Deuteronomy and Jeremiah at least partially within Levitical circles, see, e.g., Cook, *Social Roots,* 59–63; Mark Leuchter, *The Polemics of Exile in Jeremiah 26–45* (Cambridge: Cambridge University Press, 2008), 174, 265–66 n. 19; and now S. Dean McBride Jr., "Jeremiah and the Levitical Priests of Anathoth," in *Thus Says the Lord: Essays on the Former and Latter Prophets in Honor of Robert R. Wilson* (ed. S. L. Cook and J. J. Ahn; LHBOTS 502; New York: T&T Clark, 2009), 187–89. Among other evidence, McBride notes how Jer

Agrarian societies are the middle-range link between the preliterate technologically undeveloped societies and the modern industrial societies that have received the most attention in classical social-scientific investigations. The presence of the plow is the minimal criterion for the designation "agrarian society." Iron tools and weapons signal an "*advanced* agrarian society."[5]

Fitting Lenski's theory, Israelite society evolved as an advanced agrarian system over time. Textual, archaeological, and comparative evidence attests that preexilic Israel began as a society based on acephalous, segmentary tribal structures. Later, as state formation progressed, the society developed into an advanced, stratified agrarian monarchy. With social change came increasing pressure on traditional values and ways of life that were rooted in village and tribe.

The Levites were among those groups most seriously affected by the pressures of social change that Lenski describes. As society expanded and developed, their traditional, local roles of performing cultic service, arbitrating judicial matters, and fostering societal harmony became increasingly irrelevant. Evolving societies inevitably create new organizational structures for themselves that are not based on ties of family systems.[6] As the newer structures unfold, local and lineage-based worship paradigms lose power while centralized national faiths find increased strength. Under

---

33:17–22 unqualifiedly supports God's covenant with the Levites (cf. Mal 2:4). Discussion of Jeremiah and Deuteronomy resumes below shortly.

5. See Lenski, *Human Societies,* 25, 125. Lenski remarks that the scholarly tradition up until "recent years" was for sociologists to study modern industrial societies and anthropologists to concentrate on "primitive" preliterate societies. However, he does take note of contemporary work (then considered "new") by scholars in both disciplines on "middle range" societies in Southeast Asia, the Middle East, and Latin America. Although Lenski's choice of foci was part of a new trend in the 1960s, social scientists now more commonly attend to stratified agrarian societies. I am grateful to Tracy Lemos of Huron University College for bringing to my attention various works by social scientists whom she has found informative in thinking about these types of societies, including Jack Goody, *The Oriental, the Ancient and the Primitive: Systems of Marriage and the Family in the Pre-industrial Societies of Eurasia* (Studies in Literacy, Family, Culture and the State; Cambridge: Cambridge University Press, 1990); the classic 1966 work by Louis Dumont, *Homo Hierarchicus: The Caste System and Its Implications* (rev. Eng. ed.; Chicago: University of Chicago Press, 1980); and Paul K. Wason, *The Archaeology of Rank* (New Studies in Archaeology; Cambridge: Cambridge University Press, 1994).

6. Lenski, *Human Societies,* 242, 285–86.

such circumstances, tensions between official and local clerical factions may appear, sometimes eventuating in organized conflict.[7]

In the case of Israel's Levites, a traditional lineage of priests rooted in a village-based culture found itself struggling with the royal officers and state priests of an evolving new centralized society in both Judah and Israel. Rather than be swallowed up by the new monarchic system, they stubbornly contended with increasing stratification and inequities that left them consigned to a peripheral status and relative powerlessness. Though they experienced their traditional authority and supports sharply undermined in this way, they pressed hard to overcome their disenfranchisement by society's royal center.[8]

In their beginnings, the Levites belonged to that type of technologically simple society that Lenski characterizes as having little economic surplus. They knew a way of life where forces such as individualistic orientation, decree, and coercion played only small roles, and, instead, extended family systems nurtured cooperative tendencies.[9] In their radical program for society's reform laid out in Deuteronomy, the Levites attempted to recapture much of value from this earlier era, particularly its deemphasizing of force and its empowerment of the periphery.[10] This fits the pattern of Lenski's model well, in which just this sort of move is expected to occur when groups within a society work together to adopt the sort of constitu-

7. See Lenski, *Power and Privilege*, 209.

8. For discussion of Deuteronomy's laws as a response to the problem of cult centralization in Judah, now see Jeffrey Stackert, *Rewriting the Torah: Literary Revision in Deuteronomy and the Holiness Legislation* (FAT 52; Tübingen: Mohr Siebeck, 2007), e.g., 206.

9. Cf. Lenski, *Power and Privilege*, 441; idem, *Human Societies*, 246.

10. On the Levites as a significant force behind Deuteronomy, see n. 4 above; the bibliographic summary in Cook, *Social Roots*, 62 n. 39; Robert G. Boling, "Levitical History and the Role of Joshua," in *The Word of the Lord Shall Go Forth: Essays in Honor of David Noel Freedman in Celebration of His Sixtieth Birthday* (ed. C. L. Meyers and M. P. O'Connor; Winona Lake, Ind.: Eisenbrauns, 1983), 242–44; and especially the trenchant arguments in Richard Elliott Friedman, *Who Wrote the Bible?* (San Francisco: Harper & Row, 1997), 120–24. For a good, recent review of Gerhard von Rad's classic, breakthrough arguments that the Levites composed Deuteronomy, see Peter T. Vogt, *Deuteronomic Theology and the Significance of Torah: A Reappraisal* (Winona Lake, Ind.: Eisenbrauns, 2006), 36–37.

tional accords that minimize violent conflict in the social order and optimize stability and harmony.[11]

Scholars of Deuteronomy are increasingly aware of the remarkable challenge that the book mounts to contemporary chauvinistic and centrist ideologies, such as that of the Assyrian monarchs. The judicial realm is a powerful case in point. In Assyria the political elite exercised exclusive control over the shape and enforcement of law and order. By contrast, as Eckart Otto observes, Deuteronomy advocates constituting Israel as an integrated, covenantal community, not a hierarchical state.[12] Deuteronomy 17:8–13 describes the final arbiters of law and order in Israel as the Levitical priests, not the king. If a legal case proves too difficult to adjudicate at the local level, then one must "go up to the place that the LORD your God will choose, where you shall consult with *the levitical priests*" (vv. 8–9 NRSV; see also 19:17).

The proposal of Deuteronomy to vest Levites with final judicial authority at society's center represents what Mark Christian has recently described as a vision of the royal state sharing power with peripheral agents and even nonagents of the monarchy.[13] The concern in Deut 17 is not propping up the royal center, but disseminating responsibility for justice and holiness. The ideal is keeping "all the people" (v. 13), the whole of "Israel" (v. 12), a holy community purged of evil at all levels (see v. 7). As with the Sabbath command in the Deuteronomic Decalogue, nothing is held more important than making the social order of the entire land just and holy (5:12–14).[14] The Levites in question are by no means at home in

11. See Lenski, *Power and Privilege*, 67, 442.

12. On Deuteronomy's challenge to Assyrian ideology, see now Mark A. Christian, "Priestly Power that Empowers: Michel Foucault, Middle-Tier Levites, and the Sociology of 'Popular Religious Groups' in Israel," *Journal of Hebrew Scriptures* 9, article 1 (2009): 52. For Otto, Deuteronomy envisions Israel as a "קהל (Deut 5,22) nicht durch Herrschaftsinstanzen eines königlichen Staates, sondern durch einen JHWH-Bund konstitutiert" (*Das Deuteronomium im Pentateuch und Hexateuch: Studien zur Literaturgeschichte von Pentateuch und Hexateuch im Lichte des Deuteronomiumrahmens* [FAT 30; Tübingen: Mohr Siebeck, 2000], 124).

13. Christian, "Middle-Tier Levites," 61 n. 216.

14. Contrary to a now common scholarly view, Deuteronomy does not aim to "secularize" the Judean countryside through centralizing worship in Jerusalem but insists on buttressing the entirety of the land's holiness. Multiple texts of Deuteronomy, such as 7:6; 14:2; 26:18–19 (cf. 4:20), make clear that all of the people of Israel must be "holy" in their observable life and work, in their daily routines out in the land

the royal capital, but offer only periodic service there. Verse 9 with its language of being "on duty at that time" (NLT) assumes a rotation system that brings Levites from peripheral locales into Jerusalem for fixed periods. The center is recognizing and empowering the periphery.

The Levites bring with them to their new federally sponsored judicial roles their vocational expertise in covenantal instruction and interpretation (17:10; cf. 17:18; 31:9, 25–26; 33:10). Time and again, Levitical prophets such as Hosea, Jeremiah, and Malachi complain about the lack of this very pedagogical competence in upper-tier, permanently central priests (Hos 4:6; Jer 2:8; Mal 2:6–7).[15] Incorporation of Levites within society's center marked a royal capitulation to the complaints of the Levitical bearers of Deuteronomic theology. Deuteronomy seeks this capitulation, advocating a new enfranchisement of country Levites. Their presence would exert covenantal leverage amid a dangerously intensifying centralization of Judah's society.

Deuteronomy's proposal of power sharing with Levites would have appeared starkly anachronistic when the Deuteronomic code took center stage during King Josiah's reign. Judah's development as a hierarchical monarchy had occurred precisely at the expense of older, lineage-based modes of societal polity to which Levitical circles were long accustomed. Gone were the days of the village era, when the Levites wielded significant mediatory and judicial power both within and between Israel's tribal seg-

---

(see 6:6–9; 28:9–10). As texts such as 5:12–15 and 14:21 attest, conduct through the land, not just in Jerusalem, is directly pertinent to the people's sacral status (see Vogt, *Deuteronomic Theology,* 95; Norbert Lohfink, "Opfer und Säkularisierung im Deuteronomium," in *Studien zu Opfer und Kult im Alten Testament mit einer Bibliographie 1969–1991 zum Opfer in der Bibel* [ed. A. Schenker; FAT 3; Tübingen: Mohr Siebeck, 1992], 36). Joshua 22:10–34 illustrates well how centralizing worship does *not* secularize Israel's periphery. Brimming with Deuteronomy's theology, the text recounts how tribes in the Transjordan insisted on a symbolic copy of the Lord's altar on their territory—a huge altar. They were insistent that their territory, as far as it was from the tabernacle, was still God's land, part of God's unique sanctuary-territory. No one seeing that altar could claim otherwise (see J. G. McConville, *Deuteronomy* [Apollos Old Testament Commentary 5; Downers Grove, Ill.: InterVarsity Press, 2002], 96).

15. On the identification of Hosea, Jeremiah, and Malachi as Levites, see n. 4 above; William L. Holladay, *Jeremiah: A Commentary on the Book of the Prophet Jeremiah* (2 vols.; Hermeneia; Minneapolis: Fortress, 1986–1989), 1:15–17; 2:71–75; Cook, *Social Roots,* 17–20, 231–66; idem, "Malachi, Book of," *The Oxford Encyclopedia of the Books of the Bible* (ed. Michael D. Coogan et al.; 2 vols.; New York: Oxford University Press, 2011), 2:34–41.

ments. Gone was the era when traditional clan heads, field commanders, and chiefs depended on the sacral support and ritual collaboration of the Levites for effectiveness. Past was the time when priestly lineages played a role in chief-making and in controlling the effectiveness of chiefs (cf. 1 Sam 15:27–28; 1 Kgs 1:19, 25; 11:29–31). But as Lenski argues in wielding his stratification theory, "in sociology, as in physics, *actions produce reactions*."[16] The new exercise of power and privilege by elites will elicit a variety of reactions among society's different segments, according to Lenski, including a clergy's assertion of its partially independent basis of power.

To Lenski's credit, he realizes that priestly groups within advanced agrarian societies often occupy a unique position of independence from the authority of the crown. As agents of a transcendent power, they may elicit the special respect of elites (cf. 1 Sam 22:17; 1 Kgs 2:26). Further, the masses may stand behind them, considering the valued services they provide (e.g., presiding over local festivals, such as the Festival of Unleavened Bread, Exod 13:6–7; Deut 16:7–8). Thus history has witnessed many priestly groups asserting their authority and entering into struggles with political elites.

On the basis of Lenski's model, we might predict that certain Levites within Israelite society would counter monarchic power with a social vision that featured their relegitimation and reenfranchisement. We might even predict the sort of new alliance that emerged between King Josiah and the Levites (Deut 18:6–8; 2 Chr 35:3–6). Lenski writes, "Usually … the result [of conflict between priests and elite] has been a compromise involving an alliance of church and state. In exchange for the ideological support of the priests, the political elite protect them against religious competition."[17]

Did the proponents of Deuteronomy's vision realize that Levitical reenfranchisement would not be a risk-free experiment? Our tradents apparently failed to anticipate that returning traditional powers to the Levites might blunt the critical edge they applied to the monarchy and allow central power to co-opt their allegiance. Careful examination of Jeremiah's language about his opponents reveals that the prophet understood some of his Levite brethren to have succumbed to just this temptation.

16. Lenski, *Power and Privilege*, 63; also see p. 67.

17. Ibid., 67; cf. p. 209; idem, *Human Societies*, 284.

Evidence associated with Jeremiah's poetic "confessions" is especially telling. The data indicate that some Levite contemporaries of the prophet fit a pattern sketched by Lenski in which political and clerical circles ally, each side drawing benefits from their being in cahoots. According to Lenski, the priests usually defend the elite, "asserting that their power had been given them by God." Agrarian rulers, in appreciation, "were often extremely generous with religious groups."[18]

But, as Lenski notes, matters often become complicated once such alliances are formed. In some cases, hostile clerical groups from the periphery, largely endogamous, struggle against the co-opted priests and the societal center that they have come to defend. "On the whole, the divisions within advanced agrarian societies were more serious than those within simple agrarian. In particular, they were much more likely to lead to violence."[19] Jeremiah confesses to being entangled in such violence.

The enemies of Jeremiah appear to have included reempowered Levites, who have essentially sold out to what Jeremiah considered very dangerous, complacent thinking in Jerusalem. Jeremiah meanwhile, at least as his editors present him, remained an unswerving Levite proponent of Deuteronomy and its vision challenging and restricting the governing class and empowering the periphery. He was the quintessential prophet like Moses of Deut 18:15–19, subject to the resistance and violence often aimed at this role (cf. Num 12:1–2 [E]; Hos 6:9). Dean McBride outlines the evidence for Jeremiah's complex interrelationship with his fellow Levites of Anathoth in an essay just published in the Robert Wilson Festschrift.[20]

McBride ruminates on the cross-referencing that Jeremiah's book makes to the story of King Solomon's banishment of chief priest Abiathar to Anathoth in the territory of Benjamin (1 Kgs 2:26). Solomon's act effectively disenfranchised, or at least demoted, the Levitical house of Eli and Shiloh, to which Abiathar belonged (1 Sam 22:18–21; 1 Kgs 2:27). The first verse of Jeremiah declares the prophet one of the priests who lived at Anathoth. Later in the book the prophet buys the field of a Levitical relative in Anathoth, having the right of redemption to buy it. Echoes of the mention

18. Lenski, *Human Societies*, 285.

19. Ibid., 288; cf. idem, *Power and Privilege*, 209. Note also *Power and Privilege*, 264, 266, where Lenski makes some very perceptive comments on priests' role as a check on the abuses of privileged classes in agrarian societies.

20. McBride, "Jeremiah and the Levitical Priests," 179–96.

of Abiathar's "field" in 1 Kgs 2:26 are hard to miss, especially since Jer 32 mentions Anathoth three times (vv. 7–9).

McBride argues persuasively that these cross-references in Jeremiah to Abiathar and Eli purposefully invite the reader to consider the book another chapter in the complex saga of the Levites of Shiloh. Favored of God (cf. Jer 33:17–22) and now back in power at Jeremiah's time, as they were both under David and (even earlier) at Shiloh, they must be vigilant lest history repeat itself. When in power, their priestly house tended to incur divine wrath. The banishment of their forebear to Anathoth represented an awful divine judgment against their family line for neglect of the covenant (1 Kgs 2:27; cf. 1 Sam 2:27–36; 3:10–14). The same judgment could fall upon them again, as we see hinted in the intertextual resonances between 1 Sam 3:11 and Jer 19:3.[21]

The Elides needed to hear this warning in Jeremiah's day because their tenacity had landed them back in power. To quote McBride, "Nothing in DtrH [the Deuteronomistic History] precludes the possibility—even the probability, as the Chronicler and other sources indicate—that at least some of Abiathar's Anathothite descendants … were brought back into … the ranks of Jerusalem's Levitical clergy and scribal officials. Among the likeliest times for their reintegration as priestly officers were the … 'Deuteronomic' reforms."[22]

The program of Deuteronomy empowered Jeremiah to press his fellow Levites to regain their critical distance from society's monarchic center. The book carves out a key role for prophets in its outline of covenantal society's ideal leadership. In a weighty section in 18:9–22, Deuteronomy insists on prophets, such as Jeremiah, exercising leadership and wielding authority in Israel alongside judges (16:18–17:13), kings (17:14–20), and altar ministers (18:1–8).

Prophets differ from other Israelite leaders in that factors such as gender, age, and lineage have little bearing on eligibility for their office (Deut 18:18; Jer 1:7, 9). Like the divine word that they bear, prophets are free of such constraints. Partaking of the pure freedom of God, they may freely challenge the status quo and all established authority. They may confront monarchic officials and deputies with impunity, insisting that they learn covenantal teaching and embrace covenantal rigor. They provide a

21. I am grateful to Jeremy Hutton, University of Wisconsin-Madison, for bringing the connection of 1 Sam 3:11 and Jer 19:3 to my attention.

22. McBride, "Jeremiah and the Levitical Priests," 188–89.

crucial check on the complacency and insolence of ensconced power holders.

The program of Deuteronomy, which the Deuteronomic reforms of Kings Hezekiah and Josiah attempted to actualize, aimed at incorporating country Levites not only into Judah's centralized judicial system but also into the central cult of the Jerusalem temple. Deuteronomy 18:1–8 insists that the whole tribe of Levi constitutes Judah's priesthood. Outlying Levites, should they desire, are allowed to perform sacrifices at the temple in Jerusalem. Verse 5 reads, "The LORD your God has chosen Levi out of all your tribes, to stand and minister in the name of the LORD, him and his sons for all time" (NRSV). According to verse 7, any Levite passionate about altar service in Jerusalem may certainly minister there, "like all his fellow-Levites who stand to minister there before the LORD."

Was Deut 18 successful on the ground in enfranchising Levites? Did Kings Hezekiah and Josiah actually incorporate Levitical priests of the high places in Jerusalem's sacrificial cult? Julius Wellhausen, for one, doubted it. In what has become a commonplace truism among historical critics, he interpreted Deut 18's vision as an ideal doomed to fail. He argued that 2 Kgs 23 directly attests to this failure and that Ezek 44 provides a moral rationale for what happened. It was out of the de facto collapse of this piece of Deuteronomic legislation, according to Wellhausen, that the present scriptural distinction between sacrificing priests and non-sacrificing Levites arose.[23]

All modern English translations understand 2 Kgs 23 as Wellhausen did, along the lines of the NRSV of verse 9, "The priests of the high places, however, did not come up to the altar of the LORD in Jerusalem, but ate unleavened bread among their kindred." But does the Hebrew say this? A quick look shows that Wellhausen has misled a majority of critics and translators. In the verse a *kî 'im* clause follows a negative statement expressed with an imperfect verb. This syntax signals an entirely different reading than the one in the NRSV, namely, an expression leaning on an "unless and until" clause, an "exceptive clause." In such a case, the initial negative statement does not express a general fact but, as Bill Arnold and John Choi explain, a situation that is *reversed* after something specific hap-

23. Julius Wellhausen, *Prolegomena to the History of Ancient Israel* (New York: Meridian, 1957; 1st German ed., 1878), 121–67. For one summary and critique of Wellhausen's position, see Stephen L. Cook, "Innerbiblical Interpretation in Ezekiel 44 and the History of Israel's Priesthood," *JBL* 114 (1995): 193–208.

pens.[24] The same syntax occurs, among other places, in Gen 32:27, where Jacob eventually *does* release God; in Lev 22:6, where the priest *does* eventually eat; and in Isa 55:10, where earth's water *does* eventually evaporate. Likewise in 2 Kgs 23:9 the Levites do eventually serve at the Lord's altar in Jerusalem.[25]

In an article on the Levites, Mark Leuchter of Temple University renders 2 Kgs 23:9 as follows: "The priests of the high places did not go up [to the altar of the LORD in Jerusalem] until they ate unleavened bread among their brethren [= fellow Israelites]."[26] As Leuchter argues, this reading fits the rhetoric of the account far better than Wellhausen's understanding. The Deuteronomists tend to gloss over Josiah's failures and would scarcely have voiced a negative evaluation of his work enfranchising the Levites.[27] This reading also explains the puzzling reference in the verse to the celebration by the Levites of Passover/Unleavened Bread.

According to 2 Kgs 23, Josiah crowned his Deuteronomistic reforms with a Passover of a kind not seen since the days of the judges (v. 22). What is more, according to Chronicles it was at this Passover that the king organized the Levites for service in Jerusalem (2 Chr 35:2–4). All this followed the precedent of King Hezekiah, who himself had held a great Passover in Jerusalem as a centerpiece of his reform and had given the Levites his patronage after they demonstrated great skill at temple service there (2 Chr 30:22; 31:2).

---

24. Bill T. Arnold and John H. Choi, *A Guide to Biblical Hebrew Syntax* (Cambridge: Cambridge University Press, 2003), 155 §4.3.4 (m); see also Ronald J. Williams, *Williams' Hebrew Syntax* (rev. John C. Beckman; 3rd ed.; Toronto: University of Toronto Press, 2007), 197 §556; Paul Joüon and T. Muraoka, *A Grammar of Biblical Hebrew* (Subsidia biblica 27; Rome: Pontifical Biblical Institute, 2006), 603 §173b; Bruce K. Waltke and M. O'Connor, *An Introduction to Biblical Hebrew Syntax* (Winona Lake, Ind.: Eisenbrauns, 1990), 642–43 §38.6.

25. It is probable that the Hebrew Bible preserves the names of two close relatives (cousins) of Jeremiah from the Levites of Anathoth who joined ranks with the priests of Jerusalem under Josiah's rule, the priests Maaseiah (Jer 35:4) and Zephaniah (21:1; 29:25–26, 29; 37:3). They were apparently the son and grandson of Jeremiah's uncle Shallum (32:7). For discussion see Robert R. Wilson, *Prophecy and Society in Ancient Israel* (Philadelphia: Fortress, 1980), 234, 246; McBride, "Jeremiah and the Levitical Priests," 192–94.

26. Mark Leuchter, "'The Levite in Your Gates': The Deuteronomic Redefinition of Levitical Authority," *JBL* 126 (2007): 429.

27. Ibid., 428 and n. 43.

As Bernard Levinson has clarified, Deuteronomy combined Passover and Unleavened Bread into a "constitutive national holiday, in which all families are incorporated into a single polity."[28] According to Chronicles, opting out of the new centralized Passover was tantamount to rejecting the covenant (2 Chr 30:8). Josiah must have made this very assumption, and restricted Levitical enfranchisement to those rural priests willing to join with fellow Israelites around the observance of eating unleavened bread. He thus insured that all his official priests embraced Deuteronomy's covenant and uniform polity. Those refusing to conform presumably fell under the same opprobrium as the idolatrous priests whom Josiah rejects and slaughters at 2 Kgs 23:19–20.[29]

Why do the Deuteronomistic authors of 2 Kgs 23:9 appear to have emphasized the dimension of "unleavened bread" within Josiah's new centralized Passover? Perhaps they wished to stress the theme of pilgrimage (cf. Exod 13:6 E), which for Deuteronomy entails a new orientation toward a central shrine where all Israel should renew its covenantal life before the Lord. The rites of Passover did not involve this theme of pilgrimage before Deuteronomy's innovations, which shape the Passover as a meal that ushers in the pilgrimage festival of Unleavened Bread (see Deut 16:3–4). They may also have had in mind how the unleavened bread had served as a pointer to a central value of every true Levite, having "the teaching/torah of the LORD … on your lips" (Exod 13:9 E). In addition, they may have been introducing a thought of renewing the Levites' priesthood. Unlike the traditional Passover meal, the Festival of Unleavened Bread was an occasion where priests presided. Unleavened bread is also the standard grain offering received and shared by priests (Exod 23:18 E; cf. Lev 2:11; 6:17).[30]

Finally, and perhaps most interestingly, the wording of 2 Kgs 23:9 may reflect a bold assertion by Josiah of royal authority to interpret Deuter-

---

28. Bernard M. Levinson, *Deuteronomy and the Hermeneutics of Legal Innovation* (New York: Oxford University Press, 1997), 95.

29. Although the NRSV at 2 Kgs 23:5 states that Josiah "deposed" idolatrous priests, the Hebrew verb *šbt* used there can also mean "exterminate" (see BDB 991 Hiph. 2, where 2 Kgs 23:5 is listed; note the translation of the NJB; cf. NET note; also cf. 2 Chr 34:5).

30. I wish to thank the panel at the "Levites and Priests in History and Tradition Consultation" session at the SBL annual meeting (New Orleans, November 2009), especially Jeremy Hutton and Diana Edelman, for helping me brainstorm these suggestions.

onomy and his insistence that the Levites bow to his control. The phrase "among their kindred" in 2 Kgs 23:9 probably refers to the assembly gathered at Jerusalem for Passover (*'aḥîm* is standard Deuteronomic diction signaling members of the covenant community; cf. Deut 1:16; 3:20; 10:9; 15:7; 17:15, etc.). A literal reading of Deut 16 would suggest that this assembly should break up to allow for a reverse pilgrimage out of Jerusalem and back home to the outlying towns for local celebrations of the Festival of Unleavened Bread (see 16:7!). In contrast to this literal reading, Josiah appears to have insisted that the covenant community remain assembled in Jerusalem for both Passover and the subsequent pilgrimage feast (see 2 Chr 35:17). He apparently demanded that all Levites wishing for his patronage observe things his way. They had to prove their loyalty to the crown by staying in Jerusalem and eating "unleavened bread among their kindred."[31]

What remains unclear is whether Deut 18 envisions a Levite moving permanently to Jerusalem for ongoing cultic service (NJB, NIV, NLT) or simply visiting periodically to perform at the altar (NAB) once he has been fully reenfranchised. The assumption of 2 Kgs 23:9 is that Deuteronomy envisions a great many former priests of the high places coming up to help officiate at sacrifices. Jerusalem would not accommodate a permanent presence of Levites in such numbers, so I suggest a more feasible interpretation of rotating Levites, as in the rota system we saw embraced in Deut 17:9.[32]

---

31. On the interpretation of Deut 16:7, see Levinson, *Hermeneutics of Legal Innovation*, 89. The idea that the Levites had to adhere to Josiah's specific form of the Unleavened Bread festival as a test of their loyalty to the crown was suggested to me by Susan Ackerman at the Brown University Moskow Symposium on "Social Theory and the Study of Israelite Religion: Retrospect and Prospect" (Providence, February 28–March 1, 2010).

32. From a later period 1 Chr 24 describes divisions of rotating courses of Levites (vv. 20–31), each serving at Jerusalem's temple for two week-long cycles every year. Josephus mentions this very system of Levitical rotation, noting that King David created 24 Levitical divisions that "came up in the same manner [as the Aaronide priests] for their courses of eight days" (*Ant.* 7.367). See also 1 Chr 9:25; 2 Chr 23:4, 8; m. Ta'an. 4:2; t. Ta'an. 4:2–3. Of course, the system of Aaronide rotation is better known than the Levitical one. It was in place "in the days of King Herod of Judea" (37–4 B.C.E.) according to Luke 1:5–25, which refers to the "priestly order of Abijah" (v. 5; see 1 Chr 24:10) being "on duty" (v. 8) at the Jerusalem sanctuary. At least nine texts from the

Jeremiah's confessions presuppose a rota system in which Jerusalem's cult officiants maintain primary residence in outlying towns. According to these texts, his challenges to the official cult first provoked death threats in his home village of Anathoth (Jer 11:21, 23; 12:6).[33] Elsewhere in the book, such threats of death are specifically associated with his prophetic attacks on the temple and God's chosen city (see Jer 26:6–9, 11, 20–21; 36:5; 38:3–4).[34] It is out in Judah that Jeremiah first faces the ire of those invested in Zion's sacral protection. His fellow villagers are surprisingly wrapped up in Jerusalem's establishment and central cult.[35] These Anathothite neighbors are the "foot-runners" who weary Jeremiah before he ever has a chance to "compete with horses" (Jer 12:5).

The Anathothite defenders of Jerusalem were likely resident priests, not currently on duty at the temple. Language about them within the first confession in Jer 11:23 parallels that directed against temple personnel committing wickedness in God's house in 23:11–12. Remembering that Anathoth was one of four towns in southern Benjamin assigned to Aaronide families according to some texts (Josh 21:17–18; 1 Chr 6:45 [NRSV

Qumran community, including calendrical legal texts, attest to an ongoing interest in the rotation of priestly courses that is worked out in 1 Chr 24.

33. On the historical setting of these verses, see Holladay, *Jeremiah*, 1:370–71, 375. Holladay lists several points in favor of the historicity of opposition to Jeremiah from the side of his Levitical kinfolk in Anathoth. For example, the specific, incidental quotes of the kinfolk in Jer 11:21 and 12:6 do not have the feel of an invented construct. What is more, it is unlikely that a later editor would invent a construct of familial strife in apparent contradiction to traditions elsewhere in Jeremiah about the prophet enjoying good relations with family and associates (32:6–15; 37:12).

34. Defenders of the Jerusalem temple appear to have been particularly offended by prophecies against Zion "in the name of the LORD" (Jer 11:21). The same phraseology about offensive use of the Lord's name resounds in their response to Jeremiah's temple sermon: "How dare you claim the LORD's authority to prophesy such things!" (26:9 NET). Also see 26:20 (the "sinister parallel" between Jeremiah's situation in his village and the earlier threat against Uriah ben Shemaiah from the side of the Jerusalem establishment has now been noted by Leslie C. Allen [*Jeremiah* (OTL; Louisville: Westminster John Knox, 2008), 147]).

35. For discussion see McBride, "Jeremiah and the Levitical Priests," 190 n. 32, 191–92; Wilson, *Prophecy and Society*, 244–46; cf. Walter Brueggemann, *A Commentary on Jeremiah: Exile and Homecoming* (Grand Rapids: Eerdmans, 1998), 117. Jeremiah's temple sermon would have provoked the particular ire of his fellow Anathothites, given the salt that it threw into their wounds about the destruction of Shiloh, their former home base (Jer 7:12–14; 26:6).

60]), one might at first suppose that Jeremiah's local foes must have been sons of Aaron, whose native traditions always differed markedly from Jeremiah's own Deuteronomic perspective. This thought is dispelled, however, by Jer 12:6, which describes the foes specifically as the Levitical kin of Jeremiah, "your brothers and your father's house" (cf. 20:10).[36]

Jeremiah's Levitical kin took his threats against the central cult very personally. Within the confessions, Jeremiah quotes their language of taking "revenge" on him (20:10). Such enmity makes sense when we recall that local shrines were now decommissioned; the Levites likely clung to their recent reintegration at Jerusalem. Just at the point when they had finally come back into power as in the old days at Shiloh and under David, their own Levitical relative was undermining the system that sanctioned their priesthood and granted them patronage.

In contrast to those Levites who appear to have sold out and adopted a blind commitment to Jerusalem's establishment, Jeremiah and like-minded Levitical purists clung to the genuine Deuteronomic vision. They refused to relinquish the ideal of a holy people undivided by artificial hierarchies, a vision of the whole land as God's sanctuary where justice and holiness must prevail. Many current scholars characterize Deuteronomy as aligned with centralized power and intent on elevating Jerusalem to the detriment of the local sphere. This understanding is erroneous.

Levites such as Jeremiah remained hard-core proponents of Deuteronomy's vision of *one people*, a brotherhood and sisterhood of co-vassals under one divine suzerain. They balked at the sociocultural cleavage between the urban sphere and the rural sphere that Lenski describes as a typical development in advanced agrarian societies.[37] According to Lenski, although the majority of people in an agrarian society always live on farms away from cities and towns, to city dwellers the rural sphere appears increasingly alien, backward, and stupid.[38]

---

36. See McBride, "Jeremiah and the Levitical Priests," 190.

37. Lenski, *Power and Privilege*, 200; idem, *Human Societies*, 246–47. On Deuteronomy's understanding of the covenant community as a brotherhood and sisterhood, see my comments above on the phrase "among their kindred [*'ăḥêhem*]" in 2 Kgs 23:9.

38. Lenski, *Human Societies*, 249, 287. We can accept that official Jerusalem's attitude toward the countryside may often have been as Lenski describes, without going farther and adopting from Lenski an assumption of the near collapse of rural life in Judah at the hands of the urban elite. Lenski describes injustice and oppression reducing rural life to the barest subsistence level in many advanced agrarian societies, but such a dire state of affairs is not attested archaeologically in monarchic Israel.

Deuteronomy, read plainly, considers the whole of Israel to be a holy community,[39] and it naturally values and upholds the rural provinces and Judah's old clans. The Levites, who are resident in Judah's towns and villages apart from their stints of service in Jerusalem, should pursue a specifically sacral ministry in the countryside. They should "minister" and "bless" there (Deut 21:5). They should teach and administer the covenant there. Enforcing the covenant and assisting clan elders in judiciary matters was part of their traditional village role (cf. Hos 4:6; Jer 2:8; 2 Chr 19:8).

Texts such as Deut 16:18–20 and 17:2–7 are attempts to counter and reform the monarchy's hierarchically organized legal system. These texts push back against a system that concentrated judicial power in a royal center. They aim to decentralize and disperse judicial power, so that most legal matters are handled locally.[40]

In Deuteronomy's ideal polity, there are to be local judges and civil servants throughout Israel's tribes, in all the towns (Deut 16:18). Their work must accord with the idiom of local, tribal wisdom (16:19b; cf. Prov 17:23; 18:5). The motivation is the people's singular pursuit of covenantal justice in God's own land (Deut 16:20; 17:2, 7). God, not the king, is the guarantor of this justice (16:20).

Deuteronomy 21:1–9 attests to the presence of Levites among the book's local judges. The immediate context pictures them functioning as juridical administrators well outside of the capital. Out among the rural communities of Judah, it is by their decision that "all cases of dispute and assault shall be settled" (v. 5). The scenario depicted in the passage fits in with much cross-cultural evidence, in which settling disputes and mediating between tribal segments is a key role of traditional priestly descent groups spread out among the segments of society.[41]

See esp. Avraham Faust, *Israelite Society in the Period of the Monarchy: An Archaeological Examination* [in Hebrew] (Jerusalem: Yad Izhak Ben-Zvi, 2005); idem, *The Archaeology of Israelite Society in the Iron Age II* (Winona Lake, Ind.: Eisenbrauns, forthcoming).

39. See n. 14 above.

40. For example, see Robert R. Wilson, "Israel's Judicial System in the Preexilic Period," *JQR* 74 (1983): 246; Stephen L. Cook, "The Tradition of Mosaic Judges: Past Approaches and New Directions," in *On the Way to Nineveh: Studies in Honor of George M. Landes* (ed. S. L. Cook and S. C. Winter; ASOR Books 4; Atlanta: Scholars Press, 1999), 286–315.

41. See Cook, *Social Roots*, 189–91.

We have a reference to village Israel's traditional judicial figures, the elders and the Levites, in the phrase *šōpĕṭîm wĕšōṭĕrîm* ("judges and magistrates") used at the start of Deut 16:18–18:22, the section of the book on public offices. Deuteronomy 1:9–18 uses these same Hebrew terms, specifying that these selfsame judges are selected specifically from among tribal lineage heads (v. 15, an inner-biblical rehearsal of Num 11:16 E, which uses the term *šōṭĕrîm*, and Exod 18:21, 25 E). At the same time, evidence for Levitical participation in these judicial roles appears in texts such as 1 Chr 23:4; 26:29; and 2 Chr 19:5–11.

Mark Leuchter has done a fine job recently bolstering the case that Levites are indeed included in the phrase "judges and magistrates," in accordance with an aim of Deuteronomy to sanction a Levitical role in regional jurisprudence, in the village gates of Judah's local communities. Leuchter notes that it would make precious little sense to give Levites authority interpreting the law at the palace (Deut 17:18) and in Jerusalem's appellate courts (17:8) unless they had backgrounds in local/regional juridical processes.[42] The deliberate cross-referencing between 21:5 and 17:8 confirms that Levites were supposed to be exercising and honing their legal skills in the gates. By citing the latter text, 21:5 makes clear that it understands the Levitical adjudication of "all cases of dispute and assault" to take place specifically in local gate settings.[43]

The various pieces of evidence adduced by this essay could be multiplied, but enough has been covered to reach some fairly assured conclusions about the history of the Levites and specifically about their place within sociocultural change in Judah. The social-scientific model of Gerhard Lenski has been of much helpful guidance in hammering out and formulating these conclusions. Aided by Lenski's model, we see between the lines of Deuteronomy and Jeremiah a group of stubborn Levites, originally based in Shiloh, insisting on a repristination of their traditional powers and privileges within old Israel's village-based, lineage-based society.[44] We also see their kinsman Jeremiah stubbornly insisting that whatever privileges they see restored to them in the wake of Josiah's revolution, the Levites must adhere to Deuteronomy's strict caveats, tempering, and cen-

42. Leuchter, "Levite in Your Gates," 423.

43. Ibid., 424–25.

44. For some keen insights on the possibility of the resurgence of older ways of life in more advanced, centralized societies, see Lenski, *Power and Privilege,* 230, 266.

sures aimed against the almost inevitable evils of an advanced, centralized, stratified monarchic society.

Deuteronomy mounted a multipronged plan for overcoming Levitical disenfranchisement, which, contrary to Wellhausen's influential reconstruction, appears to have actually been temporarily implemented on the ground. On the one hand, this plan included rotating country Levites into the capital to serve as interpreters of the covenant at the palace, to hear legal cases within appellate courts, and to serve as altar priests at the temple. On the other hand, the plan lent official sanction to the traditional Levitical role of enforcing the covenant in the countryside. Federalizing their traditional role, the plan included granting the Levites official authority in Judah's city gates, the traditional seats of local jurisprudence. In this way it resisted any vision of centralized monarchy to devalue and secularize the periphery.

Away from Ritual: The Prophetic Critique

Ronald Hendel

A prophetic oracle in Amos 5:21–24 conveys a judgment against the contemporary ritual practices of ancient Israel.[1] The poetry of the oracle is terse and emphatic:

śānēʾtî māʾastî ḥaggêkem	21 I hate, I reject your festivals,
wĕlōʾ ʾārîaḥ bĕʿaṣṣĕrōtêkem	I do not delight in your assemblies.
kî ʾim taʿălû lî ʿōlôt ûminḥōtêkem	22 For when you offer burnt offerings and your grain gifts,[2]

1. This essay is a rethinking of issues previously treated in "Prophets, Priests, and the Efficacy of Ritual," in *Pomegranates and Golden Bells: Studies in Biblical, Jewish, and Near Eastern Ritual, Law, and Literature in Honor of Jacob Milgrom* (ed. David P. Wright, David N. Freedman, and Avi Hurvitz; Winona Lake, Ind.; Eisenbrauns, 1995), 185–98. Recent contributions from which I benefited include Alexander B. Ernst, *Weisheitliche Kultkritik: Zu Theologie und Ethik des Sprüchebuchs und der Prophetie des 8. Jahrhunderts* (Neukirchen-Vluyn: Neukirchener, 1994); John Barton, "The Prophets and the Cult," in *Temple and Worship in Biblical Israel* (ed. John Day; LHBOTS 422; London: T&T Clark, 2005), 111–22; Thomas Krüger, "Erwägungen zur prophetischen Kultkritik," in *Die unwiderstehliche Wahrheit: Studien zur alttestamentlichen Prophetie: Festschrift für Arndt Meinhold* (ed. Rüdiger Lux and Ernst-Joachim Waschke; Leipzig: Evangelische Verlaganstalt, 2006), 37–55; and Jonathan Klawans, "Rethinking the Prophetic Critique," in *Purity, Sacrifice, and the Temple: Symbolism and Supersessionism in the Study of Ancient Judaism* (New York: Oxford University Press, 2006), 75–100.

2. Hebrew *mĕnāḥôt* ("gifts") can refer to sacrifices in general or to grain offerings in particular. In the context of the two major types of (non-Priestly) meat offerings, the latter meaning seems more suitable; cf. the collocation *ʿōlâ ûminḥâ* in Jer 14:12 and the discussion in Shalom M. Paul, *Amos* (Hermeneia; Minneapolis: Fortress, 1991), 190.

lō' 'erṣeh	I do not accept them,
wěšelem měrî'ěkem	And well-being offerings of your fatlings,
lō' 'abbîṭ	I do not regard them.
hāsēr mē'ālay hămôn šīrêkā	23 Turn away from me the noise of your songs,
wězimrat něbālêkā lō' 'ešmā'	And the music of your lyres, I do not hear.
wěyiggal kammayim mišpāṭ	24 But let justice roll like water,
ûṣědāqâ kěnaḥal 'ētān	And righteousness like an eternal stream.

This famous poem—whose last lines are among the most quoted from the Hebrew Bible—is an example of the poetry of prophetic critique, in which ordinary practices are exposed to withering rejection. I will explore the nuances of this and related texts, and will attempt to situate them in their social contexts in order better to understand their practical, institutional, and conceptual claims. The theory of Mary Douglas on the social relations that are conducive to the discourse of antiritualism will inform the scope and substance of my inquiry.

Let us consider first this poem's rhetoric and verbal texture. As is the general rule for biblical poetry, its effects are ordered by what Robert Alter calls structures of intensification.[3] These effects occur between the parallel lines in a verse, but also within a single line. For instance, the first word, *śānē'tî* ("I hate"), an emotive term, is immediately intensified by *mā'astî* ("I reject"), which is its cognitive and practical consequence. In the sound pattern of the verse, the two verbs in sequence, each with three syllables and ending with *tî*, create a rhythmic and emphatic sequence. In the parallel line (v. 21b), these verbs are heightened and explicated by a verb with a technical ritual sense, *'ārîaḥ* (lit. "I smell"), which here has the extended meaning of "delight (in)." In these "festivals"/"assemblies," the central rite is sacrifice, which Yhwh customarily "smells" and "delights (in)." But this customary response is reversed and negated here. The ritual sense of "I do not smell (the sacrifices)" is activated retrospectively by the mention of

3. Robert Alter, *The Art of Biblical Poetry* (New York: Basic Books, 1985), 62–84.

sacrifices in the following verse (v. 22). Rather than smell the sweet aroma and delight in the festivals dedicated to him, Yhwh refuses to inhale.

By withholding his positive reception of these rites, he nullifies their effectiveness. They become empty gestures, gifts with no recipient and no reciprocity. Yhwh's rejection of the festivals, which is concretized and intensified by his privation of his sense of smell, is expanded in the following verses, where he sequentially shuts off his other senses. In verse 22 his rejection of sacrifices, *lō' 'erṣeh* ("I do not accept"), is intensified by the parallel verb, in which he withholds his sense of sight: *lō' 'abbîṭ* ("I do not see, regard"). In verse 23 the command to "turn away" your songs and music is intensified by the parallel verb, where Yhwh shuts off his sense of hearing: *lō' 'ešmāʿ* ("I do not hear"). The fourfold sequence of negated verbs (*lō'*-X) creates a rhythmic refrain of Yhwh's rejection of the Israelites' rites, in which the general statements of rejection are made vivid and concrete by his sequential withholding of his senses of smell, sight, and hearing. Yhwh declares himself to be insensible to their ritual practices, which are now solipsistic dramas performed to an empty house.

In the final verse (v. 24), the prophet deliberately contrasts the elaborate sights, smells, and sounds of Israelite ritual with the simple practices of justice and social morality. This is the briefest verse of the poem, and is, interestingly, the only place where the poem employs metaphors. The ordinary phrase, *mišpāṭ ûṣĕdāqâ* ("justice and righteousness") is broken up across the juncture between the two poetic lines, creating a chiastic parallel. This break-up of the formulaic phrase defamiliarizes it by giving each term a separate syntactic focus, while intensifying them in the "doubling" of poetic parallelism. The verb that governs both terms, *wĕyiggal* ("roll," intransitive), includes a play on the word *gal* ("wave"), which is activated by the subsequent images of "water" and "stream." The striking metaphor of justice rolling like water is intensified in the second line where the general noun "water" is seconded by the concrete image of a *naḥal 'êtān* ("eternal stream"), a river that does not dry up after the rainy season (an important feature in a semi-arid climate). The concrete image of an "eternal stream" is lifted out of the register of ordinary speech by its adjective *'êtān* ("eternal"), which in the discourse of poetry activates a mythic resonance. The simple practice of justice and righteousness is heightened by this composite metaphorical vehicle, in which the water becomes an eternal stream. The senses of sight and sound evoked by the eternally flowing river (of justice) provide a dramatic contrast with Yhwh's privation of his senses, in response to Israelite rituals, in the previous verses.

The metaphorical image of the eternal river represents the social practice of justice as if it were a feature of nature. This naturalization of ethics is the counterpoint to the representation of ritual as a social convention, which Yhwh will neither see, hear, nor smell. His positive command, "Let justice roll," grammatically reverses his negation of his senses, "I do not (delight/smell, accept, see, hear)." The sounds and senses of the river of justice replace the hated cacophony of ritual practice. With his command he dramatically changes the subject from customary ritual to the simple practice of morality. The contrast is absolute: one set of practices Yhwh hates, whereas the other is—or should be—a fundamental feature of the world. There is no suggestion that Yhwh's rejection of ritual and his privation of senses are reversible or temporary. The last verse is not a revision or reformation of ritual, but a change of subject to a different category, and it is spoken in the imperative mood, as a divine categorical imperative. The strong rhetorical contrast between the subjects of verses 21–23 and verse 24 seems irreconcilable, incapable of mediation.

There is a relational directness in the poetic language that points to and implicitly interrogates the human agents. That is, as many commentators have noted, the poem is not a blanket rejection of ritual as such, but a rejection of the practices of the interpellated "you." In verses 21–22 the pronominal suffix *-kem* ("your," plural) occurs four times—"your festivals," "your assemblies," "your gifts," and "your fatlings"—each at the end of a line, creating a rhythm and rhyme of collective indictment. In verse 23 the focus narrows to the individual Israelite, with the repeated pronominal suffix *-kā* ("your," singular) in "your songs" and "your lyres," which are in chiastic parallel. The movement from plural to singular creates a rhetorical intensification of the critique—Yhwh's rejection singles out first the group and then each participant. In the final verse, the tense interpellation relaxes. There is no direct addressee, but a divine volition that focuses on the ideal practice of justice and morality. The people are implicitly commanded to practice justice rather than ritual, but there is no guilt, interrogation, or even human agency in this rhetorical climax, only the powerful good of right conduct.

Ritual as *Doxa*

This prophetic poem contests ritual practices that ordinarily were not contestable in Israelite culture. This text belongs to a small circle of prophetic texts, composed primarily in the eighth and seventh centuries

B.C.E.,[4] that bring these practices into question. Prior to these prophetic critiques it was uncommon—or perhaps even unthinkable—to question the validity of customary Israelite rituals, including festivals, sacrifices, prayers, and hymns. These practices belonged to the domain of what the sociologist Pierre Bourdieu calls *doxa* (Greek for "opinion, notion, expectation"). The *doxa* of a culture are the unquestioned assumptions and practices of everyday life, which since they are unspoken are not subject to argument or dispute. Bourdieu writes: "Because the subjective necessity and self-evidence of the commonsense world are validated by the objective consensus on the sense of the world, what is essential *goes without saying because it comes without saying*."[5]

The habits of thought and practice that no one questions are the background assumptions of everyday life. These silent hypotheses are described by Mary Douglas as "implicit meanings," which only those whose assumptions differ can easily interrogate. Douglas argues for a strong bond between the self-evident practices of everyday life and the social relations that validate and support them: "the logical patterning in which social relations are ordered affords a bias ... [in which] is to be found the confident intuition of self-evident truth. ... Only one who feels coolly towards that society can question its self-evident propositions."[6]

The eighth-century classical prophets are examples of those who "feel coolly" toward the self-evident truths of ordinary Israelite ritual practices. Accordingly, following Douglas's line of thinking, we may suppose that they are able to question these self-evident propositions because they have a slightly different set of *doxa*, which are supported by their particular pattern of social relations. We will explore these issues below.

First let us first consider the evidence for festivals, sacrifices, and hymns as unquestioned *doxa* in ancient Israel. If we grant the validity of the anthropological view that myths often function as charters for social action and institutions,[7] then we might expect the introduction of these ritual practices in the Pentateuch to provide such a charter or justification.

---

4. See the studies cited in n. 1 above.

5. Pierre Bourdieu, *Outline of a Theory of Practice* (Cambridge: Cambridge University Press, 1977), 167.

6. Mary Douglas, *Implicit Meanings: Essays in Anthropology* (London: Routledge & Kegan Paul, 1975), 209.

7. The social utility of myth was emphasized by Bronislaw Malinowski, *Magic, Science and Religion and Other Essays* (Garden City, N.Y.: Doubleday, 1954), 100–101;

(Or in terms more familiar to biblicists, an etiology.) For the practices in question, however, no charter or etiology is given, since there is apparently no need to explain or justify them. In Genesis the first sacrifices are those of Cain and Abel, but no reason or justifications are given for this practice: "Cain brought from the fruit of the soil an offering (*minḥâ*) for Yhwh," and Abel too brought his offering from flocks (Gen 4:3–4). Unlike such matters as childbirth and agriculture, sacrificial ritual needs no justification; in Bourdieu's phrase, it "*goes without saying because it comes without saying*." As *doxa*, sacrificial offerings in Genesis are simply part of ordinary practice, an unquestioned norm of the commonsense world, a self-evident proposition.

The second round of sacrifice is undertaken by Noah after exiting the ark. His first act on dry land is to build an altar and offer sacrifice (Gen 8:20). Without any explanation or justification—because it goes without saying—"Yhwh smelled the sweet savor," whereupon Yhwh renews his bond with humans and nature. The practice of sacrifice, including the human offering and the divine response, does not receive any kind of announcement or justification. These sacrificial texts, both from the J source, do not require explanation or etiology. Similarly, in the P source, where the sacrificial system does have a specific origin in the laws that Yhwh commands at Sinai, no explanation or reason is given for the rites. Yhwh simply commands, and Moses disposes. There is nothing that counts as explanation for the sacrifices, festivals, and related rites. For these pentateuchal sources, the implicit meanings of ritual practices are not verbalized, because as *doxa* they do not rise to the level of self-conscious discourse.

The closest thing to a rationale for sacrifice in the Pentateuch is found in a single verse in the preamble to the Covenant Code, where Yhwh gives a law for constructing altars: "An altar of earth you shall make for me, and on it you shall sacrifice your burnt offerings and your well-being offerings of your flocks and your herds. In every place where you remember[8] my name, I will come to you and bless you" (Exod 20:21). This command

---

see more recently Robert A. Segal, *Myth: A Very Short Introduction* (New York: Oxford University Press, 2004), 27–29, 126–27.

8. Reading *tazkîr* with the Syriac Peshiṭta and a rabbinic *'al tiqre'*; MT has *'azkîr*, "I will cause (my name) to be remembered." Yair Zakovitch plausibly argues that *tazkîr* is the original reading, which was secondarily assimilated to Deuteronomistic language: "The Book of the Covenant Interprets the Book of the Covenant: The 'Boomerang

assumes that burnt offerings (*ʿōlôt*) and well-being offerings (*šĕlāmîm*) are already customary ritual practices; its focus is to specify what kind of altars the Israelites must construct. The coda to this command states Yhwh's response to the proper construction of altars and the performance of sacrificial offerings: "I will come to you and bless you." This response is an exegesis of what it means for God to "smell the sweet aroma" of the sacrifice, as in the story of Noah's sacrifices. It leaves out the reasons for the origin and form of sacrificial ritual, because these are *doxa* and are simply assumed without saying.

These sacrificial practices are *doxa* in other West Semitic cultures as well. The Ugaritic epics do not explain why Kirta and Danel offer sacrifices to El, Baal, and Asherah, except to record the presence or absence of the desired response: the blessing of the gods. The same goes for other Ugaritic and Phoenician sacrificial and ritual texts. In this respect there is no difference in the *doxa* of such rites between Israel and its predecessors and neighbors.[9] These are self-evident practices in ancient West Semitic cultures. The eighth-century prophets interrupt this chain of self-evidence.

It is instructive to note that in the narratives of the Pentateuch and Former Prophets, prophets participate in the *doxa* of sacrificial ritual. Abraham, Moses, Samuel, and Elijah—prophets all—perform sacrifices. The ritual activities of Abraham and Samuel are particularly instructive. Abraham is explicitly a prophet in the E source (Gen 20:7), and in Gen 22 (E) God commands Abraham to build an altar and sacrifice a burnt offering—the sacrificial victim being his son, Isaac. Abraham demonstrates that he is a "God-fearer" (*yĕrēʾ ʾĕlōhîm*) by passing this test of obedience, and in the end he sacrifices a ram. In this story, Abraham's virtue is precisely his obedience in performing the sacrificial rite.

The sacrificial activities of Samuel have a similar message. Samuel rejects Saul as king precisely because Saul fails to follow the proper instructions for sacrifice. In 1 Sam 13:8–14 Saul offers burnt offerings and well-being offerings without waiting for Samuel—who is both prophet and priest—to offer them (see Samuel's instructions to Saul in 10:8). As a result of this improper sacrifice, Samuel proclaims: "If[10] you had obeyed the

---

Phenomenon'" [Hebrew], in *Texts, Temples, and Traditions: A Tribute to Menahem Haran* (ed. Michael V. Fox et al.; Winona Lake, Ind.: Eisenbrauns, 1996), 60*.

9. See, e.g., Dennis Pardee, *Ritual and Cult at Ugarit* (SBLWAW 10; Atlanta: Society of Biblical Literature, 2002), 233–41.

10. Reading *lūʾ* (the particle for contrary-to-fact conditional) rather than the Mas-

command of Yhwh your God that he commanded you, now Yhwh would have established your kingship over Israel forever. But now your kingship shall not stand" (13:13–14).

Saul's dynasty is rejected because he violated proper sacrificial procedure. In the follow-up episode in 1 Sam 15, Samuel declares that Yhwh has rejected Saul as king because of another sacrificial transgression. Saul spared King Agag of Amalek and the choicest of the Amalekites' flocks and herds from the command of *ḥērem* (dedication by destruction), because, he tells Samuel, the soldiers wanted "to sacrifice to Yhwh, your God, at Gilgal" (15:21). Samuel replies with a withering poetic utterance:

> Is Yhwh pleased with burnt offerings and sacrifices
> as much as obeying the voice of Yhwh?
>
> For obedience is better than sacrifice,
> To hearken, than the fat of rams. (15:22)

He follows with a tit-for-tat judgment:

> Because you have rejected the word of Yhwh,
> He has rejected you as king. (15:23)

Saul's improper performance of rituals—including sacrifice and ritual destruction (*ḥērem*) earns him the rejection of his dynasty and his rule as king. Notice that the *doxa* of ritual is not questioned in Samuel's poetic discourse. Yhwh does not reject "burnt offerings and sacrifices"; rather, obedience to his command is a higher value.

In 1 Sam 15:22 "burnt offerings and sacrifices" (*ʿōlôt ûzĕbāḥîm*) are in antithetical parallelism with "obeying [lit. 'hearing'] the voice of Yhwh" (*šĕmōaʿ bĕqôl yhwh*), a contrast that is often compared with Amos's binary opposition of ritual and ethical practices. But in Samuel's poetry, both categories are objects of Yhwh's "pleasure" (*ḥēpeṣ*). Yhwh's rejection is directed at Saul, not at ritual practices. Yhwh delights in ritual sacrifices, but he delights more in obedience. The proper comparison is with the "God-fearer" Abraham, who obeys the voice of Yhwh, rather than with Amos's poem, where ritual practices are the direct objects of Yhwh's hate and rejec-

---

oretic reading *lōʾ*; see P. Kyle McCarter, *I Samuel* (AB 8; Garden City, N.Y.: Doubleday, 1980), 226.

tion. In other words, ritual is still *doxa* in Samuel's speech and actions, even though it has comparatively less value than obedience to God's commands. Samuel's position is consonant with the position of the E source regarding Abraham's sacrifice, and is consonant with the Deuteronomistic position generally, in which sacrificial ritual is necessary, but is relatively less valued than obedience to God's commandments. This is in line with what Moshe Weinfeld characterized as the "secularizing trend," perhaps derived from scribal wisdom traditions, in Deuteronomic literature.[11]

The wisdom books, as scholars have noted, have a relatively low view of ritual. But, as I have indicated, this view is more in line with the "obedience is better" position than a rejection of the value or efficacy of ritual. In other words, ritual is *doxa* in wisdom literature too, even if it is not a particular focus of wisdom instruction. Alexander Ernst has recently made a strong case that the critique of cult in wisdom literature is presupposed by the eighth-century prophets.[12] This may be so, but I would suggest that the wisdom critique is milder than he indicates, and is consonant with Samuel's (Deuteronomistic) position in 1 Sam 15. The two strongest examples from Proverbs are the following:

> The sacrifice of the wicked is an abomination to Yhwh
> And the prayer of the upright is his pleasure. (Prov 15:8)
>
> Doing justice and righteousness
> is more acceptable to Yhwh than sacrifice. (Prov 21:3)

The poetic antithesis of sacrifice and right behavior, as above, serves to draw a scale of values in which righteousness is higher than sacrifice. Sacrifice as such is explicitly acceptable to Yhwh, but doing justice and righteousness is *more* acceptable (*nibḥār*, lit. "choicer"). In the first proverb, being wicked overcomes the value of sacrifice, while in the antithetical parallel line, a lesser rite—prayer—is the more valuable because its offerer is upright. This does not differ from the sense of Samuel's judgment.

---

11. Moshe Weinfeld, *Deuteronomy and the Deuteronomic School* (Oxford: Clarendon, 1972), 190–243; see further Ernest Nicholson, "Deuteronomy's Vision of Israel," in *Storia e tradizioni di Israele: Scritte in onore di J. Alberto Soggin* (ed. D. Garrone and F. Israel; Brescia: Paideia, 1991), 191–203, which draws on Mary Douglas's theory of antiritualism.

12. Ernst, *Weisheitliche Kultkritik*.

In these proverbs, I suggest, the *doxa* of sacrifice still goes without saying. Its self-evident truth serves as a standard that allows the sage to exalt the higher imperative of moral behavior. In the intensity of its rejection of all rituals—including sacrifices, hymns, and festivals—the poetic judgment in Amos 5 is of a different order. To be sure, the people are wicked, but ritual practice falls off of Yhwh's scale of values altogether. He now "hates" the rites and "rejects" them. The antithesis, doing justice and righteousness, is not *more* acceptable than sacrifice, but is the *only* acceptable practice. If Amos is aware of this wisdom stance, he radicalizes it utterly.

Theory and Practice of Antiritualism

Amos's rejection of the ritual practices of his contemporaries is seconded by later preexilic prophets. Isaiah's denunciation of rituals in Isa 1:10–17—including festivals, sacrifice, and prayer—contains echoes of the diction of Amos 5:21–24.

ḥodšêkem ûmôʿădêkem	14 Your new moons and your set festivals
śānĕʾâ napšî	My soul hates.
hāyû ʿālay lāṭōraḥ	They have become a burden to me,
nilʾêtî nĕśōʾ	I am weary of bearing them.
ûbĕpāriśkem kappêkem	15 And when you stretch out your hands (in prayer),
ʾaʿlîm ʿênay mikkem	I hide my eyes from you.
gam kî tarbû tĕpillâ	Though you increase prayer,
ʾênennî šōmēaʿ	I do not hear.

The combination of Yhwh's "hate" (*śnʾ*) with his privation of senses—"I hide my eyes," "I do not hear"—seems to reprise the rhetoric of Amos 5.[13]

---

13. On the relationship between these two texts, see Ernst, *Weisheitliche Kultkritik*, 161–68; Paul, *Amos*, 189; and H. G. M. Williamson, *A Critical and Exegetical Commentary on Isaiah 1–27*, vol. 1: *Commentary on Isaiah 1–5* (ICC; London: T&T Clark, 2006), 84–85.

The repetition of the suffix "your" (*-kem*, plural) five times in two verses, some in quick succession ("your new moons and your set festivals," "your stretching out of your hands")—also recalls the rhetoric of interrogation in the Amos oracle. Isaiah's audience is called into this denunciation, and finally exhorted to practice justice instead of rituals:

ḥidlû hārēaʿ	16 Cease to do evil,
limdû hêṭēb	17 Learn to do good.
diršû mišpāṭ	Seek justice,
ʾaššĕrû ḥāmôṣ	Set right the ruthless.
šipṭû yātôm	Judge the orphan,
rîbû ʾalmānâ	Plead for the widow.

The rapid-fire repetition of these six terse commands, with the internal rhyme of the second-person plural imperative (with the echoing vowel sequence: *i–û*),[14] makes plain the verdict on the people. Rather than their worthless ritual practices, Yhwh requires the practices of social justice.

Similar passages in Hosea, Micah, and Jeremiah indicate that these prophetic figures and books (it is often hard to make a firm distinction) share a family relationship on this issue.[15] They seem to agree that the ritual practices of their contemporaries are worthless. Each makes a strong contrast between ritual and ethics, such that the *doxa* of ritual is not only brought into question, but is rejected in contrast to the ethical virtues that Yhwh requires. This strong binary contrast between ritual and ethical practices is a striking feature of these prophetic texts.

Commentators tend to regard this stance as either a revolutionary idea or a rhetorical exaggeration. Nineteenth-century scholars tended to praise these texts as sharing (and inspiring) the spirit of Martin Luther thundering against the "dead works" of Catholicism, or Paul disavowing the burden of biblical ritual. After the Second World War, chastened by the

14. The imperative *ʾšrw*, "set right," here vocalized *ʾaššĕrû*, is elsewhere vocalized *ʾiššĕrû*, which arguably is the preferred vocalization here.

15. Hosea 6:6; 8:13; Mic 6:6–8; Jer 6:19–21.

consequences of this (often explicitly anti-Semitic) position, the scholarly consensus shifted to viewing these texts as rhetorical indulgences, which chastened the Israelites for immoral behavior but did not reject ritual practices as such. This domestication of the prophetic voice was soothing for postwar ecumenical tastes. Joseph Blenkinsopp's comments in his handbook, *A History of Prophecy in Israel*, are representative of this view:

> The idea of anyone in eighth century B.C.E. Israel rejecting worship as such in favor of a purely spiritual and ethical religion is, however, quite implausible. Rather, the point seems to be that worship was (as it still is) a very powerful way of legitimating the current political and social status quo. Quite simply, Amos was not taken in by the religiosity of his contemporaries.[16]

The sense of these texts is taken as a rejection not of ritual practice as such but of the corrupt political establishment that used such practices as a way of legitimating its power. This is an ingenious explication of the texts, drawing on a neo-Marxist theory of religion, but is in my view an ameliorating reading that fails to do justice to the texts. There is no obvious reason to think that the texts do not mean what they plainly say. As John Barton aptly responds to this interpretation: "Maybe the sinfulness of the worshippers makes the sacrifices *worse* than useless, but essentially they are useless anyway. The heart of religion consists instead in right social interaction."[17] And as Thomas Krüger similarly comments: "These thoughts are unusual in their radicality in the framework of the ancient Near East; however, these texts scarcely allow us to understand them in

16. Joseph Blenkinsopp, *A History of Prophecy in Israel* (2nd ed.; Louisville: Westminster John Knox, 1996), 80–81; for similar statements see Rainer Albertz, *A History of Israelite Religion in the Old Testament Period* (trans. John Bowden; 2 vols.; OTL; Louisville: Westminster John Knox, 1994), 1:171: "Amos, Micah and Isaiah fundamentally reject the cultic practice of their time because it covers up the social injustice and misery in society"; and recently Bryan D. Bibb, "The Prophetic Critique of Ritual in Old Testament Theology," in *The Priests in the Prophets: The Portrayal of Priests, Prophets and Other Religious Specialists in the Latter Prophets* (ed. Lester L. Grabbe and Alice O. Bellis; JSOTSup 408; London: T&T Clark, 2004), 34: "Although Amos, Isaiah and Jeremiah denounce the cult of Israel and question its original authority, they surely are not calling for the elimination of ritual practice, are they? How could they envision a world without cult and ritual?"

17. Barton, "Prophets and the Cult," 121.

any other sense."[18] It is hard to maintain that the texts are mere rhetorical denunciations, and that they do not reject the customary rites of religious practice. In other words, it is difficult to assimilate them to the terms of Samuel's denunciation of Saul in 1 Sam 15 (see above).

The extremity of these preexilic prophetic texts should be more widely acknowledged, and we should refrain from domesticating them for modern ecumenical sensibilities. I concur with Barton that "the nineteenth-century scholars who first saw clearly that the prophets had been revolutionary in their turning away from the sacrificial cultus thus seem … in essence to have been right."[19] The prophets did step outside the *doxa* of their contemporaries and cast these conventional habits into radical doubt. But they did not step outside their century or culture altogether. As Mary Douglas's theory of antiritualism suggests, they had different habits, different social relations, that enabled them to see these *doxa* in a different light.

As Barton recommends, "For theoretical consideration I go, as Old Testament scholars do in times of need, to the work of Mary Douglas, and especially to her *Natural Symbols* (1970)."[20] As I have argued previously, Douglas's theory of antiritualism is well suited to elucidating the antiritual perspective of these prophetic texts.[21] Douglas's theory illuminates the "concordance between symbolic and social experience" that is conducive to a position of antiritualism in any culture—whether in ancient Israel or in modern tribal societies.[22]

Douglas's thesis is that certain ways of construing symbols—including the embrace and rejection of ritual—tend to vary according to the background rules of social life. That is, the social context makes certain ways of thinking about symbols seem natural. She writes: "Each social form and its accompanying style of thought restricts the self-knowledge of the individual in one way or another."[23] This is a theory of how the *doxa*,

18. Krüger, "Erwägungen," 47.

19. Ibid., 121.

20. Ibid., 117.

21. See n. 1 above.

22. Mary Douglas, *Natural Symbols: Explorations in Cosmology* (2nd ed.; New York: Random House, 1973). Douglas discusses antiritualism in several modern tribal societies, including the Navajo peyote cult, Mbuti pygmies, Nuer and Dinka pastoralists, and the Basseri nomads of Persia. She also discusses, with less sympathy, the antiritualism of 1960s youth culture and post–Vatican II Catholic clergy.

23. Ibid., 174.

the unquestioned propositions of everyday life, can differ among societies or among segments of a particular society. This type of analysis has deep roots in sociological and anthropological discourse, with an intellectual genealogy that includes Montesquieu's *On the Spirit of the Laws* (1748), Émile Durkheim's *Division of Labor in Society* (1893), and Max Weber's *Protestant Ethic and the Spirit of Capitalism* (1905). Douglas refines this field of inquiry by proposing a detailed typology of social forms and their corresponding "natural" or "self-evident" styles of thought.

She argues that antiritualism is a natural perspective for agents in a social field with lax rules of behavior and porous group boundaries. In Douglas's terms, this is a social field with "low grid" (viz., lax rules of behavior) and "low group" (viz., porous group boundaries). From the clues one can glean from their eponymous books, the social interactions of Amos, Hosea, Isaiah, and Jeremiah belong to this type. There are few constraints on prophetic behavior in these books, and there are few boundary conditions for their social position. Regarding their behavioral rules, Hosea marries a prostitute, Isaiah goes naked for three years, Amos threatens a royal priest, and Jeremiah wears an ox yoke and continually provokes the royal court. Clearly their behavior is improvisational and independent of habitual norms. Regarding their group boundaries, Amos famously denies the role of "prophet" (*nābîʾ*), although he does admit that Yhwh called him to "prophesy" (*hinnābēʾ*, Amos 7:14–15). To echo Buckminster Fuller (another radical individual), Amos views his social identity as a verb rather than a noun. In Max Weber's terminology, the prophet achieves his status as a result of personal charisma, by persuading others that one hears Yhwh's word. In other words, to be a prophet is an achieved, not an ascribed, status. The classical prophets are, as Weber observed, intellectuals, political demogogues, and pamphleteers (and I would add, poets) who stood aslant from conventional social rules and roles.[24]

In contrast, the role of priest, soldier, or king in ancient Israel was an ascribed status—it depended on one's place in a clearly defined hierarchy, which classified its members according to ascribed criteria such as birth and seniority. These individuals derive their social authority from what Weber calls "office charisma" (*Amtscharisma*), which is the inverse of the prophets' personal charisma. The mechanism of office charisma is a fixed

24. Max Weber, *Ancient Judaism* (trans. Hans H. Gerth and Don Martindale; Glencoe, Ill.: Free Press, 1952), 267.

system independent of the individual, whereas personal charisma is a willed agency of the individual, involving persuasion and negotiation. The biblical text knows of prophets who derive some portion their authority from office charisma (e.g., Nathan in the court of King David), or who are members of prophetic groups (*běnê hanněbîʾîm*, "the sons of the prophets" in 2 Kgs 2, presumably disciples of Elijah), or who are cultic officials (what scholars call the "cultic prophets").[25] However, the protagonists of the preexilic prophetic books are not members of these groups. Amos explicitly seems to dissociate himself from these groups when he says, "I am not a prophet or a prophet's disciple (*ben nābîʾ*)" (Amos 7:14). In their writings, as Barton observes, "[t]he classical prophets … refer disparagingly to 'the prophets' as a group distinct from themselves."[26]

As the examples of Amos, Isaiah, and Jeremiah particularly attest, to be a prophet (with the qualification that this is not their self-designation) one must have a transformative inner experience, with God's speech heard like a lion's roar (Amos 1:2; 3:8), or like a fire burning in one's heart (Jer 20:9). Isaiah has a vision that initiates him into his new identity by a near-death experience in the heavenly temple (Isa 6). These are not people who inhabit offices with strict rules of initiation and decorum. Their social relations are aptly characterized, in Douglas's terms, as low group and low grid.

Having established the loose grip of institutional rules on these classical prophets, let us consider the characteristic features of antiritualism that tend to seem self-evident from this social location. Douglas observes that this social position, which tends to produce "alienation from the current social values," correlates with the following biases: "a denunciation not only of irrelevant rituals, but of ritualism as such; exaltation of the inner experience and denigration of its standardized expressions; preference for intuitive and instant forms of knowledge; rejection of mediating institutions, rejection of any tendency to allow habit to provide the basis of a new symbolic system."[27]

This configuration of what Douglas calls "cultural bias" is aptly illustrated by the writings of the preexilic classical prophets. Each of these

25. See John W. Hilber, *Cultic Prophecy in the Psalms* (BZAW 352; New York: de Gruyter, 2005).

26. Barton, "Prophets and the Cult," 118.

27. Ibid., 40.

features may be discerned in another illustrative text, from Isaiah of Jerusalem:

wayyōmer 'ădōnāy[28]	13 My Lord said:
ya'an kî niggaš[29] *bĕpîw*	Because they approach me with their mouths,
ûbiśĕpātāyw kibbĕdûnî	and with their lips they honor me,
wĕlibbô riḥaq mimmennî	but their hearts they distance from me;
wattĕhî yir'ātām 'ōtî	and their worship of me
miṣwat 'ănāšîm mĕlummādâ	is a human commandment that is taught;
lākēn hinĕnî yôsīp	14 therefore I am going to multiply
lĕhaplî' haplē' wāpele'	wonderful and terrible wonders.
wĕ'ābĕdâ ḥokmat ḥăkāmāyw	And the wisdom of their wise shall perish,
ûbînat nĕbōnāyw tistattār	and the intelligence of their intelligent ones shall be hidden. (Isa 29:13–14)

Douglas's first trait, "denunciation not only of irrelevant rituals, but of ritualism as such," is clear in this text. The key line is in verse 13: "and their worship of me / is a human commandment that is taught." This critique of Israelite religious practice perhaps goes beyond the texts considered above by explicitly labeling these religious practices as human cre-

28. Some MSS read *yhwh*, which may be original, but 1QIsa[a] and the older MT codices read *'dny*. For textual issues, see Hans Wildberger, *Isaiah 28–39* (trans. Thomas H. Trapp; CC; Minneapolis: Fortress, 2002), 86–87.

29. Bracketing *hā'ām hazzeh* ("this people") in vv. 13 and 14 as an explicating gloss. The phrase conflicts with the plural verbs and suffixes in v. 13b, and without it the poetry is balanced and characteristically artful, especially v. 14: *lĕhaplî' haplē' wāpele'*.

ations. The phrase *yir'ātām 'ōtî*, "their worship [lit. 'fear'] of me," is God's rendering of the familiar expression, "fear of God," which denotes religious virtue. In the parallel line, this phrase is unpacked in two parts—it is "a commandment of humans," not a commandment of God, and it is something "that is taught" (by humans), not revealed by God. This is a shocking exegesis of the forms of Israelite worship. The rituals are worthless because they are human creations, taught by humans and not by God. This is a powerful indictment of the origin and insignificance of the practices of Israelite worship.

While it is clear that some of these denunciations of ritual are aimed at the wealthy class, who are guilty of oppressing the poor, there is no hint that the rituals of the poor or the just are exempt from this critique. Appeals to the memory of the wilderness period, when there was no ritual practice, argue against this supposition. For instance, a prose addendum in Amos 5:25 clarifies the scope of the preceding poetic oracle (vv. 17–24): "Did you offer me sacrifices and grain gifts in the wilderness for forty years, O house of Israel?" The redactor who added this prose expansion (which may possibly be a citation of Amos) clearly understood the prophet's position to be a denunciation of ritual as such.

Douglas's second trait, "Exaltation of the inner experience and denigration of its standardized expressions," is also evident in this text. The first poetic tricolon is key: "Because they approach me with their mouths, / and with their lips they honor me, / but their hearts they distance from me." The parallelism from "their mouths" to "their lips," which progressively narrows the focus on their external organ of speech, is contrasted in the third line with "their hearts." The standardized expressions of hymns and prayer, mouthed by the people's lips, is opposed to their inner experience. With external standard expressions "they approach me," but their interior experience "they distance from me." These vivid contrasts and inversions create a classic statement of the primacy of inner experience over standardized ritual practices.

In these preexilic prophetic texts, the goal is interior perception of God's word—what Hosea calls "knowledge of God" (*da'at 'ĕlōhîm*, Hos 4:1; 6:6; etc.), which produces a life of ethical deeds and purpose. No standardized expressions of this knowledge are acceptable other than doing what is right and just. The book of Jeremiah accordingly speaks of a circumcision of the heart (Jer 4:4), and of a "new covenant," which Yhwh will inscribe within the people's hearts (30:31–34). With this new interior perception of God's word, "all of them will know me, from the least to the greatest, declares Yhwh" (31:34). With these texts, the exaltation of individual interiority becomes a key religious virtue.

Douglas's third trait, a "preference for intuitive and instant forms of knowledge," is supported by the self-authenticating source of these classical prophetic oracles: God's voice. The prophet's knowledge is intuitive and instant—it comes directly from a perception of God's divine words, unmediated by preparatory rituals or other procedures. This seems to distinguish the classical prophets from the prophetic state produced by music and other rites in the depictions of the "ecstatic" prophets of 1 Sam 10:5 and 1 Kgs 18:26–29, or in the sacrificial rites that accompany Balaam's prophecies in Num 23. The classical prophets perceive God's word directly, as if they "have stood in the council of Yhwh / and heard my word" (Jer 23:22). The valorization of direct and unmediated knowledge of God naturally inclines the prophets to mistrust conventional ritualized forms of sacred knowledge.

Douglas's fourth trait, a "rejection of mediating institutions, rejection of any tendency to allow habit to provide the basis of a new symbolic system," is evident in the rejection of traditional worship and even traditional wisdom: "And the wisdom of their wise shall perish, / and the intelligence of their intelligent ones shall be hidden" (v. 14). Mediating institutions are castigated, whether based on the wisdom of sages and counselors, the ritual knowledge of priests, or the oracles of the conventional prophets. Hosea goes so far as to denounce the institution of kingship: "They made kings, but not by me" (Hos 8:4). As noted above, Amos refuses to call himself a prophet—he rejects identification with any mediating institution. Isaiah and Jeremiah treat with kings, and so they implicitly grant the king institutional authority. But they consistently denounce the existing social institutions as morally corrupt, particularly the religious mediators, the priests and prophets. In Isaiah's memorable depiction, the priests and prophets are worthless drunks:

kōhēn wĕnābîʾ šāgû baššēkār	Priest and prophet stagger from strong drink,
niblĕʿû min hayyayin	they are confused [lit. "swallowed"] by wine.
tāʿû min haššēkār	They reel from strong drink,

šāgû bārōʾeh	stagger in seeing,
pāqû pĕlîlîyâ	totter in judgment.
kî kol šulḥānôt mālĕʾû qîʾ	For all their tables are full of vomit,
ṣōʾâ bĕlî māqôm	filth, without any place left. (Isa 28:7–8)

The graphic rejection of the priests and prophets in this poem is unequivocal. They are filthy drunks—their bodies totter and leak; they are out of control, they create vomit and filth rather than right judgments. In Douglas's terms, they *are* dirt, people out of place. The natural symbol of the body becomes a vehicle to express their corrupt status. As a consequence of their shameful stupor—in which they "totter in judgment" both literally and figuratively—the prophet and priest are stripped of their legitimacy. As commentators note, this critique may reflect an actual occasion of revelry, but the implications go beyond the particular moment to a general—and bitingly satirical—indictment of these standard institutions.

In sum, the social and conceptual traits of antiritualism that Douglas diagnoses are clearly exemplified in the words and behaviors of the classical prophets. Their denunciation of the ritual *doxa* of their time is a radical departure from the norm, in part because their practices and social status depart from the norm. They see differently because they inhabit a social and conceptual space that provides the possibility of seeing differently. Their critique encompasses more than sacrifice—it includes the religious institutions of prophets and priests, and the panoply of ritual practices and objects, including cultic sites and iconography (extending to the Jerusalem temple; see Jer 7). Whether their contemporaries understood what they said is another question. What is clear is that the views they first articulated became a basis for subsequent conceptualizations of religion, ritual, and social ethics in biblical and postbiblical traditions. In other words, they invented the conceptual lenses that have since become, at least in part, our *doxa*.

Conclusions

It is important to emphasize that the antiritualism of these preexilic prophets is consonant with their critique of the ills of contemporary society, without it being reducible to a rhetorical reflex of the latter. That is, we should assume that they meant what they said and wrote, even if the implications were novel or radical at the time. We should not domesticate prophetic speech to suit our modern ecumenical tastes. They were in their day (and perhaps remain in our day) religious radicals and eccentrics.[30]

At the same time, as Douglas emphasizes, "Ritual and anti-ritual are the idiom which natural systems of symbols afford for acting out theories of society."[31] The critical discourse of these prophets about ritual is of a piece with their critical discourse about society. Whereas those with ascribed authority will naturally be conservative with respect to habitual practices and institutions, the classical prophets, with their distinctive mode of personal authority, embraced a utopian ideal of a just society, where people only seek what is good. This utopian view of a society of moral individuals provides the seedbed of the utopian eschatological future, which is—primarily in postexilic times—written into these prophetic books.[32] That is, their antiritualism is wedded to their theory of an ideal society, which is nurtured by their own social contexts as independent and relatively unfettered moral agents. The consonance between these prophets' form of life and their style of thought yields a utopian vision of a society in which ritual symbols are no longer needed.[33] With the simple practice of justice, the people will walk in the "way of Yhwh" and will "know Yhwh." Of course, their books include other visions of the future that are more dystopic, involving irreversible judgment and destruction. But antiritualism persists, which, in Douglas's words, "reject[s] … any tendency to allow habit to provide the basis of a new symbolic system."

It is difficult for biblical scholars to accommodate a theory that situates the prophets in a conceptual-causal nexus that involves their social status

---

30. Hence the mocking epithet *měšuggāʿ* ("crazy one," Hos 9:7; Jer 29:26; 2 Kgs 9:11).

31. Barton, "Prophets and the Cult," 179.

32. See Ronald Hendel, "Isaiah and the Transition from Prophecy to Apocalyptic," in *Birkat Shalom: Studies in the Bible, Ancient Near Eastern Literature, and Postbiblical Judaism Presented to Shalom M. Paul* (ed. Chaim Cohen et al.; Winona Lake, Ind.: Eisenbrauns, 2008), 261–79.

33. See Baruch Halpern's suggestive remarks on the epistemology of the preexilic prophetic critique ("'Brisker Pipes than Poetry': The Development of Israelite Monotheism," in *Judaic Perspectives on Ancient Israel* [ed. Jacob Neusner, Baruch A. Levine, and Ernest S. Frerichs; Philadelphia: Fortress, 1987], 96): "The prophetic critique [was] based on the isolation of the symbol from the represented reality."

and behavioral norms. We are accustomed to read their texts as theological discourse, unmoored from the conditions that made their discourse thinkable. The chief reason that we do this is that their words remain a part of our *doxa*, the furniture of our implicit knowledge, which is difficult to question. I submit that Douglas's theory of cultural bias provides a vocabulary that opens up this conceptual space. Her theory shows that the classical prophets were speaking from a particular situation, which in some respects resonates with the individualist social forms and assumptions of our modern culture. That is, we share many of the biases of the classical prophets, in part because they invented some of the conditions of our thought. Prophets such as Amos and Jeremiah were arguably architects of the "individual," in whom religion is primarily an interior ethical disposition. The literary legacy of these biblical writers has shaped our own sense of self, through their canonical texts and through such later intermediaries as Augustine, Dante, Luther, Montaigne, and Spinoza.

The classical preexilic prophets' forms of social life informed their perspective on the *doxa* of customary ritual practice, precisely because their social forms were already at variance with the social forms of the majority. They could call these habits into question because they saw them as habits, and not as the self-evident basis of everyday life. Their everyday life was different, and so they could see these practices differently. Through their poetic discourse they defamiliarized these habits, and, for those who could see and hear (e.g., their followers and support groups) they exposed these practices as "mere" conventions. Once a customary practice is exposed as a convention, it is no longer *doxa*. It becomes subject to question and debate. An inevitable implication of Douglas's theory is that we are forced to turn to our own concordances of social forms and styles of thought, to discern our own conceptual and cultural biases—as she says, to "make the process visible." This is a refinement not only of Durkheim and Weber, but also, more distantly, of the critical practice of the preexilic prophets.

"They Have Become Women": Judean Diaspora and Postcolonial Theories of Gender and Migration*

T. M. Lemos

"I am an Oriental. And being an Oriental,
I could never be completely a man."
—*M. Butterfly*[1]

"How rich our mutability, how easily we change (and are changed) from one thing to another, how unstable our place—and all because of the missing foundation of our existence, the lost ground of our origin, the broken link with our land and our past."
—Edward Said, *After the Last Sky*[2]

"et il est place pour tous au rendez-vous de la conquête
et nous savons maintenant que le soleil tourne
autour de notre terre éclairant la parcelle qu'a fixé
notre volonté seule et que toute étoile chute de ciel

---

* Jeremiah 51:30 reads: "The warriors of Babylon have ceased from fighting, they remain in their strongholds. / Their strength has failed, they have become women." (Translations are my own unless otherwise noted.) As we shall see, this verse seems rather ironic in light of Ezekiel's portrayal of the conquered Israelites.

I thank Brent Nongbri, Andrea Stevenson Allen, Chaya Halberstam, and William Danaher for their helpful comments on earlier versions of this essay, as well as those present at the Moskow Symposium held at Brown University—both fellow participants and audience members—who made suggestions and comments about the paper.

1. Quoted in David L. Eng, *Racial Castration: Managing Masculinity in Asian America* (Durham, N.C.: Duke University Press, 2001), 1. The author of the play is David Henry Hwang; the character who is speaking here is Song Liling.

2. Edward Said, *After the Last Sky: Palestinian Lives* (2nd ed.; New York: Columbia University Press, 1999), 26.

en terre à notre commandement sans limite."
—Aimé Césaire, *Cahier d'un retour au pays natal*[3]

Postcolonial studies is, one might say, distinctly a product of our contemporary period of empires in decline and fallen, of decolonization, migration, and globalization. At the same time, postcolonial studies, with its revival of interests historical and diachronic, transcends the contemporary moment, attending to a wide set of interests, problems, and cultural settings. Postcolonial studies, for roughly three decades now, has been so popular in certain academic disciplines as to seem at times faddish; it perhaps even approaches the status of *passé*. Despite this, it is really only since the mid-1990s that biblical scholars have begun to utilize ideas put forth by postcolonial theorists.[4] One might ask, however, what we as biblical schol-

3. Quoted in Said, *Culture and Imperialism* (New York: Vintage, 1994), 231.

4. Though the time period is short, one might nonetheless say that there has been an explosion of work done in this area. Daniel Smith-Christopher has been particularly prolific. See Smith-Christopher, "The Book of Daniel," in *The New Interpreter's Bible* (ed. Leander E. Keck; Nashville: Abingdon, 1996), 7:17–152; idem, "Ezekiel on Fanon's Couch: A Postcolonialist Critique in Dialogue with David Halperin's *Seeking Ezekiel*," in *Peace and Justice Shall Embrace: Power and Theopolitics in the Bible* (ed. Ted Grimsrud and Loren L. Johns; Telford, Pa.: Pandora, 1999), 108–44; idem, "Prayers and Dreams: Power and Diaspora Identities in the Social Setting of the Daniel Tales," in *The Book of Daniel: Composition and Reception* (ed. John J. Collins and Peter W. Flint; 2 vols.; VTSup 83; Leiden: Brill, 2001), 1:266–90; idem, "Ezekiel in Abu Ghraib: Rereading Ezekiel 16:37–39 in the Context of Imperial Conquest," in *Ezekiel's Hierarchical World: Wrestling with a Tiered Reality* (ed. Stephen L. Cook and Corrine L. Patton; SBLSymS 31; Atlanta: Society of Biblical Literature, 2004), 141–58; idem, *A Biblical Theology of Exile* (Minneapolis: Fortress, 2002). See also various essays in R. S. Sugirtharajah, *Voices from the Margins: Interpreting the Bible in the Third World* (3rd ed.; Maryknoll, N.Y.: Orbis, 2006; the first edition was published in 1991), though this volume is more focused on how the Bible is interpreted in "Third World" and postcolonial contexts than on applying ideas from postcolonialism to the study of ancient Palestine. This is generally the case, too, for the other volumes authored or edited by Sugirtharajah. Exceptions can be found in Sugirtharajah, ed., *The Postcolonial Biblical Reader* (Malden, Mass.: Blackwell, 2006), namely, the essays by Richard A. Horsley, Jon L. Berquist, and Werner H. Kelber. Horsley has written or edited other works relevant to this topic, as well, e.g., *Paul and Empire: Religion and Power in Roman Imperial Society* (Harrisburg: Trinity Press International, 1997); "Subverting Disciplines: The Possibilities and Limitations of Postcolonial Theory for New Testament Studies," in *Toward a New Heaven and a New Earth: Essays in Honor of Elisabeth Schüssler Fiorenza* (ed. Fernando F. Segovia; Maryknoll, N.Y.: Orbis, 2003), 90–105; *In*

ars really have to gain from this area of inquiry. Could studying French colonials or African refugees really tell us something about the Israelites? While I will say at the outset that I think this type of comparative study can contribute a great deal to our discipline, one must nonetheless be cautious—we must not assume that every idea or hypothesis from cultural studies in general or postcolonial studies in particular is applicable to the investigation of ancient peoples. What controls should we apply to the use of such theories, what methodological constraints should we establish?[5] In this paper, I will begin with an examination of these questions of method, and then proceed to discussing certain postcolonial ideas about empire, migration, and gender that I think can be responsibly and profitably utilized by ancient historians. Finally, I will consider two different responses to the problems of masculinity in an exilic or diaspora setting, those of the book of Ezekiel and the later book of Daniel.

Methodological Considerations

I have noticed two major trends operative in biblical studies in the years in which I have been involved in this area of research, and both are in my view unfortunate. On the one hand, one sees what might be characterized as an unselfconscious, or at times even knee-jerk, defensive modernism and, on the other, an overly enthusiastic and at times seemingly voguish embracing of postmodern theories of culture. Lost in these two extremes is the "militant middle ground," as Michael Herzfeld puts it, "a space that at

the Shadow of Empire: Reclaiming the Bible as a History of Faithful Resistance (Louisville: Westminster John Knox, 2008); and *Revolt of the Scribes: Resistance and Apocalyptic Origins* (Minneapolis: Fortress, 2010). The engagement of Stephen D. Moore with postcolonial "theories" is quite explicit in *Empire and Apocalypse: Postcolonialism and the New Testament* (Sheffield: Sheffield Phoenix, 2006), which contains an extremely useful and very extensive annotated bibliography of works in postcolonial studies and those in biblical studies that have made use of postcolonial ideas. His list is not exhaustive, however—the works of Smith-Christopher are not included, nor is Roger Bagnall's essay, "Decolonizing Ptolemaic Egypt," in *Hellenistic Constructs: Essays in Culture, History, and Historiography* (ed. Paul Cartledge, Peter Garnsey, and Erich Gruen; Berkeley: University of California Press, 1997), 225–41.

5. Bagnall addresses these issues also in "Decolonizing Ptolemaic Egypt." His treatment is useful, but is different from mine in various ways. For broader discussions of historiographical method, see Bagnall's very helpful work, *Reading Papyri, Writing Ancient History* (Approaching the Ancient World; New York: Routledge, 1995).

once is strongly resistant to closure and that is truly grounded in an open-ended appreciation of the empirical," one that occupies "a skeptical distance from the solipsistic extremes, the Scylla and Charybdis, of modern sociocultural theory: postmodernism and positivism in their more dogmatic excesses."[6] Part of this absence of a qualified, sophisticated empiricism in biblical studies is due, I believe, to the tendency, long afoot in this area of the academy, to trumpet historicism while at the same time rather carelessly executing the norms of modernist historiography. In short, one cannot carry out a qualified modernism made aware of itself without considering what modernist standards were in the first place.

This being so, it seems worthwhile to begin with a discussion of these standards as I comprehend them. Let me make clear that I am not advocating for a return to modernist historiography, nor am I labeling myself either a modernist or a historical positivist. I only seek to outline here what traditionalist standards of historiography were or are in order to discuss the relationship of biblical studies to these standards, as well as to consider how postcolonial studies relates to them. That said, in describing these traditional standards, one must consider first the following question: What are the expectations of modernist historiography as they relate to a scholar's use of evidence? Certain evidentiary standards are, of course, absolutely central to this historiography, and these revolve around having, ideally, a preponderance of evidence, corroboration of sources, a range of type of sources, a range of perspective of sources, and the ability to interrogate directly the sources available. That is, one needs to have a certain amount of evidence before drawing a conclusion about something for that conclusion to be seen as persuasive or even plausible. One needs to have sources that in some way corroborate each other in order to responsibly draw said conclusion. One ideally would like to have many different types of evidence (material, literary, legal, visual, etc.), and one would like to have sources that come from different social or political groups in order to be able to strengthen the corroboration of sources and thus one's conclusion. It is all the better if one can directly interrogate the reliability of these sources, if one can go to a place to gauge the accuracy of a description, if one can ask a source what he or she meant by thus-and-such, and if one can bear witness directly to a political, historical, or cultural event.

6. Herzfeld, *Anthropology: Theoretical Practice in Culture and Society* (Malden, Mass.: Blackwell, 2001), x; and *Cultural Intimacy: Social Poetics in the Nation-State* (2nd ed.; New York: Routledge, 2005), 39–41.

No historical positivist would call any of this into question. Yet, despite the tendency toward positivism in our discipline, it has been very rare for the work of biblical scholars to fulfill these norms. Part of this is that, for scholars of the ancient world, some of these norms present impossible standards—we cannot ask an Israelite priest what he meant about whatever verse in Leviticus, nor can we travel to Solomon's temple to gauge whether the splendorous description of it in Kings is accurate. Nor do we generally have the preponderance of evidence or the range of evidence for events or social or cultural phenomena that would be expected for a modern historian. These norms, if strictly upheld by biblicists, would leave us all very much hamstrung. We cannot, however, extol the virtues of positivism[7]—as I often hear biblicists and ancient historians do—and then let these norms completely fall away due to the impossibility of our keeping them. If one is a positivist historian, then one should keep to these standards as much as possible and be honest when sufficient evidence is lacking. And we have very often failed to do this. Think of source criticism. For decades, certain positions on dating and source division went unchallenged, as did the source-critical enterprise as a whole, despite the fact that so much of the work on sources would not conform to modernist historiographical standards of preponderance of and corroboration of evidence.[8] I think we must be honest with ourselves about this. The situation with redaction criticism is very much the same.

This brings me to postmodernism in biblical studies, a trend that has unfortunately brought not real caution nor a consistent employment of methodological constraints but rather an embracing of historiographical pessimism and sometimes even an overall abandonment of evidentiary standards. If I may be allowed a moment of melodrama for the sake of a field I care so deeply about: it is as if a herd of wild mustangs has gone trampling through an admittedly already arid plain, and the quest to understand the Israelites, a group that did, after all, actually exist, has been stamped down by so many galloping postmodernist hooves. Since

7. Though biblicists do not generally refer explicitly to "positivism," when they advocate for traditional approaches, it is almost always a historical positivism that they have in mind.

8. A notable exception is found in Joseph Blenkinsopp, *The Pentateuch* (ABRL; New York: Doubleday, 1992), 111–18, where he speaks with justifiable caution about what one might hope to achieve through source criticism.

"evidence" and "objectivity" are concepts ever to be encapsulated by quotation marks and a figment of the modernist imagination besides, we are necessarily on firmer ground alleging that there were no Israelites except quotation mark Israelites, whose history cannot be perfectly known and is thus completely unknowable, and no biblical text save the one received by us, whose authors cannot be known perfectly and thus whose intentions are only dishonestly studied.[9]

This characterization of postmodernism in biblical studies may seem exaggerated, and perhaps it is. What I am characterizing is the worst of postmodernism in our field, not the work of those who use postmodernism in a way that moves biblical studies toward a greater sophistication and refinement of method. It bears noting, too, that though I do not agree with the stances I have just outlined, I concede that these trends have arguably had a less pernicious effect on biblical studies than has the resistance of some scholars in our field to methodological progress of any sort. How, then, is a biblical scholar to address this situation of extremes? Biblical scholars, I believe, need to think more about methods, about our own standards, and about our own objectives. Are we, as individual biblicists, primarily historians? Then we should set historiographical standards for ourselves and keep to them. Are we primarily literary scholars, or philologists, or theologians? Then we should be familiar with the accepted standards of literary studies, of linguistics, or of philosophy, and stick to those.[10] As a social and cultural historian, I will speak in this essay to other biblicists who consider themselves social historians about how I think we can make use of cultural studies in general and postcolonial studies in particular.

---

9. One could say that the occasional and unselfconscious solipsism of modernists is thus replaced by the self-conscious solipsism of postmodernists, which as Terry Eagleton and others have pointed out, fits strikingly well with the self-centered consumerist agenda of our amoral, globalizing times. See Eagleton, *Literary Theory: An Introduction* (2nd ed.; Minneapolis: University of Minnesota Press, 1996), 204–5; and *Illusions of Postmodernism*, 14, 132–35. Even cursory introductions to postmodernism comment upon postmodernism's being "passively conservative in effect"; see Christopher Butler, *Postmodernism: A Very Short Introduction* (Oxford: Oxford University Press, 2002), 61.

10. This is not to say, I want to make clear, that one cannot utilize various methodologies in one's work, but one must be aware of the danger of using multiple methods poorly if one is not aware of what one's *primary* goals are.

We ancient historians have a fundamental problem that we must ever keep in mind and that is the problem of evidence or, to be more precise, our lack of evidence. The ethnographic methods of anthropologists and anthropological historians are impossible for us, and apart from this, we often just do not have enough evidence to make claims in a responsible fashion. How do we deal with this? We can: (1) pretend the problem does not exist and proceed in willfully ignorant bliss; (2) look toward cross-cultural evidence and social-scientific models to fill in the gaps; and (3) look toward postmodern theories to relativize the gaps, or erase the gaps, or celebrate the gaps.[11] Of these three options, I feel very strongly that the second is our best one, and I feel this way for several reasons. Again, let us consider traditional evidentiary standards. Imagine that there is a scientist who wishes to understand how a new surgical procedure will affect the human heart. The scientist cannot just try out this method on human patients willy-nilly and will thus confront the problem of incomplete evidence. Should she theorize based on the very small sample of human patients she might have at her disposal or merely on her generalized understanding of how the human heart works? No, because scientific standards would not allow for this. Clearly, the scientist would not merely pretend that she has sufficient evidence for how the procedure might affect patients, but will instead run simulations. This idea of the simulation, I think, has been somewhat forgotten by biblicists, and I would like to revive it. Continuing with the scenario of the medical researcher, this scientist, based upon her knowledge of human anatomy, would find herself another animal whose anatomy is similar to humans, and she would perform surgeries on that animal in order to gauge how the human heart might be affected by this procedure. In this way, she would expand her base of evidence—yes, imperfectly, but also significantly. For a historian, our analogous species are cross-cultural historical and ethnographic data. We must find societies that have similar social and cultural features to the Israelites and carefully examine the evidence from those societies as a simulation in order to expand, imperfectly but significantly, our base of evidence for studying ancient Israel. If we are to use explanatory schemata in this endeavor, then we should use primarily social-scientific models rather than cultural theories because these models are expected to be based upon a preponderance of evidence from a wide range of societies. We should,

11. I thank Brent Nongbri for the wording here.

however, be ready to critique these models and should not employ them without a good degree of caution.[12]

What is the problem with "theory," one might ask?[13] It is at times the case that postmodern theory is not evidentiary in basis but rather the result of semiphilosophical ruminations. This fact by itself does not necessitate that one entirely dismiss theory, for even the theory that is most divorced from modernist evidentiary standards can be "good to think with," if you will.[14] But I do believe that the theorists whose works are based more on historical or ethnographic evidence provide a sounder foundation. Two examples are Michel Foucault and Pierre Bourdieu. Although Foucault's uses of history and historical evidence have been criticized by some, the fact is that Foucault did very frequently cite historical evidence.[15] Bourdieu goes even further toward fulfilling evidentiary standards, one might say. As an anthropologist, he drew upon the ethnographic evidence he himself compiled, as well as upon historical data.[16] I think it questionable to dismiss the work of these theorists out of hand unless one dismisses *all* interdisciplinary or cross-cultural research.

All of this carries through to postcolonial studies. At its worst, postcolonial studies is like the worst of postmodernist theory more generally. As Terry Eagleton puts it, "[Postcolonial theory's] language has too often betrayed a portentous obscurantism incongruously remote from the

12. As others have stated, as well, e.g., Bagnall, "Decolonizing Ptolemaic Egypt," 228.

13. I use the term *theory* here in the cultural studies sense of the term, rather than in its strict scientific sense, which has unfortunately been forgotten by many in the humanities.

14. I refer, of course, to Claude Lévi-Strauss's famous statement that animals are "good to think with" (*bonnes à penser*). See *Totemism* (trans. Rodney Needham; Boston: Beacon, 1963), 89.

15. See, for instance, *Discipline and Punish: The Birth of the Prison* (trans. Alan Sheridan; 2nd ed.; New York: Vintage, 1995; original French ed. 1975), which utilizes a good number of both primary and secondary sources. The same is true of *The Birth of the Clinic: An Archaeology of Medical Perception* (trans. A. M. Sheridan Smith; New York: Pantheon, 1973; original French ed. 1963).

16. Among other works, see *Outline of a Theory of Practice* (trans. Richard Nice; Cambridge: Cambridge University Press, 1977; original French ed. 1972); *The Logic of Practice* (trans. Richard Nice; Stanford: Stanford University Press, 1990; original French ed. 1980); *Distinction: A Social Critique of the Judgement of Taste* (trans. Richard Nice; Cambridge: Harvard University Press, 1984; original French ed. 1979), where Bourdieu bases his analysis upon surveys of over twelve hundred people.

peoples it champions."[17] It sometimes appears that postcolonial thinkers are surprisingly uninterested in asking the subalterns of whom they write what they might feel about their own marginality, that they would rather assert the silence of the subaltern than actually attempt to give that subaltern a voice.[18] Biblical scholars are right to be suspicious of this, but it is not what postcolonial studies is in its entirety. At its best, postcolonial studies has from its inception jarred both postmodernism and anthropology into looking actively again toward the historical and diachronic. This field affirms the centrality of historical circumstances to the construction of human societies and human subjects in a way that even the most diehard of modernists should applaud. And in its treatment and examination of historical evidence from imperialist, colonialist, and postcolonialist settings, we find an abundance of comparative data for the proposed simulations that I feel we as ancient historians must run. I also believe that ethnographic studies performed by anthropologists with colonial and postcolonial interests should perhaps be the single most important source of comparative data for us in studying the conquered peoples of the ancient world. This is because anthropology as a discipline has never abandoned or retreated from a focus on evidence and because anthropologists have the benefit of being able to make use of methods such as observation, interviewing, and conversation that we as ancient historians are simply unable to utilize.

Postcolonial Studies, Gender, and Migration

But, one might ask, what specific emphases or insights from postcolonial studies might we profitably draw upon in studying ancient Israelite experiences of exile and diaspora? The options are manifold, but as this is ostensibly an essay focusing on issues of gender, I shall speak to that topic specifically. Even in the classic postcolonial works dating to a half century ago,

17. Eagleton, *Literary Theory*, 206.

18. The postmodern theorist Gilles Deleuze has written: "Reality is what actually happens in a factory, in a school, in barracks, in a prison, in a police station." Yet Deleuze was not actively engaged in the study of those places, nor, it seems, are some of the most prominent postcolonial writers. (The quote is found in Gayatri Chakravorty Spivak, "Can the Subaltern Speak?" in *Marxism and the Interpretation of Culture* [ed. Cary Nelson and Lawrence Grossberg; Champaign: University of Illinois Press, 1988], 275.)

one sees important discussions of gender-related topics. These works have in fact been critiqued for assuming a male colonized subject.[19] There is often an androcentrism or even a sexism in these works. An example may be found in Frantz Fanon's *Black Skin, White Masks*, in which Fanon is much more sympathetic toward the male colonized individual who yearns for sex with a white woman than he is toward black or mulatta women who seek white male lovers. Of these women, he speaks in fact with derision, while he clearly sees himself in the reverse scenario (and unsurprisingly so considering the realities of his life). Yet, despite the sexist or androcentric underpinnings of these early works' treatments of gender, they are nonetheless useful and point toward what later more sophisticated or openly feminist works have confirmed—the central role of sexuality in colonial contexts as a tool of domination, negotiation, and resistance.[20] These classic works and other more recent ones also suggest that women in colonial contexts are sometimes offered paradoxically more freedom of action than in precolonial or postcolonial ones, as they may have the opportunity to navigate between the norms of their own culture and that of their colonizers.[21] This is in contrast to postcolonial settings, where nationalist discourses are almost always deeply gendered, presenting a controlling male subject as the idealized citizen of the nation-state; the female is a citizen only in so far as she conforms to traditionalist norms that may have never existed in so rigid a form in the past, but which nationalism retrojects and molds in its exercises of discursive and highly "selective nostalgia."[22]

---

19. This is quite apparent in Albert Memmi's *The Colonizer and the Colonized*, for instance.

20. Among others, see Frantz Fanon, *Black Skin, White Masks* (trans. Charles Lam Markmann; New York: Grove, 1967), particularly chs. 2 and 3; Anne McClintock, *Imperial Leather: Race, Gender, and Sexuality in the Colonial Contest* (New York: Routledge, 1995); several of the essays in Anne McClintock, Aamir Mufti, and Ella Shohat, eds., *Dangerous Liaisons: Gender, Nation, and Postcolonial Perspectives* (Minneapolis: University of Minnesota Press, 1997); and works by Ann Laura Stoler, particularly *Carnal Knowledge and Imperial Power: Race and the Intimate in Colonial Rule* (Berkeley: University of California Press, 2002).

21. See, for example, Robert J. C. Young, *Postcolonialism: A Very Short Introduction* (Oxford: Oxford University Press, 2003), 97. McClintock describes this negotiation in more negative terms, however (*Imperial Leather*, 6). Stoler, *Carnal Knowledge*, 57, is also relevant.

22. Eric J. Hobsbawm uses the phrase "selective nostalgia" in *On Empire: America, War, and Global Supremacy* (New York: Pantheon, 2008), 7, though he speaks there of

Nationalism and rigid, patriarchal gender norms have very frequently gone hand in hand.[23]

This relates also to the realities of gendering in diasporic contexts. These contexts are frequently multiethnic, and men in particular must negotiate ethnic hierarchies of manhood that they may have never had to confront in their native lands.[24] This being so, and with assimilating forces threatening the stability of migrants' identities on every side, gender ideals become only more rigid, forming as it were a symbolic barricade against cultural encroachment. Women's bodies become the battleground for fighting against acculturation and against the cultural hegemony of more socially dominant groups. In these contexts, violence against women can even increase as men project the frustrations of the masculine demotions

---

the nostalgia of the nation-states that were once imperial powers for their more glorious pasts. See also the essays in Eric Hobsbawm and Terence Ranger, eds., *The Invention of Tradition* (Cambridge: Cambridge University Press, 1983); Hobsbawm, *Nations and Nationalism since 1780: Programme, Myth, Reality* (Cambridge: Cambridge University Press, 1990); and Jean Pickering, ed., *Narratives of Nostalgia, Gender, and Nationalism* (New York: New York University Press, 1997). Patricia Waugh writes on nostalgia and postmodernism in "Modernism, Postmodernism, Feminism: Gender and Autonomy Theory," in *Postmodernism: A Reader* (ed. Patricia Waugh; London: Edward Arnold, 1992), 189–204, esp. 191–92. The work of Michael Herzfeld is also relevant here; see *Cultural Intimacy*, esp. ch. 7 on "structural nostalgia."

23. In addition to works cited above, see Andrew Parker et al., eds., *Nationalisms and Sexualities* (New York: Routledge, 1992); Sita Ranchod-Nilsson and Mary Ann Tetrault, eds., *Women, States, and Nationalism: At Home in the Nation?* (London: Routledge, 2000); Lata Mani, "Contentious Traditions: The Debate on SATI in Colonial India," *Cultural Critique* 7 (1987): 119–56; Geraldine Heng and Janadas Devan, "State Fatherhood: The Politics of Nationalism, Sexuality, and Race in Singapore," in *The Gender/Sexuality Reader: Culture, History, Political Economy* (ed. Roger N. Lancaster and Micaela di Leonardo; New York: Routledge, 1997), 107–21; Young, *Postcolonialism: A Very Short Introduction*, 97; Rowena Robinson, "Boundary Battles: Muslim Women and Community Identity in the Aftermath of Violence," *Women's Studies International Forum* 33 (2010): 365–73; and others.

24. See Raymond Hibbins and Bob Pease, "Men and Masculinities on the Move," in *Migrant Men: Critical Studies of Masculinities and the Migration Experience* (ed. Mike Donaldson, et al.; New York: Routledge, 2009), 1–20, esp. 2, 11; R. W. Connell, *The Men and the Boys* (Berkeley: University of California Press, 2000), esp. 10–11, 48–50, 61, 161–62; idem, *Masculinities* (2nd ed.; Berkeley: University of California Press, 2005), xvii–xviii, xxii, 80–81, 166–67, 197–98, 264; Charlotte Hooper, "Masculinities in Transition: The Case of Globalization," in *Gender and Global Restructuring: Sightings, Sites, and Resistances* (London: Routledge, 2000), 62–64, 70.

they often experience in diasporic settings upon their wives, daughters, and sisters.[25] These women are expected to attest to their husbands' or fathers' masculine respectability by resisting acculturation into societies that in some cases would offer them a wider range of life choices, not to mention sexual and marriage partners from groups that are often presented as more desirable and more masculine than the partners available in their own ethnic communities. Men in these contexts frequently expect to maintain the dominance they could exert over women in their home societies[26] or even increase that dominance as they struggle to compensate

---

25. See Hibbins and Pease, "Men and Masculinities," 5; Ruth M. Krulfeld, "Changing Concepts of Gender Roles and Identities in Refugee Communities," in *Reconstructing Lives, Recapturing Meaning: Refugee Identity, Gender and Culture Change* (ed. Linda A. Camino and Ruth M. Krulfeld; Basel: Gordon and Breach, 1994), 71–74; Lucia Ann McSpadden, "Negotiating Masculinity in the Reconstruction of Social Place: Eritrean and Ethiopian Refugees in the United States and Canada," in *Engendering Forced Migration: Theory and Practice* (ed. Doreen Indra; New York: Bergahn, 1999), 242–60, esp. 252–53; Aylin Akpinar, "The Honour/Shame Complex Revisited: Violence against Women in the Migration Context," *Women's Studies International Forum* 26 (Sept./Oct. 2003): 425–42. Akpinar writes, "I would argue that keeping control of 'their space' by controlling 'their women' can compensate for feelings of powerlessness for some immigrant men" (435). Scott Poynting, Paul Tabar, and Greg Noble, "Looking for Respect: Lebanese Immigrant Young Men in Australia," in *Migrant Men*, 135–53, esp. 148–49, is also quite germane. Fatemeh Farahani, "Diaporic Narratives on Virginity," in *Muslim Diaspora: Gender, Culture, and Identity* (ed. Haideh Moghissi; New York: Routledge, 2006), 186–204, discusses the role of brothers in Iranian culture. Brothers are expected to help parents guard daughters against being shamed—or shaming themselves. Nonetheless, some brothers choose to diverge from this expectation and help their sisters "exercis[e] more freedom" (199). She writes: "Some women mentioned that they could meet boyfriends, go to parties or engage in political activities … by having their brothers as escorts when they wanted to do something 'inappropriate'" (199).

26. See, for example, Atsuko Matsuoka and John Sorenson, "Eritrean Canadian Refugee Households as Sites of Gender Renegotiation," in *Engendering Forced Migration*, 218–41, though they also discuss cases where men and women have different relationships than they would have in their home nation, e.g., ones in which men sometimes take on "feminine" responsibilities, such as household chores or child care, out of necessity. Unsurprisingly, there is some variation in how men (and women) respond to the realities of a new cultural and social environment. However, what generally occurs is that women continue to be responsible for all tasks gendered as feminine, in addition to working or taking on whatever roles they must in these new environments. At the same time, they are expected to act in accordance with traditional mores: "In general, the use of public space by diaspora women continues to be

for the loss of social status they generally experience in a new situation.[27] Women in these settings might, however, give the lie to the myth of male agency and female passivity by using their sexuality to negotiate privileges and a higher status for themselves.[28] Fanon's disapproval notwithstanding, women in colonial, postcolonial, and diasporic contexts are not always good girls, good wives, or good citizens of nationalist communities.[29]

But do these generalizations, drawn as they are from societies many centuries and in some cases many thousands of miles distant from the ancient Israelites, apply to the study of the latter group? On the one hand, such phenomena as transnational corporations, globalization in its modern forms, and even the nation-state as one finds it today were nonexistent in the ancient world. On the other, imperialism, warfare, migration, multiethnic communities, acculturation, and negotiation of status were all realities in the ancient world, just as they are today.[30] In addition, while the gen-

---

circumscribed by the direct exertion of control by men and through rumor, gossip, and innuendo" (227).

27. See Anne Altolppa-Niitamo, "From the Equator to the Arctic Circle: A Portrait of Somali Integration and Diasporic Consciousness in Finland," in *Rethinking Refuge and Displacement* (ed. Elżbieta M. Goździak and Dianna J. Shandy; Selected Papers on Refugees and Immigrants 8; Arlington, Va.: American Anthropological Association, 2000), 53; and McSpadden, "Negotiating Masculinity." Matsuoka and Sorenson, "Eritrean Canadian Refugee Households," remark that many Eritrean men "experienced a sharp loss of status." This is because a large number of Eritrean refugees who settled in Canada had been upper class and/or highly educated in their native land, but in Canada were sometimes unemployed or forced to hold menial positions (233, 235).

28. Stoler discusses this occurrence in colonial contexts (*Carnal Knowledge*, 57, and elsewhere).

29. Albert Memmi states in *Decolonization and the Decolonized* (trans. Robert Bononno; Minneapolis: University of Minnesota Press, 2006) that the daughters of immigrants are sometimes "wilder than the boys, freer with respect to religion and tradition: they have nothing to lose but their chains" (113). Matsuoka and Sorenson write that "a few young women stated that they regarded wage employment [in the country to which they had migrated] as an opportunity that would allow them to live independently, with less supervision from relatives" ("Eritrean Canadian Refugee Households," 227). See also Farahani, "Diasporic Narratives on Virginity." Also relevant is the collection of stories by Shahrnush Parsipur, *Women without Men* (trans. Kamran Talattof and Jocelyn Sharlet; New York: Feminist Press at the City University of New York, 2004).

30. I discuss the negotiation of status at greater length in "'Like the Eunuch Who Does Not Beget': Gender, Mutilation, and Negotiated Status in the Ancient Near East,"

eralizations made above are based on studies of a variety of time periods and cultural settings, much of the research I cite here was performed upon social groups analogous to the exiled Israelites in some specific way, for example, on migrants from cultures in which honor and shame are concepts of pivotal importance, or on migrants whose social status was high in their countries of origin but whose status dropped significantly when they became refugees.[31] Although it is clear that ancient historians must be careful in utilizing the analyses of postcolonial theorists and scholars of migration, to jettison all of them would be going too far. Doing so would eliminate for us a major way to address the fundamental problem of insufficient evidence that forever plagues us as biblicists—comparison with the modern societies that are so much more easily studied and to which we ourselves have direct access.[32] In the discussions of the books of Ezekiel and Daniel that follow, I will therefore endeavor to apply many of the ideas I summarize above. In a longer work, I would not merely summarize the evidence from modern societies, but would examine several case studies in detail; but in an essay of this length, my treatment must be abbreviated and focus merely on generalities. It is an imperfect method, but, in my view, still preferable to the alternative of limiting ourselves to evidence from the ancient Israelites or even from the ancient Near East as a whole.

Shame, Masculine Hierarchies, and the Book of Ezekiel

That said, let me turn now to discussing two different biblical texts in a postcolonial vein, beginning with the book of Ezekiel.[33] Ezekiel was

---

in *Disability and Biblical Studies* (ed. Candida Moss and Jeremy Schipper; New York: Palgrave Macmillan, 2011), 47–66.

31. To be more specific, I have cited, among other works, studies performed upon Turkish, Arab, Eritrean, and Ethiopian migrants. Migrants from the last two groups tended to be refugees and to be from upper-class backgrounds; yet very few were able to attain initially (or at all) employment as professionals in the United States or Canada and consequently suffered a steep decline in status as they were forced to take on jobs they considered menial and beneath their dignity. Racism in these countries also contributed to this loss of status.

32. Indeed, the inspiration for my comments below on masculine competition in multiethnic contexts came from my own experiences growing up in a multiethnic environment, watching and participating in the gender and cultural negotiations that transpired.

33. Of course, there is, strictly speaking, nothing postcolonial about the book

not just a migrant but an exile, a "refugee,"[34] and what has always struck me most about this book—and struck others, as well—is the almost palpable concern over masculine honor.[35] Postcolonial works refer again and again, sometimes offhandedly but quite consistently, to the shame, the humiliation experienced by the conquered *and* the migrant.[36] This

---

of Ezekiel. But it is the product of an imperialist and a diaspora setting, and "postcolonial studies" is at this point a catch-all phrase, it seems, for the study of imperialism, colonialism, and postcolonialism strictly speaking. As Bart Moore-Gilbert states, postcolonial studies is "preoccupied principally with analysis of cultural forms which mediate, challenge, or reflect upon the relation of domination and subordination … between (and often within) nations, races, or cultures" (*Postcolonial Theory: Contexts, Practices, Politics* [New York: Verso, 1997], 12; quoted in Smith-Christopher, "Prayers and Dreams," 268). I use the term *postcolonial studies* broadly here to refer even to migration studies, which often relate to and discuss decolonization in some way and quite frequently assess relations of domination and subordination between nations, cultures, and ethnic groups.

34. As Smith-Christopher has rightfully emphasized; see "Ezekiel in Abu Ghraib," esp. 148–49.

35. See also my treatment in "Shame and Mutilation of Enemies in the Hebrew Bible," *JBL* 125 (2006): 225–41, esp. 239–40; and "The Emasculation of Exile: Hypermasculinity and Feminization in the Book of Ezekiel," in *Interpreting Exile: Interdisciplinary Studies of Displacement and Deportation in Biblical and Modern Contexts* (ed. Brad E. Kelle, Frank R. Ames, and Jacob L. Wright; SBLAIL 10; Atlanta: Society of Biblical Literature, 2011), 377–93. Others who have commented on expressions of honor and shame in the book include Julie Galambush, *Jerusalem in the Book of Ezekiel: The City as Yahweh's Wife* (SBLDS 130; Atlanta: Scholars Press, 1992), 105–9, 161; Margaret S. Odell, "The Inversion of Shame and Forgiveness in Ezekiel 16:59–63," *JSOT* 56 (1992):101–12; Renita J. Weems, *Battered Love: Marriage, Sex, and Violence in the Hebrew Prophets* (Minneapolis: Fortress, 1995), 96–98; Johanna Stiebert, *The Construction of Shame in the Hebrew Bible: The Prophetic Contribution* (JSOTSup 346; London: Sheffield Academic, 2002), esp. 132–64; idem, *The Exile and the Prophet's Wife: Historic Events and Marginal Perspectives* (Collegeville, Minn.: Liturgical Press, 2005); and S. Tamar Kamionkowski, *Gender Reversal and Cosmic Chaos: A Study on the Book of Ezekiel* (JSOTSup 368; London: Sheffield Academic, 2003). However, not all of these authors emphasize the sense of shame of the *author* of the book of Ezekiel.

36. See, for example, Memmi, *Colonizer and Colonized*, x, xii, 121; idem, *Decolonization and the Decolonized*, 90–95, 133; Fanon, *Black Skin, White Masks*, 116; idem, *Wretched of the Earth* (trans. Richard Wilcox; foreword by Homi K. Bhabha; preface by Jean-Paul Sartre; New York: Grove, 2004), 87, 219, 242, and Sartre's preface, l–li; Said, *Culture and Imperialism*, 18, 210; idem, *After the Last Sky*, 121; Poynting, Tabar, and Noble, "Looking for Respect"; Akpimar, "Honour/Shame Complex Revisited"; and Julie M. Peteet, "Transforming Trust: Dispossession and Empowerment among

would be particularly pronounced for someone like Ezekiel.[37] Ezekiel was not just any Israelite man but a priest in the Jerusalem temple. In his preexilic existence, he was a member of one of the most honored classes in his society. His status was based not merely on his masculinity, but on his bloodlines and his social role. The humiliation of conquest for him and others like him, then, was not your garden-variety humiliation. Ezekiel's world was turned upside down in various ways, and one of the most central was, one gathers from a close reading of his writings, that he experienced a rapid and extreme drop in status—from honored Israelite priest to dishonored Israelite captive, marched into exile, living among his conquerors as their inferior.[38] Even if his immediate community in Babylon might have been composed primarily of Israelites, it was only those Israelites to whom all of these generalizations applied—the once elite, now vanquished, the once honored, now humiliated. One can only speculate upon what Ezekiel had to endure on his long march to Babylon, but examining the evidence for the Babylonian conquest and that of ancient Near Eastern warfare more generally, the options are

---

Palestinian Refugees," in *Mistrusting Refugees* (ed. E. Valentine Daniel and John Chr. Knudsen; Berkeley: University of California Press, 1995), 168–86, esp. 168, 179.

37. One of the major questions raised by the study of the book of Ezekiel is whether the prophet Ezekiel in fact authored the book and spoke of his own experiences, how much of the book he authored, or even whether a historical personage named Ezekiel existed at all. As one can infer from my treatment here, I do see Ezekiel as having been a real Judean man living in exile in Babylon. The trauma of the author seems so much at the surface that it is hard for me to believe that anyone apart from an exiled man could have written such texts as Ezek 8–10, 16, 23, and especially the discussion of Ezekiel's wife's death in ch. 24. However, because we have no other texts apart from the book itself that might corroborate the existence and life story of the prophet Ezekiel, anything that we can say about the relationship of the man Ezekiel to the book of Ezekiel is unfortunately based purely in speculation.

38. Corrine L. Patton makes a similar point in "'Should Our Sister Be Treated Like a Whore?': A Response to Feminist Critiques of Ezekiel 23," in *The Book of Ezekiel: Theological and Anthropological Perspectives* (ed. Margaret S. Odell and John T. Strong; SBLSymS 9; Atlanta: Society of Biblical Literature, 2000), 229, saying that the book of Ezekiel "is told from the perspective of a once-elite member of society who has been dragged off in chains to an unclean land, who sits powerless, 'dumb,' as his nation is destroyed and his world turned upside down." Gale A. Yee, *Poor Banished Children of Eve: Woman as Evil in the Hebrew Bible* (Minneapolis: Fortress, 2003), 116, writes too that "all deportees suffered a radical reduction of the elite status they possessed when they governed in Judah."

not pretty. Second Kings 25:6–7 relate to us that when the Babylonians defeated the rebellious Judean king Zedekiah, they not only destroyed Jerusalem and its temple, but slew the sons of Zedekiah in his very presence, then gouged out his eyes.[39] Other biblical texts refer to large-scale slaughter and to starvation so dire that it drove parents to consume their own children.[40] Not only Mesopotamian, but Egyptian and even Israelite accounts of warfare boast of dismembering conquered enemies, of displaying their body parts as trophies of war.[41] The archaeological evidence is consonant with the biblical and extrabiblical sources, confirming that destruction was widespread throughout Judah at this time and that the population of the region was diminished to far below what it had been previously.[42] In light of all of this, it is almost certain that Ezekiel saw countless horrors on his way to Babylon. And he, the once proud minister to Yhwh, the prophet, a man of name, was powerless to do anything. While we do not know exactly what Ezekiel endured, there is no doubt that his experience with exile was traumatizing; his trauma is clear in the book he left to us.[43] But let us pause to see in this trauma the terrible

39. See also Jer 39:6–7.

40. See, e.g., Lam 2:20; 4:10. Deuteronomy discusses the cannibalism of children by their own parents in 28:54–57, perhaps with the conditions following the Babylonian conquest of Jerusalem in mind. Yee provides a reasonable description of what those in Jerusalem in all likelihood underwent at the hands of the Babylonians (*Poor Banished Children of Eve*, 114–16).

41. I discuss this phenomenon in "Shame and Mutilation of Enemies."

42. See B. Oded, "Where Is the 'Myth of the Empty Land' to Be Found? History versus Myth," in *Judah and the Judeans in the Neo-Babylonian Period* (ed. Oded Lipschitz and Joseph Blenkinsopp; Winona Lake, Ind.: Eisenbrans, 2003), 55–74; T. M. Lemos, *Marriage Gifts and Social Change in Ancient Palestine: 1200 BCE to 200 CE* (Cambridge: Cambridge University Press, 2010), 200–203; among other works.

43. On the trauma of Ezekiel, see Daniel Smith-Christopher, "Reassessing the Historical and Sociological Impact of the Babylonian Exile (597/587–539 BCE)," in *Exile: Old Testament, Jewish, and Christian Conceptions* (ed. James M. Scott; JSJSup 56; Leiden: Brill, 1997), 7–36; idem, "Ezekiel on Fanon's Couch," esp. 134–44; idem, *Biblical Theology of Exile*, 89–94; David G. Garber Jr., "Traumatizing Ezekiel, the Exilic Prophet," in *Psychology and the Bible: A New Way to Read the Scriptures*, vol. 2: *From Genesis to Apocalyptic Vision* (ed. J. Harold Ellens and Wayne G. Rollins; Praeger Perspectives: Psychology, Religion, and Spirituality; Westport, Conn.: Praeger, 2004), 215–35; Brad E. Kelle, "Dealing with the Trauma of Defeat: The Rhetoric of the Devastation and Rejuvenation of Nature in Ezekiel," *JBL* 128 (2009): 469–90; and Nancy Bowen, *Ezekiel* (Nashville: Abingdon, 2010), esp. xv–xix, 209–10.

weight of dishonor, which postcolonial writings encourage us to bring to the forefront of our analysis. Bruises and scars in most cases fade over time, but the dishonor of living among those who conquered you, your very presence in that distant land attesting to your weakness, and unable ever to exact vengeance for yourself—that dishonor, it seems, did not fade in the mind of Ezekiel.

This dishonor instead became so central to Ezekiel's worldview that he theologizes it, projects it onto Yhwh, and portrays himself and others like him in the most lowly and degraded fashion, as whores who necessarily deserved the savage treatment that they underwent. In Ezek 16 and 23 the prophet presents his version of the marriage metaphor in which Yhwh is husband to a wayward, adulterous Jerusalem. Jerusalem's adultery represents the city's cultic infidelity, her flagrant worship of other deities. Just as Jerusalem publicly shames her husband Yhwh by her actions, so Yhwh must act publicly to restore his honor by bringing a harsh punishment against her. One finds in Ezek 16 the following passage: "I am gathering all your lovers with whom you felt pleasure, all those you loved and all those you hated; I will gather them against you from all around, and I will uncover your nakedness to them, so that they will see all your nakedness. I will judge you with the judgments of adulteresses and women who shed blood. … I will deliver you into their hands … and they will strip you of your clothes and take your beautiful objects and leave you stark naked. They will bring against you a mob, and they will stone you and cut you to pieces with their swords. They will burn your houses with fire and execute judgments against you in the sight of many women. Thus I will stop you from whoring yourself out" (16:37–41). In Ezek 16 and in the similar passage in Ezek 23, the word "whore" or some variant of it is applied to Jerusalem no fewer than twenty-eight times. And in Ezek 23 one reads of Jerusalem's nose and ears being cut off for her infidelities and of her children being seized and her survivors being "devoured by fire." There too Jerusalem is stripped naked, her lewdness met with lewdness.

Ezekiel was the victim here—sometimes biblical scholars, particularly those with feminist interests, seem to forget this. He expressed his victimhood in the most misogynistic and violent of terms, but it is at base a self-hatred he is expressing. He is like a battered wife who writes an account from the perspective of her husband, telling us, the reader, how much she deserves to be beaten. It is surprising how often readers of Ezekiel either excuse the husband or vent anger and disgust at the author, forgetting that the battered wife *is* the author.[44] It is true that Ezekiel, as a prophet, was a medium for Yhwh and that Yhwh's perspective and voice took hold of him bodily and came forth from him. In this way, he could inhabit the dominant position of the husband.[45] In fact, Ezekiel was called to be a prophet only in Babylon, after he was exiled, and this calling offered him perhaps a way of subverting his loss of status by claiming instead the voice of the mighty God of Israel.[46] Still, I think it imperative in reading this book that we not overlook that Ezekiel's primary experience, the experience with which his oracles wrestle and the one with which he dealt day after day, was that of having been conquered and of living in exile as a humiliated man.

But we may probe deeper, I think, into Ezekiel's masculine humiliation using another concept discussed in postcolonial writings and also works on migration, and that is the idea of masculine hierarchies. This concept should be obvious to anyone who has lived in the United States. These hierarchies are not rigid and are variously constructed and oftentimes even conflicting as cultural and socioeconomic groups with different ideals of masculinity come together, awkwardly projecting their standards onto others and negotiating their place in the hierarchy. To give an example, it is well known that East Asians frequently fall to the bottom of the ladder, due to both actual and perceived physical differences. Their emasculation is also attributed to certain cultural features, such as a supposed passivity and excessive deference to parental authority. One could speak, too, about the very ambivalent position of the hypermasculinized black male in this hierarchy or the position of working-class men, but I think my point is sufficiently clear.[47]

Returning to the Israelite exiles, it is important to emphasize that it is not that the Israelites found themselves living in a culture that held very different standards of masculinity from their own, necessitating that they

44. Patton, "Should Our Sister," also draws attention to Ezekiel as victim. She suggests that Ezekiel might have even been the victim of sexual violence at the hands of the Babylonians.

45. As Chaya Halberstam noted to me.

46. Robert R. Wilson's comments in *Prophecy and Society in Ancient Israel* (Philadelphia: Fortress, 1980), 70–71, are relevant here.

47. I discuss the hypermasculinization of black men in somewhat more detail in "Like the Eunuch." One of the many works that discuss this phenomenon is Lynne Segal, *Slow Motion: Changing Masculinities, Changing Men* (London: Virago, 1990), primarily ch. 7, on "Black Masculinity and the White Man's Black Man."

reconcile their ideas with the other group's. It is rather a situation in which the Israelites and Babylonians held what seem to me to be strikingly similar conceptions of manhood. Indeed, from examining biblical texts of various genres, as well as Assyrian and Babylonian royal inscriptions, reliefs, literary works such as the Epic of Gilgamesh, law codes, and even treaty curses, we can see that there were certain masculine ideals that were widely held in the ancient Near East. These ideals trumpeted a warrior masculinity tied to honor and conquest, physical prowess and physical attractiveness, control over one's household and particularly the women in one's household, and yes, fidelity to one's gods, gods who themselves were frequently presented as hypermasculine.[48] The Israelites and Babylonians were in agreement concerning what was masculine, and, according to these shared ideals, the Israelites were found wanting—they could no longer fulfill their own standards of masculinity.[49] Even worse, they were forced to live among a group who realized their Israelite standards better than they could. After all, the Babylonians were the ones who fulfilled the ideal exemplified by a figure like David—they were the conquering warriors, displaying piety toward and bringing honor to their own gods, their wives and children safe at home as they molested and enslaved the wives and children of the Israelites, burning the temple of the Israelite god to the ground.

One sees this greater masculinity of the Babylonians and even the Egyptians expressed in Ezek 16 and 23. There Yhwh is the good, kind husband, who saves Jerusalem and lifts her up from rejection to respectability; but she, so whorish and shameless, turns away from him to the well-dressed Assyrians, "warriors clothed in deep blue, all of them desirable young men, horse-riding cavalry" (23:5–6). She then lusts after the Chaldeans, whose

48. For an excellent discussion of Assyrian conceptions of masculinity, see Cynthia R. Chapman, *The Gendered Language of Warfare in the Israelite-Assyrian Encounter* (HSM 62; Winona Lake, Ind.: Eisenbrauns, 2004).

49. Yee, *Poor Banished Children*, 127, states that Ezekiel internalizes the Babylonians' presentation of themselves. I see the matter rather differently, for even biblical texts that predate the rise of the Neo-Babylonians display ideas of masculinity quite similar to those of the Babylonians (and Assyrians). In my view, placing value on a warrior masculinity tied to honor and conquest is one example of a cultural trait that the Israelites and Mesopotamians held in common. Of course they held other traits in common, though one should guard oneself against the mistaken impression that all the cultures of the ancient Near East constituted a seamless *Kulturkreis*. See my discussion in *Marriage Gifts and Social Change*, 1–16.

masculinity is so alluring that she desires them merely after seeing images of them: "She increased her whoring when she saw men graven upon the wall, images of Chaldeans engraved in crimson, belts on their loins, flowing turbans on their heads, with the appearance of chariot warriors all of them" (23:14–15). And let us not forget the lovers of her youth, the Egyptians, whose masculine appeal was even more carnal in nature to the young, hormonal Jerusalem, who could not resist the Egyptians' animal sexuality and animalized sexual members.[50] This woman Jerusalem had found herself in a multiethnic context. She had a set of choices. She could choose the path of respectability, dutifully staying with her husband. This would allow her to maintain her social status *in a certain way*. But there was another choice that also would bring with it status implications not wholly negative. Perhaps some Judean women, like the Babylonians, would have seen their conquered husbands as weak and dishonored. They could stay with them and maintain respectability among their own kind, but what does respectability even mean among a deeply humiliated people? They might be better off becoming concubines of Babylonian men, who if not in actuality more physically strapping than their Israelite husbands, certainly would tower above them in status. I am obviously speculating here about how exiled Judean women might have thought or acted. Yet the documents from Āl-Yāhudu, despite being in the early stages of publication and difficult to interpret in some ways, nonetheless do seem to provide limited evidence that a few decades after the exile, some women of Judean extraction *were* marrying foreign men.[51] Ezekiel's fears were not empty ones, perhaps. Even if he is ostensibly talking about Yhwh and Jerusalem, and cultic infidelities

50. See Ezek 23:19–21, which famously refers to the donkey-like phalluses and horse-like ejaculate of the Egyptians, as well as 16:26, which calls them *gidlê bāśār*, a phrase meaning "great of flesh," but which the NRSV translates euphemistically as "lustful." This is just one example of many where the NRSV translation essentially expurgates the MT of the book of Ezekiel. The most glaring perhaps is 16:36, where *nĕḥuštēk* is translated as "your lust" rather than "your genital fluid."

51. See particularly BM 68921/BMA no. 26 (BM 65149), the marriage contracts of a woman with a Judean father to a Babylonian with a surname and thus a respectable social status; Kathleen Abraham, "West Semitic and Judean Brides in Cuneiform Sources from the Sixth Century BCE: New Evidence from a Marriage Contract from Āl Yahudu," *Archiv für Orientforschung* 51 (2006): 198–219; and Lemos, *Marriage Gifts and Social Change*, 237–44, esp. 241–42. These works also discuss marriage contracts involving women whose ethnic background is somewhat unclear, but who were of "West Semitic" origin and possibly Judean. One of these women, [f]Nanaya-kānat,

rather than actual ones, and though his concerns were certainly theological, I argue that one should see them as being at least as centered on the Israelite exiles' lowered social status and loss of masculine privilege. This loss is so pronounced in the mind of the prophet that, in Ezek 16 and 23, the Israelites have in fact become a woman.

Daniel and Diasporic Emasculation

Let us fast-forward to the book of Daniel. While the dating of the court tales of this book is still uncertain, whether these tales were written in the Persian period or the Hellenistic is seemingly immaterial to our purposes.[52] Persian or Hellenistic, these tales date many generations after the time of Ezekiel. The apocalyptic portion of the book is of course even later. By that point, the Judeans who still lived outside Judah were used to living in a diasporic context, and Judeans as a group were well accustomed to living in an imperialistic setting. This is reflected in the book's gender ideals, which are subtly expressed, a fact that prima facie distinguishes them from those of the book of Ezekiel. Whereas in Ezekiel we saw a personality wracked by trauma and struggling to make sense of the most pressing theological and social questions, a shattered psyche, in the court tales of Daniel we hear more subtle strains of disquiet. The position of Daniel and his relations to and with his overlords are textbook colonialism—the character expresses and seems to feel real loyalty toward his rulers,[53] yet at the same time the author seemingly longs for a radical change in status, longs for the humiliation of the king to replace his own, longs for a day when the mountain cut not by human hands will fill—will rule—the whole earth.[54] The author seeks not an end to imperialism but rather to stand

seems to have married a man "from the lower class urban Babylonian families" (Abraham, "West Semitic and Judean Brides," 211).

52. See John J. Collins, *Daniel: A Commentary on the Book of Daniel* (Hermeneia; Minneapolis: Fortress, 1993), 13–18, 26–38, 47; idem, "Current Issues in the Study of Daniel," in Collins and Flint, *Book of Daniel: Composition and Reception*, 1:1–15; Jan-Wim Wesselius, "The Writing of Daniel," in Collins and Flint, *Book of Daniel: Composition and Reception*, 2:292–310; Smith-Christopher, "Prayers and Dreams," 266; Matthias Henze, *The Madness of King Nebuchadnezzar: The Ancient Near Eastern Origins and Early History of Interpretation of Daniel 4* (Leiden: Brill, 1999).

53. See particularly Dan 4:19 (MT 16); 6:21 (MT 22).

54. I refer to the vision in Dan 2:31–45. I read the mountain as symbolizing the Judeans themselves, rather than a messianic figure. These two interpretations are of

as the beneficiary of imperialism, to become an imperialist, as it were. Yet he or they cannot help, it seems, but to write Daniel as feeling a certain fondness toward his king. When Daniel realizes in chapter 4 that the king's dream foretells an ominous future for him, he is "devastated for a while. His thoughts alarmed him." He states: "My lord, may the dream be for those who hate you, and its interpretation for your enemies!" (4:19 [MT 16]). Centuries of domination, of working the imperial system, have left their mark. There is, as Daniel Smith-Christopher has argued,[55] resistance in these court tales, but there is also ambivalence, an ambivalence so typical of colonized peoples.[56]

But is Daniel masculine? Certainly, the traditional Israelite conception of masculine honor that is found in exaggerated form in Ezekiel is absent here. Where is Daniel's wife, over whom he exercises masculine control? No wife is mentioned, and some have wondered if Daniel is to be seen as a eunuch.[57] Where is the violence, the pressing need for vengeance? Compared to Ezekiel, these desires seem strangely absent. One finds only intriguing reversals—the king, who should be wise, ignorant of the meaning of his own dreams, which are interpreted by a lowly foreigner who knows his very thoughts, like a god would.[58] The arrogant king is

---

course the most prominent (see Collins, *Daniel*, 171). I prefer a nationalistic rather than messianic interpretation, because the image of a mountain covering the earth is better suited to describing a group of people, or the regime of a group of people, than an individual. Also, the statue described in the dream symbolizes four national empires, not individuals.

55. See Smith-Christopher, "Book of Daniel" and "Prayers and Dreams."

56. Norman W. Porteous, *Daniel: A Commentary* (OTL; Philadelphia: Westminster, 1965), 19, speaks of the "double attitude" present in these texts. This attitude is not atypical for those living under imperialist rule. Memmi writes in the preface to *Colonizer and Colonized*: "The sum of events which I had lived since childhood, often incoherent and contradictory on the surface, began to fall into dynamic patterns. How could the colonizer look after his workers while periodically gunning down a crowd of the colonized? … How could [the colonized] hate the colonizers and yet admire them so passionately? (I too felt this admiration in spite of myself.)" (x).

57. This was the view of Jerome and of many rabbinic texts. See Collins, *Daniel*, 135–36.

58. I refer to Dan 2 especially. While one could certainly debate whether the God of the Israelites was omniscient, certainly by the time of Ben Sira such a conception of the divine seems to have been developed, as Sir 23:19 demonstrates with its assertion that the "eyes of the Lord are ten thousand times brighter than the sun/they look upon every aspect of human behavior and see into hidden corners" (NRSV).

reduced to atavism; one is tempted to see in this an image of a king who had once conquered barbarians reduced to a state more barbarous than that of any foreign people. Daniel 6 calls to my mind the masculine image of the royal lion hunts of Assyria.[59] But Daniel does not slay lions like his forebear David had (1 Sam 17:34–36); rather, he calms them through the power of his piety. Even in the apocalyptic portion of the book, there is no masculinized hero.[60] Daniel is passive and enjoined to remain passive.[61] The author longs for a violent reversal, for vengeance on an eschatological scale, but it seems that he is somehow unable to conceive of carrying out this violence himself, that centuries of diasporic life have left him emasculated, impotent. In the agonistic context of the imperial court at which Daniel lives, the non-Judean officials resent the elevations in status that he and his friends are afforded through his skills of oneiromancy. These courtiers succeed in conspiring against them, using the Judeans' foreign customs as the basis for their allegations.[62] But Daniel does not—and cannot—*act* against them. He cannot strike back. The author of the book cannot envision this. He can only project masculine power onto angelic beings.[63] Angels become masculine pinch hitters for sidelined Israelites. The desire for violent upheaval is so profound as to become cosmic, but the author's terrible imaginings have no place for the actions of men.

---

59. See Michael B. Dick, "The Neo-Assyrian Royal Lion Hunt and Yahweh's Answer to Job," *JBL* 125 (2006): 243–70. The Persian king Darius (probably Darius I) was also portrayed as taking part in a lion hunt, as Brent A. Strawn discusses ("'A World Under Control': Isaiah 60 and the Apadana Reliefs from Persepolis," in *Approaching Yehud: New Approaches to the Study of the Persian Period* [ed. Jon L. Berquist; Semeia Studies 50; Atlanta: Society of Biblical Literature, 2007], 112–13).

60. Smith-Christopher has referred to Daniel's dream interpretation in the court tales as "wisdom warfare" (*Biblical Theology of Exile*, 183). Yet there are no physical actions involved in this "warfare," and one must wonder if it would have been recognizable as "warfare" to earlier biblical writers. However, Smith-Christopher's discussion of the "wisdom warrior" does make clear that Wisdom literature provides a different model of masculinity, one based less upon brute strength and control of others than upon control of oneself, than do many other biblical texts (though Smith-Christopher does not speak in terms of masculinity). This fact warrants a longer discussion, but it will have to wait for another work.

61. See esp. Dan 12:4, 9, 13; in v. 13 Daniel is even told to go on his way and "rest."

62. Dan 3:8–12; 6:3–5 (MT 4–6).

63. It bears noting that, in both the book of Ezekiel and that of Daniel, masculinity is divinized, with masculine power being projected onto Yhwh in Ezekiel and onto angelic figures in Daniel. I thank William Danaher for pointing this out to me.

Conclusions

These are brief and impressionistic treatments, but I hope they are suggestive. Certainly many others have applied ideas from postcolonial studies to their research on biblical texts—I am only adding to that list here. My greater objective in this essay was to argue not merely that comparative research is a fruitful endeavor, but more pointedly that it is a necessary one due to the limitations of our field. Specialization has become such a central feature of academia that this specialization—or hyperspecialization—often leads to disciplinary isolationism. The drawbacks of this have long been apparent, and efforts have been made in many areas to make connections between fields. At the same time, academia has become more culturally, religiously, and ethnically diverse and has been enriched by a wider range of viewpoints than were ever present before. But biblical studies is not only seemingly less diverse than most areas; it is also arguably less interdisciplinary. And this despite the fact that our task is not easier than that of historians of the modern period or of anthropologists or sociologists—the incomplete nature of our sources and the vast distance in time between us and the ancients only makes our task undoubtedly more difficult.

A more forceful turn to cross-cultural research is thus warranted. At its best, this research arms one with a greater understanding of not only human cultures in their many variations, but of the human psyche with its paralyzing frailties and weaknesses. This might seem a banal selling point for comparative research, but in fact it is not, or is no longer one in our current intellectual climate. This is because devotees of postmodernism have claimed that it is impossible truly to understand another culture, for to do so requires an objectivity that we are just not capable of, enmeshed as we are in the totalizing discourses and ever shifting webs of culturally produced signification that engender us as subjects. As Seyla Benhabib writes, summarizing postmodernist attitudes: "Transcendental guarantees of truth are dead; in the agonal struggle of language games there is no commensurability; there are no criteria of truth transcending local discourses, but only the endless struggle of local narratives vying with one another for legitimation."[64] I, like many others, have been influenced by such ideas and take to heart postmodernism's critiques of the facile assumptions modernists have so often made. Yet, in the end, I stand with those who assert that

64. Benhabib, *Situating the Self: Gender, Community, and Postmodernism in Contemporary Ethics* (New York: Routledge, 1992), 209.

there *is* nonetheless a commensurability to human experience, though it is in no way easy to achieve.[65] It is not a commensurability of ever rational agents or self-actualized individuals but one of weakness and victimhood, of greed and humiliation, and yes, of struggle and rebelliousness. However totalizing our cultural discourses might be, we are still physical beings, with physical and emotional needs of the basest varieties.[66] As historians, we must be students of these human realities if the histories we write are to be something other than projections of ourselves, something other than autobiographical fictions in the time-worn clothing of objective analysis.

Appendix: Ezekiel as "Pornography"

Considering the graphic nature of the book of Ezekiel and the seeming obsession of its author with the shame of the Israelites—a shame metaphorically represented as that of a whorish, adulterous wife—it is not surprising that feminist biblical scholars have given this difficult work a great deal of attention. Ezekiel is a "text of terror" for many feminists.[67] This book is no doubt *graphic* in its portrayal of sexuality, violence, and sexualized violence, but is it in fact *pornographic*? Various feminist scholars have deemed it so, and this term is frequently used to describe chapters 16 and 23 of the book in particular.[68] I too am a feminist, and proudly so, but I

65. See Eagleton, *Illusions of Postmodernism*, 14, who points out that the current academic trend "drastically undervalues what men and women have in common as natural, material creatures, foolishly suspects all talk of nature as insidiously mystifying, and overestimates the significance of cultural difference." On commensurability, see Stanley Jeyaraja Tambiah, *Magic, Science, Religion, and the Scope of Rationality* (Cambridge: Cambridge University Press, 1990), 111–39, whose discussion is extremely cautious, but constructive. Also very relevant to these issues are Benhabib, *Situating the Self*; and Edward Slingerland, *What Science Offers the Humanities: Integrating Body and Culture* (New York: Cambridge University Press, 2008).

66. I thank Leigh Johnson for introducing me to the concept of "weak humanism," which has informed these comments.

67. I refer here to Phyllis Trible's *Texts of Terror: Literary-Feminist Readings of Biblical Narratives* (OBT; Minneapolis: Fortress, 1984), though Trible does not discuss Ezek 16 or 23 in that work, or in *God and the Rhetoric of Sexuality* (OBT; Minneapolis: Fortress, 1978).

68. For a bibliography of feminist responses to this text, including those that see the book as "pornographic," see Patton, "Should Our Sister?" 221–24. Patton's call that we read Ezek 16 and 23 with an eye toward the historical realities of the sixth century B.C.E. is certainly a welcome one, in my view. Also highly relevant is

would like here to sound a sharp note of caution. There are many problems with applying this term to Ezekiel, and these problems in the use of this term tend to obscure, rather than illuminate, a text that is already difficult to comprehend in so many ways. The first issue—and it is not a small one—surrounds the term *pornography* itself. What qualifies as "pornographic"? The difficulty of defining pornography is such that the Supreme Court Justice Potter Stewart famously stated, "I know it when I see it," because he had trouble defining pornography otherwise. Biblical scholars tend to tie the purportedly pornographic character of Ezekiel to its violently misogynistic, debasing, objectifying portrayal of the adulterous Jerusalem. Their definitions and conceptions of pornography are clearly rooted in second-wave feminist—and more specifically "antipornography feminist"—responses to hypergraphic sexual films and images. These are exemplified by Andrea Dworkin and Catherine A. MacKinnon's definition of pornography as "the graphic sexually explicit subordination of women through pictures and/or words."[69] Yet some feminists have contested this

---

Robert P. Carroll, "Desire under the Terebinths: On Pornographic Representation in the Prophets—A Response," in *A Feminist Companion to the Latter Prophets* (ed. Athalya Brenner; Feminist Companion to the Bible 8; Sheffield: Sheffield Academic Press, 1995), 275–307, where Carroll critiques some of the major pieces of feminist biblical scholarship on the prophets. I agree with Carroll on various matters, but in the end I see him as misreading these texts, just as he characterizes such scholars as Drorah Setel and Athalya Brenner as having done. While it is true that the metaphors in Ezek 16 and 23 deal with cities, not women, the author's metaphorization of Jerusalem and Samaria is based upon certain presumptions regarding gender relations and would not make sense without these presumptions. Yes, these texts do condemn a male or male/female audience, not just women, but they do so by playing upon gender ideas and gender hierarchies that were at best androcentric, at worst misogynistic, and that certainly seem to have been normative in ancient Israel and much of the ancient world (and continue to be in much of the modern world, for that matter). By ignoring how cultural ideas of gender and shame are both manifest in and bolstered by prophetic texts, Carroll seems almost to betray a certain ignorance of ancient Israelite culture and society.

69. The quotation is from a bill introduced to the Judiciary Committee of the State of Massachusetts in 1992. The bill is based on the "Model Antipornography Civil-Rights Ordinance" that was cowritten by Dworkin and MacKinnon. See http://www.nostatusquo.com/ACLU/dworkin/OrdinanceMassComplete.html. This ordinance was voted upon in several cities in the 1980s, as Jennifer Nash discusses in "The Black Body in Ecstasy: Reading Race, Reading Pornography" (Ph.D. diss., Harvard University, 2009), 5.

definition, and there has been an attempt to nuance analyses of pornography.[70] After all, pornographic films and images have become increasingly varied over time and were never uniform to begin with. Arguably, what they share is a hypersexualization of the body—male bodies are no less "objectified" than female in graphic sexual materials—and the objective of eliciting sexual arousal (and/or accompanying sexual release). Denying that these traits are inherently misogynistic, some feminists have stated that it is inaccurate to allege that all pornographic materials subordinate women or encourage or even portray violence toward women.[71] Indeed, Jennifer Nash has convincingly shown that the instinctively negative con-

---

70. See Nash, "Black Body in Ecstasy," 1–11, for a history of feminist responses to pornography. The most prominent voice of pro-pornography feminism is perhaps that of Camille Paglia. See *Sex, Art, and American Culture: Essays* (New York: Vintage, 1992), in which Paglia writes that she is "radically pro-pornography and pro-prostitution" (11); and idem, *Vamps and Tramps* (New York: Vintage, 1994), particularly 56–66, 107–12, in which she refers to MacKinnon as a "twentieth-century puritan" and describes the "Protestant culture" in which the latter was raised as "pinched, cramped," and "body-denying" (108–9). Paglia's writing is nothing if not colorful. But more nuanced in thinking than either Paglia or the "antipornography feminists" are those in the "sex-radicalism" camp, who attempt, as Nash puts it, to "destabilize the tendency to view pornography as exclusively a site of women's subordination or a locus of women's agency. Instead, sex-radicals examine how arousal, pleasure, subordination, and dominance are co-constitutive, and emphasize the contingent and complex meanings inherent to each pornographic text" ("Black Body in Ecstasy," 7). Two prominent works of this movement are Carole S. Vance, ed., *Pleasure and Danger: Exploring Female Sexuality* (Boston: Routledge and K. Paul, 1984); and Ann Snitow, Christine Stansell, and Sharon Thompson, eds., *Powers of Desire: The Politics of Sexuality* (New York: Monthly Review Press, 1983). Another work relevant to these issues is Nadine Strossen, *Defending Pornography: Free Speech, Sex, and the Fight for Women's Rights* (New York: Scribner's, 1995).

71. To raise a few perhaps simplistic examples: what of materials that portray men as submissive and women as dominant in sadomasochistic sex, or those that portray male-male sexuality, or those that are geared toward a female audience? As Carroll writes, "In terms of pornography as domination matters are much more complicated than is implied by the [feminist] sources used in [works of feminist biblical scholarship]. We might ask, 'who dominates whom in pornography?' If women produce and consume pornography, then who is dominating whom?" ("Desire under the Terebinths," 296). Alleging that men are only used in place of women in these types of films and that the films nonetheless further power dynamics that oppress women is a weak counterargument, in my view. The porn industry seems to me amoral, making available images of whatever kind to cater to the wide variety of sexual tastes that exist.

ceptions of pornography held by many feminists do not even adequately describe a type of pornography that many have seen as being problematic in the extreme—that with racialized sexual content.[72] This is not to deny that feminists can and should take issue with much of what falls under the category of pornography in our culture. I merely wish to make the point that pornography—how it is to be defined, whether it is inherently objectionable on feminist grounds—is contested *in our own society*.[73] Thus to apply this terminology to an ancient text such as Ezekiel seems highly questionable. Moreover, this use of the term "pornographic" in biblical studies not only judges the text in question but also the reader, who is presumed to be offended by things "pornographic" and somehow morally or ideologically lacking if he or she is not. Using fraught and disputed terms to explicate—or rather impugn—difficult texts is surely a way of hiding behind our own visceral disgust, just as Ezekiel did. Ezekiel might turn our stomachs, but that reaction should be the beginning of our exploration, not the end of it.

---

72. See her excellent treatment of race and pornography, "Black Body in Ecstasy," as well as idem, "Strange Bedfellows: Black Feminism and Antipornography Feminism," *Social Text* 26.4 (2008): 51–76, where she writes in response to black feminists' assumptions about racialized pornography: "In ignoring both the possibilities of black spectatorship and non-'fetishistic' white spectatorship, the 'racial fetishism' logic suggests both that black bodies inhabit the visual field *for* white viewing pleasures, and that interracial viewing is inherently problematic as it is steeped in inequality. This theoretical framework leaves little room for white visual pleasures that are not degrading, objectifying, or fetishizing, foreclosing the possibility of white spectators gazing at, and taking pleasure in, black women's bodies without reducing the black female body to its constitutive parts" (61).

73. Carroll makes a similar point in "Desire under the Terebinths," 295.

Text Production and Destruction in Ancient Israel: Ritual and Political Dimensions

*Nathaniel B. Levtow**

The past decade has witnessed increased attention to the development of writing and literacy in ancient Israel.[1] This turn to the social world

---

*I am grateful to the participants in the 2010 Moskow Symposium for offering their insights and suggestions after hearing a version of this paper, and I thank Saul M. Olyan for providing many helpful comments while editing its drafts. I thank also Karen B. Stern and Megan H. Williams for reading an early draft of this paper. Any errors remain my responsibility alone.

1. See, e.g., Ryan Byrne, "The Refuge of Scribalism in Iron I Palestine," *BASOR* 345 (2007): 1–31; David M. Carr, *Writing on the Tablet of the Heart: Origins of Scripture and Literature* (New York: Oxford University Press, 2005); idem, "The Tel Zayit Abecedary in (Social) Context," in *Literate Culture and Tenth-Century Canaan: The Tel Zayit Abecedary in Context* (ed. Ron E. Tappy and P. Kyle McCarter; Winona Lake, Ind.: Eisenbrauns, 2008), 113–29, and the essays by Ron E. Tappy, Christopher A. Rollston, and Seth L. Sanders in the same volume; Christopher A. Rollston, "Scribal Education in Ancient Israel: The Old Hebrew Epigraphic Evidence," *BASOR* 344 (2006): 47–74; idem, *Writing and Literacy in the World of Ancient Israel: Epigraphic Evidence from the Iron Age* (SBLABS 11; Atlanta: Society of Biblical Literature, 2010); Seth L. Sanders, "What Was the Alphabet For? The Rise of Written Vernaculars and the Making of Israelite National Literature," *Maarav* 11 (2004): 25–56; idem, *The Invention of Hebrew* (Traditions; Urbana: University of Illinois Press, 2009); Joachim Schaper, "A Theology of Writing: Deuteronomy, the Oral and the Written, and God as Scribe," in *Anthropology and Biblical Studies: Avenues of Research* (ed. Louise J. Lawrence and Mario I. Aguilar; Leiden: Deo, 2004), 97–119; idem, "Exilic and Post-Exilic Prophecy and the Orality/Literacy Problem," *VT* 55 (2005): 324–42; idem, "The Death of the Prophet: The Transition from the Spoken to the Written Word of God in the Book of Ezekiel," in *Prophets, Prophecy and Prophetic Texts in Second Temple Judaism* (ed. Michael H. Floyd and Robert D. Haak; LHBOTS 427; New York: T&T Clark, 2006), 63–79; idem, "The Living Word Engraved in Stone: The Interrelationship of the Oral and the Written and the Culture of Memory in Deuteronomy and Joshua," in *Memory in the Bible*

of Israelite scribes seeks new answers to old questions concerning the history of the biblical text and the nature of Israelite authorship. Recent scholarship on Israelite scribal culture moves helpfully beyond traditional boundaries of biblical study by engaging broader methods and debates in social anthropology and by appealing to better-attested scribal traditions of ancient Mesopotamia, Egypt, and Greece. As a result, the obscure social contours of Israelite scribal activity are coming into sharper relief through a focus on individuals and social groups skilled and empowered to inscribe words upon stones, shards, and scrolls.

The emerging portrait of Israelite scribal activity is, however, surprisingly static. More specifically, the development of scribal practices in ancient Israel and Judah is often understood as a process of institutionalization and stabilization, whereby formerly unstable oral mythic and ritual traditions became textually represented and preserved by scribal specialists who served the royal and priestly hierarchies of these emerging polities. According to this view, text production is an essentially conservative activity that preserves tradition. It is not unreasonable, however, to argue the opposite point. Whether it be the violent transformation of ancient Judah's ritual, sociopolitical, and textual landscape during the reign of King Josiah, or the similarly transformative ritual, political, and textual activity that accompanied the restoration programs of Persian Yehud, or indeed the sociopolitical changes that accompanied the canon debates of Greco-Roman Christendom, text production can also be described as a socially destabilizing and transformative activity.

In this paper I argue for a view of textual activity as an agent not of cultural conservation and stability but of cultural production and change.

and Antiquity (ed. Stephen C. Barton, Loren T. Stuckenbruck, and Benjamin G. Wold; WUNT 212; Tübingen: Mohr Siebeck, 2007), 9–23; and the essays collected in Joachim Schaper, ed., *Die Textualisierung der Religion* (Tübingen: Mohr Siebeck, 2009); William M. Schniedewind, *How the Bible Became a Book: The Textualization of Ancient Israel* (Cambridge: Cambridge University Press, 2004); idem, "The Textualization of Torah in Jeremiah 8:8," in *Was ist ein Text? Alttestamentliche, ägyptologische und altorientalistische Perspektiven* (ed. Ludwig Morenz and Stefan Schorch; BZAW 362; Berlin: de Gruyter, 2007), 93–107; Karel van der Toorn, *Scribal Culture and the Making of the Hebrew Bible* (Cambridge: Harvard University Press, 2007). Aspects of these discussions were anticipated in the earlier studies of David W. Jamieson-Drake, *Scribes and Schools in Monarchic Judah: A Socio-archaeological Approach* (JSOTSup 109; Sheffield: Almond, 1991); and esp. Susan Niditch, *Oral World, Written Word: Ancient Israelite Literature* (Library of Ancient Israel; Louisville: Westminster John Knox, 1996).

I further argue that texts in ancient Israel's cultural environment may be understood as embodiments of social relations and as actors that played social roles in ritual contexts. To do so, I approach the topic of text production from the opposite angle of text destruction. In other words, I investigate the social dynamics of text production through a focus on the ritual and political dynamics of text destruction. I thereby seek to activate the portrait of Israelite scribal culture by exploring the social roles of texts and the ritual and political dimensions of textualization in ancient Israel and its wider environment.

My discussion focuses on three biblical narratives of text destruction: Jer 36, in which a scroll is cut and then burned in fire; Exod 32, in which tablets are shattered on the ground; and Jer 51, in which a scroll is thrown into water. I compare these accounts with similar acts of violence attested against texts in other Northwest and East Semitic cultural contexts. In addition, I correlate the production and destruction of texts with the production and destruction of cult images and with the making and breaking of covenant relations. I examine this range of ancient evidence and social phenomena in order to locate acts of text destruction within broader processes of ritualization, textualization, and social formation.[2] By doing so I aim to redescribe textual activity—including the production, transmission, and destruction of scrolls and inscriptions—not as a static mode of cultural conservation, but as a dynamic mode of cultural production and a socially transformative ritual and political practice in ancient West Asia.

Theoretical Perspectives

Hermann Gunkel's form-critical interests in the oral lore behind Israelite literature inclined a century of Hebrew Bible scholarship to focus on the relationship between oral and written traditions in ancient Israel.[3] Biblical

2. On these terms, see n. 19 below. The investigation of text destruction practices intersects two major subjects of debate in biblical studies today, iconoclasm and text production, and engages both fields of inquiry.

3. Hermann Gunkel, *Genesis, übersetzt und erklärt* (HKAT 1/1; Göttingen: Vandenhoeck & Ruprecht, 1901), and the introduction to this volume published separately in idem, *Die Sagen der Genesis* (Göttingen: Vandenhoeck & Ruprecht, 1901). The rise of form criticism coincided with the rise of social-scientific approaches to the study of religion, as biblical studies widened its nineteenth-century focus on documentary criticism to embrace new developments in the fields of sociology, anthropology, and ethnography. See John H. Hayes, *An Introduction to Old Testament Study* (Nashville:

scholars in the late twentieth and early twenty-first centuries have drawn particularly upon the works of Jack Goody, Walter Ong, and Eric Havelock for explanatory models of emergent literacy and writing in ancient Israel.[4] Ong issued a call to biblical studies specifically in his often-cited 1982 book *Orality and Literacy: The Technologizing of the Word*: "Orality-literacy theorems challenge biblical study perhaps more than any other field of learning."[5] Ong's challenge to locate the social dynamics of Israelite literacy in a developing relationship between the oral and the written has been taken up in a number of studies that either posit a historical transition from oral to written culture or argue for a more dynamic interplay between oral and written modes of discourse in the development of biblical traditions.[6]

Abingdon, 1979), 123–24; Robert R. Wilson, *Prophecy and Society in Ancient Israel* (Philadelphia: Fortress, 1980), 1–14; Douglas A. Knight, *Rediscovering the Traditions of Ancient Israel* (3rd ed.; SBLStBL 16; Atlanta: Society of Biblical Literature, 2006). See also nn. 1, 4, and 6 here.

4. See esp. Jack Goody and Ian P. Watt, "The Consequences of Literacy," *Comparative Studies in Society and History* 5 (1963): 304–45; Jack Goody, *The Logic of Writing and the Organization of Society* (Cambridge: Cambridge University Press, 1968); idem, *The Power of the Written Tradition* (Smithsonian Series in Ethnographic Inquiry; Washington, D.C.: Smithsonian Institution Press, 2000); Walter J. Ong, *Orality and Literacy: The Technologizing of the Word* (London: Routledge, 1982); Eric A. Havelock, *Preface to Plato* (Cambridge: Harvard University Press, 1963); idem, *The Literate Revolution in Greece and Its Cultural Consequences* (Princeton: Princeton University Press, 1982); idem, *The Muse Learns to Write: Reflections on Orality and Literacy from Antiquity to the Present* (New Haven: Yale University Press, 1988). Homeric scholarship, especially the work of Milman Parry and of Albert Lord (*The Singer of Tales* [Cambridge: Harvard University Press, 1960]), has been equally influential; see, e.g., Frank Moore Cross, "The Epic Traditions of Early Israel: Epic Narrative and the Reconstruction of Early Israelite Institutions," in *The Poet and the Historian: Essays in Literary and Historical Biblical Criticism* (ed. Richard Elliott Friedman; Chico, Calif.: Scholars Press, 1983), 14–18 (Saul M. Olyan, written correspondence); see also Joseph Russo, "Oral Theory: Its Development in Homeric Studies and Applicability to Other Literatures," in *Mesopotamian Epic Literature: Oral or Aural?* (ed. Marianna E. Vogelzang and Herman L. J. Vanstiphout; Lewiston, N.Y.: Mellen, 1992), 7–22.

5. Ong, *Orality and Literacy*, 173.

6. For discussion and critique of the orality/literacy dichotomy and its legacy in biblical studies, see Michael H. Floyd, "'Write the revelation!' (Hab 2:2): Re-imagining the Cultural History of Prophecy," in *Writings and Speech in Israelite and Ancient Near Eastern Prophecy* (ed. Ehud Ben Zvi and Michael H. Floyd; SBLSymS 10; Atlanta: Society of Biblical Literature, 2000), 103–43; Werner H. Kelber, "Orality and Biblical Stud-

When an opposition between orality and textuality is created and then bridged by theoretical models that posit transitions and interfaces between these two modes of discourse, this bridge often leads to an understanding of writing as a socially conservative practice. A focus on the relationship between the oral and the written, whether as transition or interplay, tends to portray text production as a process that preserves tradition across cultures and across time by externalizing language.[7] Text production, according to this view, separates words from the people who write them and from the social contexts within which they are written.[8] In this

ies: A Review Essay," *RBL* 12 (2007); Niditch, *Oral World*; Carr, *Writing on the Tablet*, 4–8; Sanders, *Invention of Hebrew*, 1–35, 44–45; Schaper, "Exilic and Post-exilic Prophecy"; idem, "Written Word Engraved in Stone"; William M. Schniedewind, "Orality and Literacy in Ancient Israel," *RSR* 26 (2000): 327–31; idem, *How the Bible Became a Book*, 2, 91–92. See also Deborah Tannen, "The Myth of Orality and Literacy," in *Linguistics and Literacy* (ed. William Frawley; New York: Plenum, 1982), 37–50. For further discussions of orality and textuality in biblical and ancient studies, see the essays collected in Ben Zvi and Floyd, eds., *Writings and Speech*; Jonathan A. Draper, ed., *Orality, Literacy, and Colonialism in Antiquity* (SemeiaSt 47; Atlanta: Society of Biblical Literature, 2004); Morenz and Schorch, eds., *Was ist ein Text?*; Lou H. Silberman, ed., *Orality, Aurality, and Biblical Narrative, Semeia* 39 (1987); Vogelzang and Vanstiphout, eds., *Mesopotamian Epic Literature*. On orality and literacy in medieval Europe, see M. T. Clanchy, *From Memory to Written Record: England, 1066–1307* (Cambridge: Harvard University Press, 1979), 7, 202–30; Sanders, *Invention of Hebrew*, 186 n. 39.

7. Carr points to a classic (over)statement of a sharp oral/written dichotomy in Albert Lord's description of oral and written techniques as "mutually exclusive" (*Writing on the Tablet*, 6–7, citing Lord, *Singer of Tales*, 129). Emphasizing instead the complex interplay between orality and textuality, Carr writes: "Orality and writing technology are joint means for accomplishing a common goal: accurate recall of the treasured tradition" (ibid., 7; see also 288). Van der Toorn describes a similar interplay and notes how more fluid, changeable oral traditions can eventually become subordinate to their written forms: "Once the knowledge of experts has been put down in writing, the tradition obtains an existence outside the mind of the initiate" (*Scribal Culture*, 218).

8. Ong, e.g., notes that "written words are isolated from the fuller context in which spoken words come into being," and that "words are alone in a text" (*Orality and Literacy*, 101). Ong here echoes Socrates in Plato's *Phaedrus* (§275d–e): "You know, Phaedrus, writing shares a strange feature with painting. The offsprings of painting stand there as if they are alive, but if anyone asks them anything, they remain most solemnly silent. The same is true of written words. … When it has once been written down, every discourse rolls about everywhere. … It always needs its father's support; alone, it can neither defend itself nor come to its own support" (text and trans. Alexander Nehemas and Paul Woodruff, *Plato: Complete Works* [ed. John M.

respect, any theoretical model that employs an oral/written dichotomy has the potential to turn writing into an alienating act that freezes discourse, and text production into an objectifying activity through which textualized tradition becomes separated from the dynamic social environment of its production and reception.[9]

On the other hand, social anthropologists and historians have also frequently described nonliterate (so-called traditional) societies as socially static and resistant to change, and modern literate societies as socially dynamic and given to transformative change.[10] The oral/written framework, therefore, tends to generate additional dichotomies that structure cultural description and explanation, including, for example, "traditional/nontraditional," "conservative/innovative," "canonical/noncanonical," and "static/dynamic." These dichotomies, which are all grounded in the relationship between "continuity and change," can become theoretically entrenched and understood as native categories, and are applied to either end of the oral/written spectrum to support overarching conceptions of stagnant tradition and static societies.[11]

Cooper and D. S. Hutchinson; Indianapolis: Hackett, 1997]). See also Schniedewind, *How the Bible Became a Book*, 14.

9. Goody (*Logic of Writing*, 11–12, 180–83) draws upon Weber's theory of rationalization to argue for a view of textualization as a mode of rationalization, systematization, stabilization, institutionalization, universalization, objectification, and specialization. See Max Weber, *The Protestant Ethic and the Spirit of Capitalism with Other Writings on the Rise of the West* (ed. and trans. Stephen Kalberg; Oxford: Oxford University Press, 2009), 103–23; Catherine Bell, *Ritual Theory, Ritual Practice* (New York: Oxford University Press, 1992), 131–32; Stephen Kalberg, "Max Weber's Types of Rationality: Cornerstones for the Analysis of Rationalization Processes in History," *American Journal of Sociology* 85 (1980): 1145–79; idem, "The Rationalization of Action in Max Weber's Sociology of Religion," *Sociological Theory* 8 (1990): 58–84.

10. Goody writes, "Scholars of all kinds … have looked upon preliterate societies as static, stagnant, perhaps unable to change without outside intervention" ("Canonization in Oral and Literate Traditions," in *Power of the Written Tradition*, 123); Goody here includes Max Weber, Claude Lévi-Strauss, Jürgen Habermas, Anthony Giddens, and others. In his discussion of tradition, change, and canonization, Goody challenges applications of this explanatory model to all domains of a given society, adding: "Has any age not experienced the loss as well as the gain of tradition? … In the domains of ritual and religion, oral cultures are constantly changing" (ibid., 124). See also Goody's discussion of writing as a socially transformative practice in "Writing and Revolt in Bahia," in ibid., 86–108.

11. Bell, *Ritual Theory*, 118; see also Goody, "Canonization," 123–24. The binary

The tendency in biblical studies to describe texts as objects that preserve tradition can turn texts, and the traditions they represent, into so-called dumb objects.[12] This is strikingly similar to the way cult images are often understood as objectified symbols of objectified referents. When texts and images are unmoored from the social contexts of their production and reception, they become mute objects with no fundamental, intersubjective relation to people.[13] Such an understanding of text production posits an Israelite scribal culture in which words and things possess power and meaning independent of any particular social world and cultural order.[14]

Understanding textual activity as a conservative social force that operates within an oral/written dichotomy is similar to the way ritual practice is often understood as a conservative, consolidating force that operates within an action/thought dichotomy.[15] As Bruce Lincoln, Catherine Bell,

---

classification "oral/written" has likewise been employed to promote biases either toward written traditions (due, e.g., to the role of the biblical canon in postbiblical periods) or toward oral traditions (due, e.g., to the legacy of European romanticism in the study of religion). Historians, who largely depend on written records, have also been inclined toward a bias for writing and literacy as emblematic of civilization and progress (Clanchy, *From Memory to Written Record*, 7).

12. See Leroy Vail and Landeg White, *Power and the Praise Poem: Southern African Voices in History* (Charlottesville: University Press of Virginia, 1991), xi–39; Marshall Sahlins, *How "Natives" Think: About Captain Cook, For Example* (Chicago: University of Chicago Press, 1995), 153.

13. Sahlins, *How "Natives" Think*, 153; Nathaniel B. Levtow, *Images of Others: Iconic Politics in Ancient Israel* (Biblical and Judaic Studies from the University of California, San Diego, 11; Winona Lake, Ind.: Eisenbrauns, 2008), 14–15, 20–28.

14. This theoretical framework need not fully disengage texts from contexts, but it does reposition or fix the role of the text in social formation. In this respect Carr writes of the "use of texts to achieve cultural continuity in elite classes across space and time," thereby "ensuring stable transmission of key traditions" from one generation to the next (*Writing on the Tablet*, 10, 8; see also 285). Van der Toorn writes of the scribal production, reproduction, and promotion of "streams of tradition" (*Scribal Culture*, 2–4); his classification of "scribal modes of text production" allows for different degrees of scribal engagement in broader social contexts, including, for example, the invention or adaptation of texts for specific audiences and social circumstances (ibid., 109–41). See, however, John Van Seters, "The Role of the Scribe in the Making of the Hebrew Bible," *JANER* 8 (2008): 112–15. Van der Toorn's modeling of the transition from oral to written prophecy retains an active role for textualized oracles and ultimately for the biblical canon as a whole (*Scribal Culture*, 205–32, 252–61).

15. Bell notes that "most theoretical discourse on ritual … is fundamentally organized by an underlying opposition between thought and action" (*Ritual Theory*, 47).

and others have argued, however, ritual is not simply a conservative force, it is also a socially transformative force.[16] In this respect, describing textual activity as a social activity akin to ritual practice can offer a more dynamic and culturally embedded model for understanding the production of texts in ancient contexts. As Bell writes, "The dynamic interaction of texts and rites, reading and chanting, the word fixed and the word preached are practices, not social developments of a fixed nature and significance. As practices, they continually play off each other to renegotiate tradition, authority, and the hegemonic order."[17] Describing textualization as a form of ritualization underscores the dynamic aspects of texts and rites as socially performative and formative; it also identifies textual products as representations of social relations that form and reform among the people who produce and interact with these products.[18] A redescription of writing as ritual and texts as subjects can likewise activate the idea of tradition by revealing a socially dynamic nexus between textualization, ritualization, and traditionalization.[19]

---

16. Ibid., 13–29; idem, "The Ritual Body and the Dynamics of Social Empowerment," *Journal of Ritual Studies* 4 (1990): 299–313; Bruce Lincoln, *Discourse and the Construction of Society: Comparative Studies of Myth, Ritual, and Classification* (New York: Oxford University Press, 1989), 3–5. See also David I. Kertzer, *Ritual, Politics, and Power* (New Haven: Yale University Press, 1988), 87; Levtow, *Images of Others*, 23–28; Saul M. Olyan, *Biblical Mourning: Ritual and Social Dimensions* (Oxford: Oxford University Press, 2004), 4 n. 7.

17. Bell, *Ritual Theory*, 140. Sanders writes, "neither writing nor printing causes social change in itself. Rather, it is the different assumptions and practices around texts" (*Invention of Hebrew*, 187 n. 44); see also Adrian Johns, *The Nature of the Book: Print and Knowledge in the Making* (Chicago: University of Chicago Press, 1998), noted by Sanders, *Invention of Hebrew*, 186 n. 39.

18. On performative textuality, see James W. Watts, "The Three Dimensions of Scripture," *Postscripts* 2 (2006): 135–59; see also n. 29 below.

19. On the interplay between textualization, ritualization, and traditionalization, see Bell, *Ritual Theory*, 118–42; idem, "Ritualization of Texts and Textualization of Ritual in the Codification of Taoist Liturgy," *History of Religions* 27 (1988): 366–92. Bell defines "ritualization" as "the orchestration of ritual activities to serve as the medium of interaction for a particular set of social relations"; "textualization" she defines as "the generation of textual objects that structure social interaction around their use and transmission"; Bell writes of "processes of 'ritualization' and 'textualization' that altered rather than merely reflected" a given social milieu ("Ritualization of Texts," 390). "Traditionalization" Bell describes as "a practical logic of explanatory categories for rendering the new orthodox and canonical"; it is a legitimizing process that makes social innovation appear normative and natural (*Ritual Theory*, 138; Levtow, *Images*

Attention to the correlations between ritual and textual activity introduces new social-theoretical possibilities for the study of writing in ancient Israel. Furthermore, a focus not only on the social roles of ancient scribes but also on the social roles of the texts they produced makes available a range of theoretical perspectives that would otherwise remain obscured if one embraces a view of writing as the preservation of objectified tradition. "By viewing the text as an entity that merely expresses a particular perspective on its time," writes Bell, "we may miss how the text is an *actor* in those times."[20] Emphasizing the privileged social roles of scribes *and* scribal products illuminates textual activity as a kind of ritual activity. Textualization, according to this view, becomes a form of what Bell calls the "production of ritualized acts," which she describes as "the strategic production of expedient schemes that structure an environment in such a way that the environment appears to be the source of the schemes and their values."[21] Seth Sanders has similarly argued for a view of writing in ancient Israel as "an essentially *generative* mode of political communication that helps create its audience by the very means through which it addresses it."[22]

In this paper I build upon these perspectives on rites and writing to argue for the socially generative, ritualized role of texts in Israelite cultural contexts. In particular, I argue for the utility of Bell's categories of "ritualization" and "textualization" over the categories of "orality" and "literacy" as analytic tools for explaining the dynamics of writing in ancient Israel. Bell's

---

of Others, 34). See also Schniedewind's description of textualization as a process that entails "transferring the abstract into the real, and then … imbuing this written artifact with hierarchical value ("Textualization of Torah," 95). On "social formation," see Burton L. Mack, "Social Formation," in *Guide to the Study of Religion* (ed. Willi Braun and Russel T. McCutcheon; London: Cassell, 2000), 283–96. Mack describes social formation as a concept that "emphasizes the complex interplay of many human interests that develop systems of signs and patterns of practice, as well as institutions for their communication, maintenance and reproduction" (ibid., 283).

20. Bell, "Ritualization of Texts," 368. Although the social roles played by texts in ancient Israel are obscure and difficult for the modern interpreter to access, I argue that they can be better illuminated through a focus on text destruction practices.

21. Bell, *Ritual Theory*, 140. On ritual hierarchies of status and power, see Jonathan Z. Smith, *To Take Place: Toward Theory in Ritual* (Chicago: University of Chicago Press, 1987), 47–73.

22. Sanders, *Invention of Hebrew*, 171. Sanders argues for the socially dynamic and transformative power of Iron Age Levantine writing practices, emphasizing the "politically constitutive dimension of language" and the "highly developed culture of *poiesis*, cultural creation through text-making" (3, 146).

emphasis on an interplay between "textualization" and "ritualization" is, I suggest, a more helpful, locally embedded model for understanding textual activity in ancient Israel's monistic cultural and ontological environment in which rites, texts, and their dynamic social contexts were bound and inseparable. I focus on biblical narratives of text destruction to show how textualization in ancient Israel signified not the fixed transmission of objectified tradition but the ritualized transformation of embodied social relations.

Cutting and Burning a Scroll: Jeremiah 36

I begin my discussion of Hebrew biblical texts with Jer 36:1–26, a remarkable narrative of prophetic intermediation that focuses on the production, transmission, and destruction of an oracle scroll. This process is vividly depicted through at least eleven stages:

1. Jeremiah receives an oracle from Yhwh instructing him to take a scroll (*mĕgillat-sēper*) and write on it "all the words" that Yhwh has spoken to him concerning Israel, Judah, and other nations (v. 2).[23]
2. Jeremiah dictates all of Yhwh's words to the scribe (*sōpēr*) Baruch (v. 4).
3. Baruch writes Jeremiah's dictation on a scroll (*wayyiktōb bārûk mippî yirmĕyāhû*, lit. "Baruch wrote from the mouth of Jeremiah"; v. 4).
4. Jeremiah instructs Baruch to go to the Jerusalem temple and read the scroll aloud to the temple officials and to all the people of Judah who have come up to Jerusalem for a pilgrimage fast (vv. 5–6).
5. Baruch reads the scroll aloud in the temple chamber of Gemariah, son of Shaphan the scribe, "in the hearing of all the people" (vv. 8–10).
6. Micaiah (son of Gemariah and grandson of Shaphan) hears all that Baruch reads aloud from the scroll in the temple, and reports everything he hears to the scribes and officials gathered in the scribal chamber of the palace (vv. 11–13).

23. See Menachem Haran, "Book-Scrolls in Israel in Pre-Exilic Times," *JJS* 33 (1982): 161–73.

7. The royal scribes send the palace official Jehudi to Baruch to have him bring the scroll to them (v. 14).
8. Baruch goes to the palace scribal chamber and reads the scroll to the royal scribes and officials gathered there (vv. 15–16).
9. The royal scribes deposit the scroll in the palace scribal chamber, go to the royal court, and report all of its contents to the king (Jehoiakim) (v. 20).
10. The king sends Jehudi to fetch the scroll and read it aloud to him and his royal attendants (v. 21).
11. Jehudi reads the scroll to Jehoiakim; as he does so, columns of the scroll are torn away with a penknife (*taʿar hassōpēr*) and thrown into the king's brazier "until the entire scroll was consumed in the fire" (v. 23).[24]

One additional stage of transmission exists outside the narrative of Jer 36, and that is the production of the narrative itself. Because this narrative represents a process of text production in such rich detail, many discussions of Jer 36 mine this text for clues to the authorship and development of the book of Jeremiah and focus on the relationship between the oral and the written transmission of Israelite prophetic traditions.[25] My interest is in the way the narrative itself depicts ritual and political dimensions of textual activity within the context of the formation of social relations in general and covenant relations in particular.

The complex process of social intermediation and textual transmission depicted in Jer 36 is framed by an account of the creation and destruction of a scroll. The superscription to this narrative sets these events in a wider political context that concerns the creation and destruction of social relations. The fourth regnal year of Jehoiakim (Jer 36:1) witnessed Jehoiakim's Egyptian suzerain defeated by Babylon at Carchemish in 605 B.C.E. In response to Babylonian hegemony Jehoiakim transferred Judah's vassalage from Egypt to Babylon, only to rebel against Babylon three years later.

24. Jer 36:23 does not specify whether Jehudi or Jehoiakim cuts and burns the scroll. If Jehudi does so, it is in the royal palace and presence, at the instruction of the king, who sits before the brazier; vv. 24–26 clearly indicate that the king is responsible.

25. For references, discussion, and textual notes, see Jack R. Lundbom, *Jeremiah 21–36: A New Translation with Introduction and Commentary* (AB 21B; New York: Doubleday, 2004), 582–607. See also Carr, *Writing on the Tablet*, 146–47; van der Toorn, *Scribal Culture*, 184–88.

This same date of 605 is also attached to the oracles of exile collected in Jer 25. In each text (Jer 25 and 36) the consequences of Jehoiakim's vacillating vassalage between earthly powers are linked to a greater social and ritual rebellion against Yhwh.

In Jer 36 Jehoiakim is read a scroll that warns him of the violent consequences of breaking covenant relations with Yhwh (vv. 3, 7, 29). The king responds to this warning with violence against the scroll itself. When Jeremiah's scroll is then rewritten in the narrative's conclusion (vv. 27–32), Jeremiah is instructed by Yhwh to deliver the following oracle against Jehoiakim: "Thus says Yhwh: 'You have burned this scroll, saying, "Why have you written on it that the king of Babylon will surely come and destroy this land and cessate [*hišbît*] from it humans and animals?"'" (36:29).

Jeremiah's oracle then warns of the violent consequences of Jehoiakim's action against the scroll and his concomitant rejection of its content: there will be no heir to the throne of David after Jehoiakim's corpse is cast outside "to the parching heat by day and the frost by night," and the entire Davidic court, together with the inhabitants of Jerusalem and Judah, will experience "all the calamities of which Yhwh spoke to them and they ignored"; that is, they will experience the curses of the covenant invoked by the oracles of Jeremiah (36:30–31).[26]

Links to covenant curses are evident also in the account of Jeremiah's earlier visit to the Jerusalem temple (Jer 7; cf. Jer 26). Jeremiah there pits Deuteronomic covenant traditions associated with Moses and the exodus (7:6, 9, 22–26) against royal traditions associated with Jerusalem and David (7:4, 10; cf. 2 Sam 7:12–16; Ps 132:13–14). Within this framework Jeremiah issues an oracular warning similar to that of Jer 36:30–31:

> The corpses of this people will become food for the birds of the sky and for the animals of the earth and none shall frighten them away. I will cessate [*hišbît*] from the cities of Judah and from the streets of Jerusalem the sound of joy and the sound of gladness, the voice of bridegroom and the voice of bride, and the land shall turn to ruin. (Jer 7:33–34; cf. Deut 28:26)

26. See also the closely linked narrative of Jer 26, where Jehoiakim "cast out the corpse" of the prophet Uriah (26:23), whose oracles against Jerusalem were "just like the words of Jeremiah" (26:20). See also 7:20. Cf. Deut 28:26: "Your corpse will become food for every bird of the sky and animal of the earth, and none shall frighten them away."

The transformation of joy into mourning (Jer 7:34; cf. 7:29) is expressed also in the closely related text of Jer 25, in which Yhwh is said to "blot out" (*haʾăbadtî*) the sound of joy and the sound of gladness, the voice of bridegroom and the voice of bride" (25:10).[27] As noted above, the oracles of exile in Jer 25 share the same superscription and international historical context as those in Jer 36. The king's responsibility for turning joy into mourning is, in Jer 36, a consequence of his tearing and burning a scroll that invokes covenant curses. In this respect, Jehoiakim's violence against the scroll contrasts with his father Josiah's response to hearing the "book of torah" read aloud to him in 2 Kgs 22:11. When the scribe Shaphan reads the "book of torah" to Josiah, the king tears his garment in a public display of penitential mourning (2 Kgs 22:10–11); but when Shaphan's son Gemariah and grandson Micaiah bring Jeremiah's scroll to the attention of Josiah's son Jehoiakim, "neither the king nor any of his servants were in dread, nor did they tear their garments" (Jer 36:24). Instead, the king tears the scroll itself.

The public, performative aspects of mourning rituals are therefore linked in Jer 7, 25, 26, and 36 to the production, promulgation, and destruction of a scroll. These public acts recall the political and ritual dynamics of making and breaking covenants; they represent the formation of social relations actualized by covenant rites and texts and the violence done to human bodies and cities when those relations are broken. Jehoiakim's tearing of the scroll, for example, resembles the bodily dismemberment and cutting associated with covenant rituals and curse formulas, as attested in Jer 34:18 ("I will make the men who transgressed [*ʿbr*] my covenant, who did not carry out the words of the covenant which they cut before me, [like] the calf that they cut in two and between whose pieces they passed [*ʿbr*]") and in the Sefire inscriptions ("Just as this calf is cut in two, so may Matiʿel be cut in two, and may his nobles be cut in two").[28] Joachim

---

27. On the binary pairing of joy and mourning, see Gary A. Anderson, *A Time to Mourn, a Time to Dance: The Expression of Grief and Joy in Israelite Religion* (University Park: Pennsylvania State University Press, 1991); Olyan, *Biblical Mourning*.

28. I A 40 (cf. Gen 15:9–10); Joseph A. Fitzmyer, *The Aramaic Inscriptions of Sefire* (rev. ed.; BibOr 19; Rome: Pontifical Biblical Institute, 1995), 46–47. Saul M. Olyan, written correspondence; see also idem, "Honor, Shame, and Covenant Relations in Ancient Israel and Its Environment," *JBL* 115 (1996): 214 n. 42; Levtow; *Images of Others*, 141; Lundbom, *Jeremiah 21–36*, 564–66. Cf. the burning rites invoked in the Sefire inscriptions (I A 37) and in Esarhaddon's succession treaties (ll. 608–11), on which see n. 69 below.

Schaper has in this respect called attention to the binding power of the scribal documentation and public promulgation of the scroll in Jer 36.[29] As Schaper notes, the importance of accurately fixing the oracles in writing before they were read aloud publicly is indicated by the question asked of Baruch by the palace scribes in 36:17, "How did you write all of these words, was it at his dictation (*mippîw*)?"[30] The publication of an oracle that specifically invokes covenant curses is in this way an extension of the public aspects of covenant rites and texts themselves, including the identification of witnesses and the public nature of the violence enacted as a consequence of covenant violations.[31]

The shadow of Josiah and the curses of the Deuteronomic covenant hover thickly over the linked narratives of Jer 7, 25, 26, and 36. The cycle of violence involving kings (and their palaces), gods (and their temples), peoples (and their cities), and texts (and their authors and audiences) mirrors the formation, reformation, and destruction of social relations during the high and low points of Davidic rule in Jerusalem. The passage from Josiah to Jehoiakim, reform to exile, and covenant making to covenant breaking is represented in Jer 36 through an account of text production

---

29. Joachim Schaper, "On Writing and Reciting in Jeremiah 36," in *Prophecy in the Book of Jeremiah* (ed. Hans M. Barstad and Reinhard G. Kratz; BZAW 388; Berlin: de Gruyter, 2009), 137–47. See also Alan Millard, "Oral Proclamation and Written Word: Spreading and Preserving Information in Ancient Israel," in *Michael: Historical, Epigraphical, and Biblical Studies in Honor of Prof. Michael Heltzer* (ed. Yitzhak Avishur and Robert Deutsch; Tel Aviv: Archaeological Center Publications, 1999), 237–41; Seth L. Sanders, "Performative Utterances and Divine Language in Ugarit," *JNES* 63 (2004): 161–81.

30. Schaper, "Writing and Reciting in Jeremiah 36," 139 and passim. Cf. the term *ša pî*, which is used to refer to authors in the Neo-Assyrian "Catalogue of Texts and Authors" (van der Toorn, *Scribal Culture*, 43, 281 n. 30; W. G. Lambert, "A Catalogue of Texts and Authors," *JCS* 16 [1962]: 59–77). On dictation and proclamation, see Clanchy, *From Memory to Written Record*, 212–20, esp. 218: "Just as reading was linked in the medieval mind with hearing rather than seeing, writing (in its modern sense of composition) was associated with dictating rather than manipulating a pen. Reading and writing (in the sense of composition) were therefore both extensions of speaking and were not inseparably coupled with each other, as they are today" (and see 97, 183). See also Daniel Boyarin, "Placing Reading: Ancient Israel and Medieval Europe," in *The Ethnography of Reading* (ed. Jonathan Boyarin; Berkeley: University of California Press, 1993), 10–37; Sanders, *Invention of Hebrew*, 147, 169, 224 n. 18.

31. Olyan, "Honor, Shame, and Covenant Relations," 204; Levtow, *Images of Others*, 65–66.

and destruction. The violence done to the scroll in Jer 36 tears at the relationship between the king and people of Judah and their divine suzerain. Cutting the scroll uncuts the covenant; burning the scroll burns the palace, temple, and city.

Smashing Tablets: Exodus 32

Correlations between making and breaking covenants, and making and breaking texts, are explicit also in Exod 32, where Moses smashes (*yĕšabbēr*, 32:19) the tablets of testimony in response to a covenant violation. Tablet breaking of the sort depicted in Exod 32 is attested in Mesopotamian traditions dating back to the third millennium B.C.E., and these acts effectively nullified the contracts and other obligatory social relationships represented in inscribed tablets.[32] Esarhaddon's succession treaties, for example, curse anyone who would transgress, transform, erase, or in any way damage or destroy the treaty oaths, thereby equating violations of treaty tablets with violations of treaty stipulations.[33] These tablets appear to have been purposefully smashed and burned before a throne of the Assyrian king in a ritual and political act associated with the destruction of Nimrud (ancient Kalḫu) in 614 B.C.E.[34]

---

32. See examples cited in *CAD* 6, s.v. *ḫepû* (1b, 2a, b, c, d, e, f). I discuss these traditions at greater length in "Text Destruction and Iconoclasm in the Hebrew Bible and the Ancient Near East," in *Iconoclasm and Text Destruction in the Ancient Near East and Beyond* (ed. Natalie N. May; Oriental Institute Seminars 8; Chicago: Oriental Institute of the University of Chicago, 2012). On the destruction of loan tablets, see Steven J. Garfinkle, "Shepherds, Merchants, and Credit: Some Observations on Lending Practices in Ur III Mesopotamia," *JESHO* 47 (2004): 20–21; see also Piotr Steinkeller, "Money Lending Practices in Ur III Babylonia: The Issue of Economic Motivation," in *Debt and Economic Renewal in the Ancient Near East* (ed. Michael Hudson and Marc Van de Mieroop; Bethesda: CDL, 2002), 109–31. I thank Seth F. C. Richardson for his assistance with these and other Assyriological references in this paper.

33. Lines 397–413; text and trans. Simo Parpola and Kazuko Watanabe, eds., *Neo-Assyrian Treaties and Loyalty Oaths* (SAA 2; Helsinki: Neo-Assyrian Text Corpus Project, 1988), 44–45; see also D. J. Wiseman, "The Vassal-Treaties of Esarhaddon," *Iraq* 20 (1958): 57–60.

34. The agents of text destruction at Nimrud were most likely Medes; see M. E. L. Mallowan, "The Excavations at Nimrud (Kalhu), 1955," *Iraq* 18 (1956): 1–21; idem, "The Excavations at Nimrud (Kalhu), 1956," *Iraq* 19 (1957): 5–6; idem, foreword to Wiseman, "Vassal-Treaties of Esarhaddon," i–ii; idem, *Nimrud and Its Remains* (3 vols.; London: Collins, 1966), 1:241–49. See also Mario Liverani, "The Medes at Esar-

The act of text destruction narrated in Exod 32:19 is represented as a response to a specific covenant violation: the casting and worship of a cult image. Associations between making and breaking texts, images, and covenants appear across many ancient West Asian ritual and political traditions. Texts and images were two highly privileged modes of representation in Assyria and Babylonia, both produced in the ritualized workshop environment (*bīt mummi*). Both forms of representation served as a focus for the creation and destruction of social relations through the creation and destruction of these products themselves. The incantation rites for newly created cult images in Assyria and Babylonia, for example, invoke a divine origin by stating that the image was the work not of its human craftsmen but of the gods of the craftsmen ("I did not make [the statue], Ninagal who is EA god of the smith made it"),[35] just as Moses' tablets "were God's work, and the writing was God's writing, engraved upon the tablets" (Exod 32:16).[36] The links between texts, images, and social relations are evident also in the material record from Nimrud, where the smashing and burning of Assyrian treaty tablets appears to have been accompanied by

haddon's Court," *JCS* 47 (1995): 57–62, esp. 62 with n. 33. Liverani identifies these tablets as loyalty oaths for palace guards, not vassal treaties; Seth F. C. Richardson, oral correspondence.

35. Babylonian *Mīs Pî* Ritual Text (BM 45749), line 52; text and trans. Christopher B. F. Walker and Michael B. Dick, *The Induction of the Cult Image in Ancient Mesopotamia: The Mesopotamian Mīs Pî Ritual* (SAALT 1; Helsinki: Neo-Assyrian Text Corpus Project, 2001), 70–82; Levtow, *Images of Others*, 94, 96.

36. "Engraved" (Exod 32:16): *ḥārût* (on which see William H. C. Propp, *Exodus 19–40: A New Translation with Introduction and Commentary* [AB 2A; New York: Doubleday, 2006], 556); cf. Exod 31:18 and 32:32; note also 32:4, where Aaron forms an image of a calf with an engraving tool (*yāṣar ʾōtô baḥereṭ*) (on *ḥereṭ*, see ibid., 549–50). On divine writing in Exodus and Deuteronomy, see Schaper, "Theology of Writing"; Schniedewind, *How the Bible Became a Book*, 130–34; and Jean-Pierre Sonnet, *The Book within the Book: Writing in Deuteronomy* (Leiden: Brill, 1997). On iconic aspects of Scripture, see Karel van der Toorn, "The Iconic Book: Analogies between the Babylonian Cult of Images and the Veneration of the Torah," in *The Image and the Book: Iconic Cults, Aniconism, and the Rise of Book Religion in the Ancient Near East* (ed. Karel van der Toorn; CBET 21; Leuven: Peeters, 1997), 229–48; the "Iconic Books Project" of James W. Watts and Dorina Miller Parmenter (http://jameswwatts.net/iconicbooks); and Dorina Miller Parmenter, "The Bible as Icon: Myths of the Divine Origins of Scripture," in *Jewish and Christian Scripture as Artifact and Canon* (ed. Craig A. Evans and H. Daniel Zacharias; London: T&T Clark, 2009), 298–310.

the destruction of the images of those formerly bound by the loyalty oaths inscribed on these tablets.[37]

In addition to Esarhaddon's succession treaties, many ancient West Asian monumental and statuary inscriptions that represent the formation of social relations include curse formulas warning against acts of text destruction, erasure, and reinscription.[38] The curse formulas of the Sefire inscriptions, for example, warn that "whoever will not observe the words of the inscription which is on this stele or will say 'I shall efface some of its words' … may the gods overturn that man and his house and all that is in it. … May his scion inherit no name."[39] Elsewhere the Sefire inscriptions similarly warn that if anyone should "give orders to efface these inscriptions … and say, 'I shall destroy (*'uha'bid*) these inscriptions and … destroy KTK and its king,' … may he and his son die in oppressive torment."[40] These curses recall the violent threat to dynastic succession invoked in Jeremiah's oracles against Jehoiakim after his acts of text destruction and covenant violation (Jer 36:30–31). The Laws of Hammurabi likewise equate violations of Hammurabi's laws with violations of the law-code inscriptions themselves; they specifically invoke curses against anyone who would alter the engraved words or image of Hammurabi or who would erase Hammurabi's name and replace it with his own.[41] It is also within this context of ritualized violence against texts, images, and engraved names that Esarhaddon inscribed his own name, together with that of his deity Aššur, upon the cult images he returned to a rebellious king in the west, a practice that may be compared to the injunction in Deut 12:1–5 to "completely destroy" (*'abbēd tĕ'abbĕdûn*) Canaanite cult sites, to "smash (*šibbartem*) their standing stones, burn their sacred trees in fire,

37. Wiseman, "Vassal-Treaties of Esarhaddon," 5 and pl. 6:1; Mallowan, "Excavations at Nimrud (Kalhu), 1955," 14; idem, "Excavations at Nimrud (Kalhu), 1956." See also Liverani, "Medes at Esarhaddon's Court" (see n. 34 above).

38. For additional examples, see Levtow, "Text Destruction and Iconoclasm" (forthcoming). On the manipulation of statuary inscriptions in Assyria and Babylonia, see Zainab Bahrani, *The Graven Image, Representation in Babylonia and Assyria* (Philadelphia: University of Pennsylvania Press, 2003), 156–84; Levtow, *Images of Others*, 105, 110, 148.

39. I C 17–24; text, trans. modified from Fitzmyer, *Aramaic Inscriptions of Sefire*, 55, with commentary.

40. II C 1–17; ibid., 125 with commentary. *'uha'bid*: Haphel of *'bd* (ibid., 132).

41. Epilogue xlix.18–44; Martha T. Roth, *Law Collections from Mesopotamia and Asia Minor* (2nd ed.; SBLWAW 6; Atlanta: Scholars Press, 1997), 136.

hew down the statues of their gods, and destroy (*'ibbadtem*) their name from that place" so that Yhwh may "put his name there."[42] In light of these associations between violence against texts and violence against images, it is not unreasonable to also see a connection between the Judahite scribes' concern about Jehoiakim throwing Jeremiah's written Yahwistic oracles into fire (Jer 36:25) and Hezekiah's concern about the kings of Assyria hurling the gods of their enemies into fire (2 Kgs 19:19).[43] So too may Moses' smashing of tablets in Exod 32:19 be compared to what Sennacherib claims was done to the cult images of Babylon during his conquest of that city in 689 B.C.E.: "The gods who dwell therein—the hands of my people seized and smashed (*ušabbiru*) them."[44]

Texts and images both played remarkably dynamic roles in ancient West Asian societies. Whereas the destruction of images has received much scholarly attention in recent years, less attention has been paid to the destruction of texts.[45] These correlations between texts and images helpfully illuminate text production as a socially formative activity in ancient Israel's cultural environment. Both texts and images were products of skilled, elite social groups rooted in palace and temple traditions. Both were constructed in ritual and royal workshops and destroyed in cultic and political contexts associated with the formation of social relations.

Sinking a Scroll: Jeremiah 51

An intriguing corollary to the burning of the scroll in Jer 36 is the sinking of a scroll in Jer 51. Whereas Jer 36 depicts a scroll containing Jeremi-

42. Esarhaddon text: Rykle Borger, *Die Inschriften Asarhaddons, Königs von Assyrien* (AfOB 9; Osnabrück: Biblio-Verlag, 1967), §27 Nin. Episode 14: A IV 1–14; see Steven W. Holloway, *Aššur Is King! Aššur Is King! Religion in the Exercise of Power in the Neo-Assyrian Empire* (Leiden: Brill, 2002), 279 n. 182, 140 and n. 203; Levtow, *Images of Others*, 110, 148, 167. On the power of inscribed names, see n. 76 below.

43. Cf. Sefire inscriptions (I A 37) and Esarhaddon's succession treaties (ll. 608–11); see n. 69 below.

44. Daniel David Luckenbill, *The Annals of Sennacherib* (OIP 2; Chicago: University of Chicago Press, 1924), 83:48 and 137:36–37; Holloway, *Aššur Is King*, 118 n. 143; Levtow, *Images of Others*, 106.

45. One exception is the attention given in biblical scholarship to Egyptian execration texts, on which see Robert Kriech Ritner, *The Mechanics of Ancient Egyptian Magical Practice* (Studies in Ancient Oriental Civilization 54; Chicago: Oriental Institute of the University of Chicago, 1993), 136–90.

ah's Yahwistic oracles against Jerusalem thrown by its recipient into fire, 51:59–64 depicts a scroll containing Jeremiah's Yahwistic oracles against Babylon thrown by its deliverer into water. As was the case with the other acts of text production and destruction I have discussed above, this brief narrative indicates the dynamic role played by texts in ancient West Asian social contexts.

Jeremiah 51:59–64 narrates how a scroll invoking the destruction of Babylon is created by a prophet and scribe in Judah and then destroyed in the waters of the Euphrates: Baruch's brother Seraiah is instructed to take a scroll containing "all these words that are written concerning Babylon" to the city of Babylon itself, read it aloud there publicly, and then "tie a stone to it and throw it into the midst of the Euphrates." The associations in this account between creation, destruction, water, and Babylon suggestively recall cosmogonic conflict myths such as *Enuma Elish*, and these mythic associations are more explicit in the oracles against Babylon collected in the preceding verses of Jer 51. The oracles of vengeance in 50:1–51:58 may be understood as the content of Seraiah's scroll itself, the immediate referent of a scroll upon which Jeremiah wrote "all the calamities that will befall Babylon" and which contained "all these words that are written concerning Babylon" (51:60).[46] These oracles are rich in mythic conflict imagery, including 51:34–36: "King Nebuchadrezzar of Babylon has devoured me … he has swallowed me like a sea monster [*tannîn*].… Therefore thus says Yhwh: I will defend your case and avenge you. I will dry up her sea and make her fountain dry." Similarly, 51:42: "The sea has risen over Babylon; she has been covered by its turbulent waves."

This cosmogonic conflict imagery in Jer 51, when paired with the symbolic act of throwing these words into the river, links the creation and destruction of a text to the creation and destruction of political relationships, cities, cult images, and the world itself.[47] A corollary to the immer-

46. Cf. Jer 36:31. Note also correlations between the punishment against Judah invoked in the account of Baruch's scroll (36:29) and the punishment against Babylon invoked in the account of Seraiah's scroll (51:62).

47. Note the Akkadian verb *ḫepû* (commonly employed with reference to tablet breaking) attested in *Enuma Elish* IV 137: "(Marduk) *split* (*iḫpišima*) her (Tiamat) in two like a dried fish" (*CAD* 6, s.v. *ḫepû* [5]; Philippe Talon, *The Standard Babylonian Creation Myth Enūma Eliš: Introduction, Cuneiform Text, Transliteration, and Sign List with a Translation and Glossary in French* [SAACT 4; Helsinki: Neo-Assyrian Text Corpus Project, 2005], 56).

sion of the scroll in Jer 51 may be seen, for example, in the actions of Assyrian soldiers during Sennacherib's conquest and destruction of Babylon a century earlier, when Babylon's cult images were thrown into the city's flooded canals.[48] Sennacherib claims in his annals to have made Babylon's destruction "more complete than that by a flood," suggestively returning Babylon to an antediluvian state in a cosmogonic reversal that uncreates the city the way Seraiah uncreates the scroll.[49] These associations between Seraiah's immersion of the scroll and Sennacherib's immersion of Babylon and its cult images are further enhanced when Jeremiah, in his last words, instructs Seraiah that after he sinks the scroll in the river he is to say, "Thus shall Babylon sink, never to rise, because of the calamities I am bringing upon her" (Jer 51:64).

Correlations between the sinking of the scroll in Jer 51:59–64, the sinking of cult images in the annals of Sennacherib, and the cosmogonic representations of the sinking of Babylon in both accounts, are evident elsewhere in Jer 51. For example, 51:15-19 includes a hymn to Yhwh paired with an attack against Babylonian cult images: "Maker of Earth with his power, establisher of the world with his wisdom, with his understanding he stretched out the heavens. When his voice thunders, there is a roar of waters in the heavens; he raises the mists from the ends of the earth; he makes lightning for rain, and brings forth wind [*rûaḥ*] from his storehouses" (51:15–16).[50]

The following verses of this poem (51:17–19) claim that Babylonian cult images have no breath (*rûaḥ*), much like the "drowned" scroll upon which this poem is said to have been written.[51] The creation and destruc-

48. Luckenbill, *Annals of Sennacherib*, 83–84:43–56. So too were Babylon's temples destroyed; the creation and destruction of cult sites was another link in this chain of cultural production and destruction, also indicated through the recollection of the Shilonite sanctuary in Jer 7:12.

49. "Cosmogonic reversal": Holloway, *Aššur Is King*, 122; see also Levtow, *Images of Others*, 106–7.

50. Cf. Jer 10:12–16 and 51:42.

51. I borrow here from the discussion of Jer 51 as an instance of "drowning" a scroll in Seth L. Sanders, "Three Drowned Books: Jeremiah 51 and the Cultural 'Nature' of Textuality," presented at the SBL annual meeting, New Orleans, November 2009. Sanders draws upon an interesting analog to Jer 51 in the accounts of Tukaram, a seventeenth-century devotional poet from Maharashtra in western India, which describe how his manuscripts were thrown into the Indrayani River by his persecutors and, miraculously, floated and survived. See Richard M. Eaton, *A Social History*

tion of texts is thereby linked to the creation and destruction of cult images, people, cities, and the cosmos in ways that play richly upon the association of writing with death and immortality.[52]

The account of creation and destruction (textual, iconic, and civic) in Jer 51 also invokes the breaking of covenant relations, through references to the shame conferred upon covenant violators.[53] The shame conferred upon Israel as a result of her covenant violation is recalled in 51:51 ("We are ashamed, for we have heard a reproach; humiliation has covered our faces, for strangers have come into the sacred places of Yhwh's house").[54] Israel's shame is, however, transferred to Babylon ("I will punish the divine statues of Babylon, and her entire land will be ashamed" [51:47]), as Yhwh comes to destroy the city and the "waves roar like great waters" (51:55). The context of covenant violation thus drives the inversion of honor and shame in Jer 51 in the same way that it drives the inversion of joy and mourning in Jer 7 and 25.

The writing of a scroll in Jer 51 does not, therefore, depict the creation of an immortal text meant to preserve the oracles of Jeremiah and stabilize their accurate transmission for future generations of scribes. This narrative does not portray text production as a conservative activity that preserves tradition. On the contrary, the role of the scroll in Jer 51 signifies the entire range of possibilities open to Israelite social groups for the formation of their social relations. The creation and destruction of the text in Jer 51 represents the creation and destruction of people, gods, cities, and the world, and serves to transform social relationships by making, shaping, and breaking social bonds. The dynamics of social formation, and

---

of the Deccan, 1300–1761: Eight Indian Lives (New Cambridge History of India 1.8; Cambridge: Cambridge University Press, 2005), 134–36; J. Nelson Fraser and James F. Edwards, *The Life and Teaching of Tukaram* (Madras: CLS, 1922), 97; Justin E. Abbott, trans., *Life of Tukaram, Translation from Mahipati's Bhaktalilamrita, Chapters 25 to 40* (1930; repr., Delhi: Motilal Banarsidass, 2000), 203–5. I thank Ruth Vanita for bringing the accounts of Tukaram to my attention as well. See also n. 58 below.

52. On writing, memory, and death, see Schaper, "Living Word Engraved in Stone," 16–20, with references.

53. See Olyan, "Honor, Shame, and Covenant Relations," 201–18; Levtow, *Images of Others*, 64–66.

54. "Reproach": *ḥrp*; cf. Hezekiah's petition to Yhwh in 2 Kgs 19:16–18: "Hear the words of Sennacherib, which he has sent to reproach the living god. Truly, Yhwh, the kings of Assyria have laid waste to the nations and their lands and sent their gods into the fire."

of covenant relations in particular, are in this light represented throughout the book of Jeremiah by the creation, transmission, and destruction of words. This prophet was, after all, called upon "to destroy and to tear down, to build and to plant" (1:10), in a wider narrative framed by acts of creation and destruction—in its beginning, of the prophet himself in the womb (1:5), and at its end, of the prophetic text itself by the rivers of Babylon (51:63).

Conclusion

Esarhaddon's succession treaties conclude with curses against those who violate the treaty tablets by consigning them to fire, burying them in the earth, or throwing them into water.[55] Violence against the treaty tablets is equated with violations of the treaty oaths.[56] The biblical narratives I have discussed, in which texts are burned in fire, smashed on the earth, and thrown into water, similarly equate violence against texts with violations of social relationships represented in those texts.[57]

---

55. "If you should remove it, consign it to the fire, throw it into the water, [bury] it in the earth or destroy it by any cunning device, annihilate or deface it" (lines 410–413); Parpola and Watanabe, *Neo-Assyrian Treaties and Loyalty Oaths*, 45. Common clay tablets were generally not fired and would dissolve in water (David P. Wright, oral communication). For additional examples of text destruction traditions of this sort, see Levtow, "Text Destruction and Iconoclasm."

56. As noted above (n. 34), these tablets were eventually smashed and burned during the conquest of Kalḫu by Medes and Babylonians, 75 years after the city, sanctuaries, and cult images of Babylon were inundated by the Assyrian assault.

57. These correspondences between violence against texts and violations of social orders represented in texts may also be understood as a form of ritual analogy, on which see David P. Wright, "Ritual Analogy in Psalm 109," *JBL* 113 (1994): 385–404. I thank David Wright for bringing this perspective on these texts to my attention. In his analogical analysis of Ps 109, Wright argues that "figurative elements in this and other psalms can and are to be understood from a ritual and not just a literary point of view" (ibid., 386). Wright discusses a range of texts including the curse formulas in Esarhaddon's succession treaties and the Sefire inscriptions in support of his corollary observation that "analogy pervades all ritual" (385, 389). Wright further notes that "analogical meaning may also inhere in materials used in a ritual" (387). In these respects, the representations of text destruction I have discussed in this paper might be described as cases of what Wright identifies as "*transformative* analogy" (391).

The dynamic roles played by texts in Israelite social contexts suggest that text production was not a primarily conservative social activity meant to stabilize oral tradition and achieve cultural continuity. On the contrary, a focus on the roles texts play in biblical narratives and in the wider ancient West Asian ritual and political environment illuminates the way writing served to form and reform social relations through the production, transmission, promulgation, and destruction of tablets and scrolls.

One need only follow the fate of Jeremiah's dictated scrolls to find exception to the claim that written texts traveled well and more stably than oral traditions, or to the claim that writing, unlike people, is immortal.[58] The potential instability and mortality of a text may however be read as a ritually and politically pregnant stage in its life. Text production, like cult image construction, could provide the means with which and the mode through which ancient West Asian social groups embodied identities and formed social relationships.[59] Textual activity was never far from ritual and political activity, just as scribal culture was never far from temple and

58. Bell, *Ritual Theory*, 166–67 n. 270; see also Carr, *Writing on the Tablet*, 10; Schaper, "Living Word," 16–20; and the essays collected in Kristina Myrvold, ed., *The Death of Sacred Texts: Ritual Disposal and Renovation of Texts in World Religions* (Surrey: Ashgate, 2010). The disposal of an oracle scroll did not necessitate the permanent loss of its contents. This is indicated, e.g., in Jer 36:27–32, where Baruch retranscribes Jeremiah's oracles after the first scroll was consumed by fire. So too, presumably, do Jeremiah's sunken oracles against Babylon survive in the preserved text of Jer 51. Cf. the accounts of Tukaram discussed in n. 51 above. Redelivery of a consumed scroll is also depicted in Ezek 2:8–3:4, where Ezekiel eats a written scroll prior to delivering it orally. As Carr (*Writing on the Tablet*, 149) and Schaper ("Exilic and Post-exilic Prophecy," 331–32) note, Jer 36 and Ezek 3 together indicate great fluidity with respect to the relative priority of writing and speaking in the transmission of Israelite prophetic traditions.

59. With respect to the destruction of prophetic texts depicted in Jer 36 and 51, Sanders writes: "In these passages … the inherent text of the prophecy generates the writing, but the materiality of the writing is merely a theatrical prop for the prophecy's ritual performance, to help it take effect" (*Invention of Hebrew*, 147). If "text" here refers to semantic content, then the production of inscribed material may be described similarly as the *presencing* of content. Sanders notes, in this respect, the "high level of imagined intimacy and intertwining between writing, speech, and presence" in Hebrew biblical ideologies of reading, and how the West Semitic root *qr'* "is used by gods and ritual participants to invoke the presence of other beings" (ibid.). In this sense, the "materiality of writing" may indeed be described as a "theatrical prop," as a bull is a theatrical prop in the performance of sacrificial cult and a cult image is a prop in the theater of iconolatry.

palace culture.[60] Scribal activity in ancient Israel was a ritualized mode of cultural production through which texts were created and destroyed together with the social worlds they represented.

The different modes of text destruction I have discussed in this essay are linked in an Israelite continuum of textualization, ritualization, and social formation. Within this continuum, the manipulation of texts through cutting and burning is not categorically distinct from the manipulation of flesh and blood in rites of alimentary sacrifice. Both patterns of practice achieve unification and division through ritualized action upon embodiments of social relations.[61] The cutting and burning of Jeremiah's oracles is, after all, what actualizes the oracles themselves (Jer 36:29–31). A similar effect is achieved, in a very different sense, when Ezekiel consumes an oracle through ingestion: a scroll invoking consequences of covenant violation (lamentation, mourning, woe) is embodied by the prophet, transformed into words from his mouth, and spoken to an audience that suffers the realization of its semantic content upon their own bodies and city (Ezek 2:9–3:3).[62] Consuming a text through ingestion or incineration thus achieves the unification and separation that, as Nancy Jay notes with respect to communal and expiatory sacrifice, are "two aspects of one process."[63]

When a scroll invoking rites of cutting and burning is itself cut and burned, the textualization of covenant rites merges with the ritualization

60. On West Asian craft scribalism inside and outside of royal courts, see Sanders, *Invention of Hebrew*, 120, 131–32.

61. See Nancy Jay, *Throughout Your Generations Forever: Sacrifice, Religion, and Paternity* (Chicago: University of Chicago Press, 1992), 17–19, on the "joining and separating aspects of sacrifice." Jay grounds her description of the "logic of sacrifice" in this opposition between unification and differentiation which, she notes, informs the common classification of sacrificial practices as "conjunctive and disjunctive," "collective and piacular," or "communal and expiatory" (ibid.).

62. Exod 32, Jer 51, and Ezek 3 all depict texts being lost (smashed, immersed, consumed) by the same agents responsible for their production or promulgation. This is unlike Jer 36, in which the text's intended recipient becomes the agent of its destruction. All four biblical accounts of text destruction, however, signify manifest violations and realizations of inscribed content. See also n. 58 above.

63. Jay, *Throughout Your Generations Forever*, 18–19. The Akkadian verb *qalû* is employed for burning stelae (*CAD* 13, s.v. *qalû* [2e]) as well as sacrificial animals (s.v. [3]).

of covenant texts.[64] This interplay between textualization and ritualization parallels traditions discussed by Bell in which the ritual burning ("sacrifice") of texts is likened to lighting a lamp through their semantic dimensions.[65] In these respects, the role of texts in ritual contexts unites what James Watts refers to as the semantic, iconic, and performative dimensions of sacred texts.[66] "This perspective," writes Bell, "assumes that the study of religion can go beyond deciphering texts and rites as cultural artifacts and begin to analyze them as strategic dynamics in the very production of culture."[67]

The integration and differentiation of social and semantic realms in ancient West Asia was achieved through the ritualized manipulation of tablets and scrolls, as well as of cult images and animal and human bodies. In this environment the distinction between text production and destruction blurs, because both practices entail an interplay between textualiza-

---

64. See Bell, "Ritualization of Texts." Breaking treaty tablets in this way breaks the social bonds represented and embodied by those tablets.

65. Bell examines these correlations between texts and rites in her discussion of the fifth-century C.E. codification of Daoist *lingbao* ("Numinous Treasure" or "Spiritual Treasure") scriptures and their associated *zhai* rituals, in which the codification of these scriptures coincides with the codification of their ritual use ("Ritualization of Texts"). Bell describes how the study of these Daoist texts is subordinated to their ritual manipulation; to study the former without performing the latter is said to be "like traveling blindly at night without burning a lamp" (ibid., 387 n. 75, and see also 379 n. 49). Bell writes that "both the ritual medium and the textual medium strategically moderated each other, each reorchestrating the social ramifications of the other" (ibid., 392). See Fabrizio Pregadio, *Encyclopedia of Taoism* (Oxford: Routledge, 2008), 663–78.

66. Watts, "Three Dimensions of Scripture"; idem, "Disposing of Non-Disposable Texts: Conclusions and Prospects for Further Study," in *Death of Sacred Texts*, ed. Myrvold, 151–52. Watts calls attention to the frequent association of texts with bodies (for example, with respect to burial and disposal rituals) and identifies the mind-body dichotomy as a potential theoretical issue in discussions of textuality, noting the "contrast between transcendent contents and immanent material form" (153). A dichotomy of this sort may, however, be problematic as an analytic tool for understanding textual dynamics in ancient West Asian ritual contexts that assume an identity between symbol and referent. See Bahrani, *Graven Image*, 134, 147–48.

67. Bell, "Ritualization of Texts," 392. See also Sanders (*Invention of Hebrew*, 3): "Fixing texts firmly in dead, ancient contexts paints a satisfying but static picture. It does not explain how new texts or contexts emerge. But if language helps create people's social contexts, then it has a fundamental dynamic dimension: people can act to change their contexts through language."

tion and ritualization in processes of social formation. The same may said of the distinction between iconism and iconoclasm: both constellations of practices configure social relations through the ritualized manipulation of their iconic embodiments.[68] These correlations between texts and images as embodiments of social relations are invoked in the concluding curses of Esarhaddon's succession treaties ("Just as an image of wax is burnt in the fire and one of clay is dissolved in water, (so) may your figure be burnt in the fire and sunk in water").[69] Crafting, inscribing, cutting, burning, breaking, and sinking tablets and scrolls may in these respects be located within a broad continuum of ritualized social dynamics associated with cult image construction and destruction, treaty formation and warfare, and birth and burial.[70]

---

68. It is within this ritualized framework of iconism and textuality that scripturalized revelations of aniconic legislation and iconoclastic oracles are attributed to the intermediaries of Israel's creation and destruction. Before Israel's conquest of Canaan, Moses delivers Yahwistic legislation forbidding the construction and worship of Canaanite engraved statuary (Exod 20:4/Deut 5:8; Exod 20:23; 34:17; Lev 19:4; 26:1; Deut 4:15–25; 27:15). Before Jerusalem's conquest by Babylon, Jeremiah delivers Yahwistic oracles targeting Babylonian cult images (Jer 51:17–19). These divine expressions of aniconism and iconoclasm are inscribed on documents that, remarkably, these same intermediaries then destroy.

69. Lines 608–11 (Parpola and Watanabe, *Neo-Assyrian Treaties and Loyalty Oaths*, 55). Cf. the Sefire inscriptions (I A 37): "Just as this wax is burned by fire, so may Mati['el be burned by fi]re!" (Fitzmyer, *Aramaic Inscriptions of Sefîre*, 47, 95). (On unfired clay tablets dissolving in water, see n. 55 above.) This may also suggest possible correlations with a ritualized use of wax writing tablets. On wax writing tablets in Mesopotamia, see M. E. L. Mallowan, "The Excavations at Nimrud (Kalḫu), 1953," *Iraq* 16 (1954): 98–110, pls. xxii, xxiii; D. J. Wiseman, "Assyrian Writing Boards," *Iraq* 17 (1955): 3–13; Margaret Howard, "Technical Description of the Ivory Writing-Boards from Nimrud," *Iraq* 17 (1955): 14–20. See also *CAD* 6, s.v. ḫepû (2a) (citing TCL 13 160:13): "their wax tablets are erased, their (clay) tablets broken."

70. See, e.g., Z. Bahrani, *Rituals of War: The Body and Violence in Mesopotamia* (New York: Zone, 2008); Walker and Dick, *Induction of the Cult Image*, 29; D. Max Moerman, "The Death of the Dharma: Buddhist Sutra Burials in Early Medieval Japan," in *Death of Sacred Texts*, ed. Myrvold, 71–90; Måns Broo, "Rites of Burial and Immersion: Hindu Ritual Practices on Disposing of Sacred Texts in Vrindavan," in ibid., 91–106; Nalini Balbir, "Is a Manuscript an Object or a Living Being? Jain Views on the Life and Use of Sacred Texts," in ibid., 107–24; and Kristina Myrvold, "Making the Scripture a Person: Reinventing Death Rituals of Guru Granth Sahib in Sikhism," in ibid., 125–46.

Over the course of the past century, biblical scholarship has fruitfully employed orality/literacy theorems to explain aspects of scribal activity and text production in ancient Israel. This analytic framework should, however, be applied with a critical awareness of its tendency to generate misleading dichotomies concerning cultural continuity and change, which in turn support conceptions of static societies and objectified tradition as well as cultural biases toward either end of the oral/written spectrum. I do not dispute that scribes in ancient Israel fixed oral and ritual traditions, along with the social relations they represented, in textual form.[71] I argue instead that the textual form did not itself then remain fixed and static in Israelite social contexts. Israelite scribal products served as the focus for a range of social practices in which oral, aural, visual, and written modes of communication and representation were ritually integrated.[72] Texts in ancient Israel ought therefore to be viewed "not simply as expressions or reflections of changing social situations but as dynamic *agents of change*."[73] In other words, through the interplay between textualization and ritualization, the mediator (the scribe) creates the medium (the text) and "the medium is the message."[74] The textualized acts of violence I have discussed

71. The processes of textualization, ritualization, and social formation discussed in this paper concern all modes of scribal activity; on distinctions between scribes as copyists and scribes as authors and editors, see van der Toorn, *Scribal Culture*, 109–10, 125–26.

72. On hearing, seeing, writing, and "symbolic objects," see Clanchy, *From Memory to Written Record*, 203–26. Describing ceremonies for the conveyance of property in early medieval England, Clanchy writes that "the witnesses 'heard' the donor utter the words of the grant and 'saw' him make the transfer by a symbolic object, such as a knife or turf of land" as well as a Gospels text, a charter, or an inscribed object such as an ivory whip handle or knife (203–7). As Clanchy notes, Bibles are still used in legal oath-swearing ceremonies today (205).

73. Bell, "Ritualization of Texts," 369. On the agency of inscribed monuments in Mesopotamia, see Irene J. Winter, "Agency Marked, Agency Ascribed: The Affective Object in Ancient Mesopotamia," in *On Art in the Ancient Near East*, vol. 2: *From the Third Millennium B.C.E.* (ed. Irene J. Winter; Culture and History of the Ancient Near East 34.2; Leiden: Brill, 2010), 307–31; idem, "After the Battle Is Over: The Stele of the Vultures and the Beginning of Historical Narrative in the Ancient Near East," in ibid., 28–29, 38.

74. Marshall McLuhan, *Understanding Media: The Extensions of Man* (Cambridge: MIT Press, 1994), 7–21; Bell, "Ritualization of Texts," 369; Bill Brown, "Thing Theory," *Critical Inquiry* 28 (2001): 1–22; I thank Ronald S. Hendel for suggesting the potential utility of "thing theory" to describe the social agency of texts in antiquity. See

in this essay may all be described as ritualized acts of cultural production.[75] Attention to such acts highlights the role texts played in the formation of social relations, as embodiments of these relations and as dynamic agents of their change.

In the monistic cultural and ontological environment of ancient West Asia, words embodied the presence and power of the gods and humans who wrote them. As such they were burned and broken, smashed and sunk in ways that richly illuminate what has been called the "numinous power of writing" in antiquity.[76] Ancient texts were never simply objectified, passive representations of their content and context as they have

---

also van der Toorn's discussion of prophetic textualization in *Scribal Culture*, 205–32, and Carr's support of "sociological and anthropological approaches to the Bible that stress … the social dimensions of visual and material aspects" of scribal products and practices (*Writing on the Tablet*, 292).

75. On the strategic deployment of violence, see Saul M. Olyan's essay in the present volume; see also Bahrani, *Rituals of War*.

76. Schniedewind, *How the Bible Became a Book*, 24–34; Niditch, *Oral World*, 78–88. My focus in this paper on covenant contexts need not be read into all examples of text destruction (Daniel E. Fleming, oral communication). The same identity between social relations and their textualized representations obtained for a much wider range of ancient West Asian and Mediterranean texts and contexts including, e.g., loan documents, censuses, and curse formulas (see n. 32 above). Schniedewind, e.g., cites Num 5:23–24 as an instance of written language becoming a ritual "ingredient" and describes the writing of names as "a dangerous objectification of the essence of a person," citing Exod 30:11–16, Num 1:47–53, and 2 Sam 24 ("Textualization of Torah," 95–96); cf. burning and imbibing the golden calf in Exod 32:20. Note also the political role of seals in antiquity (as well as in the medieval period, on which see Clanchy, *From Memory to Written Record*, 207), and the legally binding power of signatures to this day. On "numinous" or "magical" aspects of words and writing in antiquity, see Bahrani, *Rituals of War*, 59–64; idem, *Graven Image*, 96–120; Jean Bottéro, *Mesopotamia: Writing, Reasoning, and the Gods* (trans. Zainab Bahrani and Marc Van de Mieroop; Chicago: University of Chicago Press, 1992), 87–102; Niek Veldhuis, "The Poetry of Magic," in *Mesopotamian Magic: Textual, Historical, and Interpretative Perspectives* (ed. Tzvi Abusch and Karel van der Toorn; Groningen: Styx, 1999), 35–48; Susan Ackerman, "Household Religion in Ancient Israel," in *Household and Family Religion in Antiquity* (ed. John Bodel and Saul M. Olyan; Ancient World: Comparative Histories; Oxford: Blackwell, 2008), 137; John G. Gager, *Curse Tablets and Binding Spells from the Ancient World* (Oxford: Oxford University Press, 1992); Joseph Naveh and Shaul Shaked, *Magic Spells and Formulae: Aramaic Incantations of Late Antiquity* (Jerusalem: Magnes, 1993); idem, *Amulets and Magic Bowls: Aramaic Incantations of Late Antiquity* (Jerusalem: Magnes, 1998); Hans Dieter Betz, ed., *The Greek Magical Papyri in Translation* (Chicago: University of Chicago Press, 1992); David Frankfurter,

become for their modern readers. On the contrary, writings were subjectified and writing practices were intersubjective. To disembed Israelite texts from their active roles in ancient social contexts is therefore to ignore a primary component of textual evidence itself. Text artifacts purposefully damaged in antiquity retain a value beyond their lost semantic content as source materials for modern reconstructions of ancient societies.

Religion in Roman Egypt (Princeton: Princeton University Press, 1998), 198–264; Ritner, *Mechanics of Ancient Egyptian Magical Practice*, 4–72.

The Function of Feasts: An Anthropological Perspective on Israelite Religious Festivals

Carol Meyers

Periodic gatherings for the consumption of food and drink characterize human societies everywhere. From prehistoric times to the present, around the globe, people have assembled to partake of special meals marking a variety of occasions. The ubiquity of shared repasts across cultures and the concomitant availability of social-science analysis of those events provide an opportunity to examine the festive occasions of ancient Israel.[1] Doing so can illuminate aspects of Israelite society not otherwise visible.

Let me begin with a note about terminology, specifically, about the relationship of the words *festivals* and *feasts* in the title of this paper. Both come from the Old Latin via Old French.[2] "Feast" derives from *festa*, meaning "holidays, feasts," which itself is derived from the plural of *festus* ("festive, joyful, merry"), which is also the root of "festival." Both are related to *feriæ*, "holiday," and *fanum*, "temple." When these English terms originated in the thirteenth century C.E., they were not only synonymous but also signified religious events. In the biblical past too, festivals were generally celebrations with ritual components that typically involved feasting. Indeed, social scientists consider feasting itself a powerful form of ritual activity,[3] and a festival without feasting would not have been a festal occa-

1. "Israel" and "Israelite" are used here in a general cultural, rather than a specific political or geographical, sense.

2. See the *Online Etymological Dictionary*: http://www.etymonline.com/index.php?term=feast.

3. Michael Dietler, "Feasts and Commensal Politics in the Political Economy: Food, Power, and Status in Prehistoric Europe," in *Food and the Status Quest: An Interdisciplinary Perspective* (ed. Polly Wiessner and Wulf Schiefenhövel; Providence: Berghahn, 1996), 89. See also idem, "Theorizing the Feast: Rituals of Consumption,

sion. Thus, with respect to ancient Israel, the two English words (*festivals* and *feasts*) are roughly interchangeable; and biblical scholars sometimes use them synonymously.[4]

There are many different kinds of feasts, and anthropologists have classified them in different ways, as noted briefly below in the third section. But for the purposes of this paper, the relevant classification is whether the feasts were held on an ad hoc or regular basis. The former are typically those associated with life-cycle events such as births, weddings, and deaths. Ad hoc feasts can also be held at other opportune moments for a variety of reasons; for example, they can serve as crisis interventions, mark the dedication of a temple or other building, celebrate a military victory, foster political gain, or create cooperation among groups. The ad hoc feasts of ancient Israel certainly deserve more social-science analysis than they have received, notwithstanding some recent attention to political feasting.[5] But the focus of this study is on the feasting that is associated with ancient Israel's regular or calendrical festivals, which are also understudied from a social-science perspective. Those feasts, it is important to note, have a community dimension; that is, they involved feasting that transcended individual households.

This essay has four parts: (1) discussion of past social-science analysis of festivals mentioned in the Bible and the general lack of such research in contemporary biblical scholarship; (2) identification of the regular Israelite feasts as known from biblical texts, and consideration of the validity of using biblical data as sources for Israelite festal occasions; (3) the characteristics of feasts as described in recent anthropological literature, and reasons for the affective power of feasts in ancient Israel; (4) proposals, based on anthropological research, for the social (and socioeconomic) and political (and politico-economic) functions of Israelite festivals.

Commensal Politics, and Power in African Contexts," in *Feasts: Archaeological and Ethnographic Perspectives on Food, Politics, and Power* (ed. Michael Dietler and Brian Hayden; Smithsonian Series in Archaeological Inquiry; Washington, D.C.: Smithsonian Institution Press, 2003), 65–70.

4. For example, James C. Vanderkam, "Feasts and Fasts," *New Interpreter's Dictionary of the Bible* (ed. Katharine Doob Sakenfeld; Nashville: Abingdon, 2007), 2:443–47.

5. Nathan MacDonald, *Not Bread Alone: The Uses of Food in the Old Testament* (Oxford: Oxford University Press, 2008); see esp. his ch. 2 on feasting in relation to the rise of the monarchy.

Biblical Festivals in Anthropological Research

The prominence of regularly occurring festivals in the Pentateuch, as well as their sporadic appearance in the Deuteronomic History and in prophecy, has produced a wealth of scholarship. The attention to these festivals, all of which entail sacrifice, has been a major way of both accessing and assessing Israelite religion. Indeed, a recent survey of Israelite religion claims that it is "probably considered more often in the context of sacrifice than of any other concept."[6] Publications examining Israelite religion and especially priestly sources invariably include reference to and sometimes extensive treatment of the *môʿădîm* and *ḥaggîm*.[7]

However, in the past century this scholarship has rarely engaged anthropological literature. Rather, it has focused on the history of the festivals, the differences among biblical sources that mention them, their location in the ancient Hebrew calendar, and the nature of the associated sacrifices. For example, Jacob Milgrom's masterful Anchor Bible volume on Lev 23–27 includes six essays on the list of festivals in the Holiness Code (Lev 23); but these essays deal mainly with source-critical issues and with the relation of the Leviticus list to passages about festivals in other biblical books, in Qumran texts, and in ancient Near Eastern literature.[8] A similar focus characterizes the six essays on the festival calendar of Num 28–29 in Baruch Levine's equally masterful Anchor Bible volume on Num 21–36.[9] Older, mid-twentieth-century scholarship—such as Hans-Joachim Kraus's *Worship in Israel* and Roland de Vaux's *Ancient Israel*[10]—tends to be taxo-

---

6. Richard Hess, *Israelite Religions: An Archaeological and Biblical Survey* (Grand Rapids: Baker Academic, 2007), 179.

7. The *môʿădîm* were the major feasts as well as new moons and the Sabbath, all calculated according to the movement of heavenly bodies; see Klaus Koch, "*môʿēd*," *TDOT* 8:169–79. This term is often found in synonymous parallelism with the closely related term *ḥaggîm*, which designates a community festival, especially the three major ones, and is never used for a family celebration; see Benjamin Kedar-Kopfstein and G. Johannes Botterweck, "*chagh*; *ḥgg*," *TDOT* 4:205–9.

8. Jacob Milgrom, *Leviticus 23–27: A New Translation with Introduction and Commentary* (AB 3B; New York: Doubleday, 2001), 2054–80.

9. Baruch A. Levine, *Numbers 21–36: A New Translation with Introduction and Commentary* (AB 4A; New York: Doubleday, 2000), 394–422. Levine does devote somewhat more attention than does Milgrom to the history of the festivals.

10. Hans-Joachim Kraus, *Worship in Israel: A Cultic History of the Old Testament* (trans. Geoffrey Buswell; Richmond: Knox, 1965); Roland de Vaux, *Ancient Israel: Its*

nomic while also discussing the origins of the festivals and their relation to the corresponding events of other ancient Near Eastern cultures. To be sure, de Vaux does probe the meaning of sacrifice; but he does so only by suggesting the relationship of sacrifice to deity. The implications of the feasting component of festivals for the participating individuals and for the community of celebrants were largely ignored.

This has not always been the case. Some 120 years ago William Robertson Smith asserted, "The sacrificial meal ... was a social act...; the very act of eating and drinking [together] was a symbol and a confirmation of fellowship and mutual social obligation.... Those who sit at meat together are united for all social effects."[11] These words are from *The Religion of the Semites*, a classic work in the use of anthropological data for understanding the religion and culture of the Israelites.[12] Indeed, as part of the "first wave" of the use of social theory in the study of Israelite religion,[13] Robertson Smith's work is arguably the prototype of social-science approaches in biblical studies. Although anthropological paradigms and data have consistently been present in biblical scholarship, especially in the last forty years as part of a second wave of biblical scholarship informed by the social sciences, they have rarely been used for the study of festivals. Even Ronald Hendel's welcome anthropological approach to Israelite sacrifice and foodways, which draws especially on Victor Turner's work with respect to Exod 24[14] and on Mary Douglas's work in reference to P,[15] focuses more on symbolic meanings than on

---

Life and Institutions (trans. John McHugh; New York: McGraw-Hill, 1961; original in French, 1958), 484–506.

11. William Robertson Smith, *The Religion of the Semites: The Fundamental Institutions* (1889; repr., New York: Meridian, 1956), 269.

12. See Naomi Steinberg, "Social-Scientific Criticism," in *Methods of Biblical Interpretation* (excerpted from the *Dictionary of Biblical Interpretation*; Nashville: Abingdon, 2004), 275.

13. So Robert Wilson in his contribution to this volume. First-wave social-science biblical scholarship dates from the late nineteenth century to the end of World War II.

14. Victor W. Turner, *Dramas, Fields, and Metaphors: Symbolic Action in Human Society* (Ithaca, N.Y.: Cornell University Press, 1974); and Victor W. Turner and Edith Turner, *Image and Pilgrimage in Christian Culture: Anthropological Perspectives* (New York: Columbia University Press, 1978).

15. Mary Douglas, *Purity and Danger: An Analysis of the Concepts of Pollution and Taboo* (London: Routledge, 1966); idem, "Deciphering a Meal," in *Implicit Mean-*

experiential functions.[16] Similarly, Gillian Feeley-Harnick's summary of a thematic issue of the *JAAR* highlights anthropological perspectives on religion and food but, like the articles that are the basis for her discussion, is concerned more with the symbolic or structural role of food than with the function of the food events themselves and how they may have been experienced by the participants.[17]

Now, well into the twenty-first century, new developments in anthropological research can perhaps rectify the dearth of biblical scholarship examining feasting as part of the lived religion of the Israelites. In the last two decades, anthropologists have given considerable attention to the topic of festal eating and its cultural importance.[18] Ethnographers have explored the dynamics of feasting, and archaeological anthropologists have identified its archaeological correlates.[19] This recent scholarship provides important new resources for understanding the function of festivals for people and their communities. To be sure, there are wide cross-cultural variations in feasting patterns. Yet certain attributes of festal meals, which are described in the third part of this essay, appear consistently and thus can be used with reasonable certainty in considering Israelite feasts. Just as important, much of the recent anthropological research by ethnographers and archaeologists has focused on agrarian peoples, from Pre-Pottery Neolithic settlements to contemporary premodern subsistence farmers. Thus we are now better situated to analyze Israelite feasting in social-science

---

ings (London: Routledge, 1975), 249–75; idem, "The Forbidden Animals in Leviticus," *JSOT* 59 (1993): 3–23.

16. Ronald Hendel, "Sacrifice as a Cultural System: The Ritual Symbolism of Exodus 24:3–8," *ZAW* 101 (1989): 366–90; idem, "Table and Altar: The Anthropology of Food in the Priestly Torah," in *To Break Every Yoke: Essays in Honor of Marvin L. Chaney* (ed. Robert B. Coote and Norman K. Gottwald; SWBA 2/3; Sheffield: Sheffield Phoenix Press, 2007), 131–48.

17. Gillian Feeley-Harnick, "Religion and Food: An Anthropological Perspective," *JAAR* 63 (1995): 565–82.

18. See, e.g., Martin Jones, *Feast: Why Humans Share Food* (Oxford: Oxford University Press, 2007); the contributions and bibliographies in Polly Wiessner and Wulf Schiefenhövel, eds., *Food and the Status Quest: An Interdisciplinary Perspective* (Providence: Berghahn, 1996); and the contributions and bibliographies in Dietler and Hayden, *Feasts*. See also the various individual studies referenced in this paper.

19. See, e.g., the correlates listed in Katheryn C. Twiss, "Transformations in an Early Agricultural Society: Feasting in the Southern Levantine Pre-Pottery Neolithic," *Journal of Anthropological Archaeology* 27 (2008): 419–24.

terms than was Robertson Smith, whose comparative anthropology, laudable in many ways, was flawed in its reliance on the practices of nomadic bedouin in Palestine or the Arabian Peninsula. Following Julius Wellhausen and other nineteenth-century orientalists, his assumption, no longer tenable, was that the Israelites were originally pastoralists.

In the last few years the new anthropological scholarship on feasting has surfaced on the fringes of biblical archaeology.[20] It has appeared in the study of the Aegean world; for example, a recent (2004) issue of *Hesperia* is devoted to Minoan feasting.[21] It has also influenced the work of several archaeologists working in the historical periods of the southern Levant. These researchers have sought to identify aspects of festal eating that can be recognized in the material culture. Ann Killebrew and Justin Lev-Tov, for example, have studied Iron Age I feasting and cuisine in Philistia—but not in neighboring Israel; and, in highlighting archaeologically retrieved correlates of feasting, they limit their conclusions to issues of ethnicity and do not address the broader functions of feasting.[22] Another recent study, by Lev-Tov and Kevin McGeough, does explore the sociopolitical aspects of religious feasting; but it deals with Late Bronze and not Iron Age sites.[23] Similarly, Sharon Zuckerman's study of feasting at Hazor looks only at Bronze Age evidence.[24] Their work, promising as it is, has not shed

---

20. *Biblical archaeology* is a contested term, and I use it here simply to refer to archaeological research related to biblical materials or the study of ancient Israel or both. See William G. Dever, "Biblical Archaeology," *OEANE* 1:315–19.

21. James C. Wright, ed., *The Mycenaean Feast* (*Hesperia* 73.2; Princeton: American School of Classical Studies at Athens, 2004). However, most of the studies in that anthology deal with prehistory, as do those in another 2004 publication in Aegean studies: Paul Halstead and John C. Barnett, eds., *Food, Cuisine and Society in Prehistoric Greece* (Sheffield Studies in Aegean Archaeology 5; Oxford: Oxbow Books, 2004).

22. Ann E. Killebrew and Justin Lev-Tov, "Early Iron Age Feasting and Cuisine: An Indicator of Philistine-Aegean Connectivity?" in *Dais: The Aegean Feast: Proceedings of the 12th International Aegean Conference University of Melbourne, Centre for Classics and Archaeology, 25–29 March 2008* (ed. Louise A. Hitchcock, Robert Laffineur, and Janice Crowley; *Aegaeum* 29; Liège: University of Liège, 2008), 339–49.

23. Justin Lev-Tov and Kevin McGeough, "Examing [*sic*] Feasting in Late Bronze Age Syro-Palestine Through Ancient Texts and Bones," in *The Archaeology of Food and Identity* (ed. Katheryn C. Twiss; Occasional Papers 34; Carbondale: Southern Illinois Press, 2007), 85–111.

24. Sharon Zuckerman, "'Slaying Oxen and Killing Sheep, Eating Flesh and Drinking Wine': Feasting in Late Bronze Age Hazor," *PEQ* 139 (2007): 186–204.

light on sites or epochs of Syria-Palestine directly related to the periods of the Hebrew Bible.

Nor, to the best of my knowledge, has the recent anthropological scholarship on feasting had an impact on biblical studies—with one notable exception: Nathan MacDonald's book *Not Bread Alone: The Uses of Food in the Old Testament*,[25] which was adumbrated somewhat by the 1990s analysis of ceramics, architecture, and faunal remains of Iron I Shiloh.[26] MacDonald explicitly incorporates both anthropological methodologies and archaeological discoveries in his study of a number of biblical texts in which food plays a role. He examines ad hoc political feasting and its role in the establishment of the monarchy; and he also explores some literary use of food motifs in Judges, in Second Temple novellas, and in other parts of the Hebrew Bible. Yet MacDonald considers his book, which is admirable for its broad scope and its multidisciplinary approach, a preliminary study; moreover, he examines only one aspect of regular feasting, namely, the role of the three main feasts in the communal commemoration of a remembered experience according to texts in the book of Deuteronomy.[27] Clearly it is time for the regular Israelite feasts to emerge from the shadow of the sacrificial context in which they appear in the Hebrew Bible and be recognized as events that served important functions for the participants and their communities. First, however, it is important to identify those feasts and explain why the biblical data likely reflect Israelite reality.

Regular Religious Feasting in Ancient Israel

The Hebrew Bible is our main source of information about the regular or calendrical feast days of the Israelites. These communal celebrations comprised the three annual (pilgrim) festivals (Passover/Matzot, Weeks/Shavuot, and Booths/Sukkot) and the monthly or lunar ones. The weekly Sabbath should also be considered a regular feast transcending individual households.[28] As noted above, biblical scholarship treats these festivals

25. See also MacDonald's book for the general reader, *What Did the Ancient Israelite Eat? Diet in Biblical Times* (Grand Rapids: Eerdmans, 2008).

26. Israel Finkelstein, ed., *Shiloh: The Archaeology of a Biblical Site* (Monograph Series 10; Tel Aviv: Institute of Archaeology of Tel Aviv University, 1993).

27. In the chapter on "Chewing the Cud: Food and Memory in Deuteronomy" in *Not Bread Alone*, 70–99.

28. Reasons for considering the Sabbath, whenever and for whatever reasons it

descriptively, theologically, or phenomenologically and seeks to understand their symbolism or discover their origins; but the functions of the festival experience itself are not considered.

Before proceeding, two methodological issues must be addressed. The first concerns whether relatively late biblical texts are reliable sources of information about the Israelites throughout the Iron Age. Most of the biblical information about regular feasts appears in Priestly and Deuteronomic texts dating to the late monarchic, exilic, or postexilic periods. These texts likely encode practices that are centuries older and were widely observed; yet it is also possible that the P and D materials prescribe new or narrowly practiced behaviors that became widespread only in Second Temple times if at all. However, even if all the festivals mentioned in the Hebrew Bible were not actually practiced throughout the entire Iron Age as well as in the Second Temple period, it seems relatively certain, for three reasons, that at least some of them were held for much if not all of those epochs.

For one thing, archaeological remains from many types of Iron Age communal shrines, as Rüdiger Schmitt shows in his typological study of cult places,[29] invariably include not only explicitly ritual items, such as incense stands, altars, and figurines, but also utilitarian vessels for food preparation and consumption. Most typologies of Iron Age shrines—for example, those of John Holladay,[30] William Dever,[31] Wolfgang Zwickel,[32] and Ziony Zevit[33]—have focused on the former (ritual items) virtually to

---

was instituted, a communal festival are presented in my article, "Feast Days and Foodways: Religious Dimensions of Household Life," in *Family and Household Religion: Toward a Synthesis of Old Testament Studies, Archaeology, Epigraphy, and Cultural Studies* (ed. Rainer Albertz, Beth Alpert Nakhai, Saul M. Olyan, and Rüdiger Schmitt; Winona Lake, Ind.: Eisenbrauns, forthcoming).

29. Rüdiger Schmitt, "A Typology of Ancient Israelite Cult Places," in Albertz et al., eds., *Family and Household Religion* (forthcoming).

30. John S. Holladay Jr., "Religion in Israel and Judah under the Monarchy: An Explicitly Archaeological Approach," in *Ancient Israelite Religion: Essays in Honor of Frank Moore Cross* (ed. Patrick D. Miller Jr., Paul D. Hanson, and S. Dean McBride; Philadelphia: Fortress, 1987), 249–302.

31. William G. Dever, *Did God Have a Wife? Archaeology and Folk Religion in Ancient Israel* (Grand Rapids: Eerdmans, 2005), 110–75.

32. Wolfgang Zwickel, *Der Tempelkult in Kanaan und Israel: Studien zur Kultgeschichte Palästinas von der Mittelbronzezeit zum Untergang Judas* (FAT 10; Tübingen: Mohr Siebeck, 1994), 9 and passim.

33. Ziony Zevit, *The Religions of Ancient Israel: A Synthesis of Parallactic Approaches* (London: Continuum, 2001), 123–266.

the exclusion of the latter (utilitarian objects). Schmitt's work is important not only because it notes the presence of vessels used for preparing and serving comestibles but also because it indicates that these archaeological correlates of feasting are present throughout the Iron Age.

Another reason is that many of the festal occasions found in P and D also appear in the eighth-century prophets and in Psalms, thus signifying their existence prior to the end of the monarchy. For example, both Hosea (2:11 [MT 13]) and Amos (8:5) mention new moons and sabbaths together with festivals.[34] Moreover, the instructions for Passover rituals in Exod 12 apparently preserve a pre-Priestly tradition of a household-based communal (at the clan level) sacrificial event that was celebrated long before the emergence of the festival's historicized traditions, such as the consumption of unleavened bread and a lamb.[35] It is also possible that Exod 12 is a late text, setting an old custom that still dominates—a household Passover—in a time before the existence of centralized temple cult.[36] Similar arguments could be made for the other pilgrim festivals.

Finally, ethnographic data support the likelihood that regular festivals, at least the three annual ones, were part of Israelite culture throughout the Iron Age. Seasonal celebrations are virtually ubiquitous in traditional agrarian societies, where they are keyed to critical moments in subsistence patterns. These three events are all agricultural festivals tied to major harvests and can be coordinated with the harvest seasons mentioned in the tenth-century B.C.E. Gezer calendar.[37] In short, even without the biblical references, we would have to posit that people living in the

---

34. See also Isa 1:13–14; 29:1; Hos 2:13 (MT 15); 9:5; Ps 81:3 (MT 4).

35. See Naomi Steinberg, "Exodus 12 in Light of Ancestral Cult Practices," in *The Family in Life and in Death: The Family in Ancient Israel: Sociological and Archaeological Perspectives* (ed. Patricia Dutcher-Walls; LHBOTS 504; New York: T&T Clark, 2009), 89–103. Steinberg argues that the blood manipulation in the Passover sacrifice originates in ancestral cultic practices. For a brief summary of other research on the history of the Passover, see Eckart Otto, "*pāsaḥ, pesaḥ*," *TDOT* 12:9–14; and Carol Meyers, *Exodus* (NCBC; Cambridge: Cambridge University Press, 2005), 94–100, 103–7. Some scholars (e.g., Tamara Prosic, "Origin of Passover," *SJOT* 13 [1999]: 78–94), however, argue that the Passover originated during the exile.

36. Susan Niditch, *Folklore and the Hebrew Bible* (GBSOT; Minneapolis: Fortress, 1993), 65.

37. See Jan A. Wagenaar, *Origin and Transformation of the Ancient Israelite Festival Calendar* (BZABR 6; Wiesbaden: Harrassowitz, 2005), 7–21.

highlands of Palestine in the Iron Age engaged in recurrent feasts marking harvests and the moving of herd animals.

The second issue involves the question of who the celebrants were. One of the features of feasts, as will be noted in the next section, is their corporate nature. A feast is a meal writ large, in that it involved groups of people: households, clans, or even national communities. And festivals could be local, regional, or larger events, for the archaeological correlates of feasting have been found at neighborhood, village, and regional shrines and at supraregional (state) shrines, high places, and temples.[38] However, it is impossible to determine the level of participation. For example, would every member of every household have traveled to regional shrines for a new moon celebration, or would they have been more likely to gather at village shrines? And different festal events may have had different levels of participation, with Passover, for example, being more popular than a new moon celebration. Thus it is likely that there would have been variability from event to event and from year to year as well as across the centuries.

Another issue related to the level of participation is that of class, age, and gender. Would servants, children, and women as well as men have been among the participants? Would they have been present at some or all festal occasions? Biblical data, especially the Deuteronomic texts prescribing the three seasonal festivals, seem to contain conflicting information. Susan Ackerman provides a thorough review of the Deuteronomic materials and concludes that wives were not necessarily present at all the festivals, perhaps because child-rearing responsibilities precluded their participation, and that the Passover festival at the central shrine seems to have constrained the presence of all but male householders.[39] Nonetheless, because these biblical materials are concerned with the central shrine and are probably from late in the Iron Age, they should not be regarded as indicative of Israelite festal practices throughout the Iron Age. Moreover, those texts generally do not preclude the participation of children and servants, both male and female; and the more comprehensive list in Deut 16:14 includes "strangers, orphans, and widows." Other biblical pas-

---

38. Schmitt, "Typology." Note, however, that the existence of temples outside Jerusalem in the Iron II period, except perhaps for Arad, is doubtful; see Avraham Faust, "The Archaeology of the Israelite Cult: Questioning the Consensus," *BASOR* 360 (2010): 23–35.

39. Susan Ackerman, "Only Men Are Created Equal," *Journal of Hebrew Scriptures* 10 (2010): 15–23.

sages (e.g., Exod 12:3–4, 45–49; 2 Sam 6:19; cf. Deut 31:10–12) indicate inclusivity. Given the preponderance of ethnographic materials indicating gender inclusivity in community feasts and the information about the role of Israelite women in food preparation, women in social reality (as opposed to biblical texts) were likely to have been frequent participants in festivals, which were food events.[40] Thus, although some degree of inclusivity for women, children, servants, and socially marginal groups can be conjectured, especially because of all the positive attributes of feasting (see the next section), it is not certain that inclusive participation characterized all festivals in all places at all times.

Nor is it likely that everyone in ancient Israel would have celebrated and experienced seasonal festivals in exactly the same ways. Feast days would have had different meanings and functions for ordinary agrarian households than they did for priestly and political elites on the one hand or sojourners and servants on the other. Also, festivals in larger settlements were probably more elaborate than those held in rural or regional cult centers. Although a core of similar cultic feasting practices can be posited for various locations and diverse social groups, most of the functions known from recent anthropological research and described in the fourth part of this paper are likely to be ones experienced by the nonelite agrarian majority.

Feasting in Recent Anthropological Research

Although feasts have been relatively understudied and undertheorized by social scientists in the past, many anthropologists now regard the study of feasts to be essential for understanding numerous cultural processes of premodern societies.[41] Collective consumption is considered a significant

40. For gender identification of Israelite bread production, see Carol Meyers, "From Field Crops to Food: Attributing Gender and Meaning to Bread Production in Iron Age Israel," in *The Archaeology of Difference: Gender, Ethnicity, Class and the "Other" in Antiquity: Studies in Honor of Eric M. Meyers* (ed. Douglas R. Edwards and C. Thomas McCollough; AASOR 6/61; Boston: American Schools of Oriental Research, 2007), 72–75. A similar argument could be made for the preparation of other foodstuffs, although the archaeological data that contribute to gender identification are relatively scanty.

41. Michael Dietler and Brian Hayden, "Digesting the Feast: Good to Eat, Good to Drink, Good to Think: An Introduction," in Dietler and Hayden, *Feasts*, 1–2; see also the other contributions to the Dietler and Hayden volume.

factor in various aspects of community life. As a cultural phenomenon, it is a category of human experience that is found virtually everywhere—it is as much a part of human societies as are kinship and language. Feasting involves food, which satisfies a basic and ongoing human need for nutrition; as such it is embedded in a wide array of cultural elaborations. Feasting is thus a central cultural practice. Rather than being instances of unnecessary self-indulgence, as they are often perceived in the modern world, feasts were essential for the functioning if not the very survival of premodern societies. Anthropologists have shown them to be powerful arenas for establishing, maintaining, or even changing cultural identities and ideologies; they can also be strong mechanisms for establishing and maintaining political dominance. Because feasts entail a considerable expenditure of time and energy as well as resources, there surely were benefits for the participants and their society.[42] At the same time, some aspects of feasting may have served the interests of elites more than the people as a whole. Before considering what those benefits and liabilities were—that is, how feasts functioned for some or all of the participants—it is important to note the essential qualities of feasting as understood by anthropologists.

The term *feast* can include a widely diverse set of cultural events, and it is not surprising that anthropologists define and categorize feasts in different ways. The ad hoc versus regular distinction has already been used to specify which Israelite festivals are to be considered here. Anthropologists draw on many other features of feasts to organize their study of these events. Categories include work feasts, penalty feasts, competitive feasts, and others, depending on the organizing principles of individual scholars. For example, one of the leading theorists of feasts divides them into three main types: alliance and cooperative, economic, and diacritical; and another anthropologist proposes eight different types.[43] The very variety of suggested feasting typologies may indicate that imposing taxonomies

42. Brian Hayden, "Feasting Research"; online: http://www2.sfu.ca/archaeology-old/dept/fac_bio/hayden/curres/feast.htm.

43. For the three types, see Brian Hayden, "Fabulous Feasts: Prolegomenon to the Importance of Feasting," in Dietler and Hayden, *Feasts*, 35–40; and for the eight, see James R. Perodie, "Feasting for Prosperity: A Study of Northwest Coast Feasting," in Dietler and Hayden, *Feasts*, 189–91. Most of these categories classify specially called feasts rather than life cycle and seasonal ones, but their features and functions are present broadly in all kinds of festal events.

on feasts provides methodological convenience at the price of oversimplifying a diverse, complex, and rich set of behaviors.[44]

Thus no specific typology is adopted here, other than that regularly occurring calendrical festivals rather than ad hoc ones are being considered.[45] However, several prominent characteristics are consistently ascribed to all kinds of feasts and serve to define them generically; and they are relevant to a consideration of regular Israelites festivals:[46] (1) A feast is commensal; that is, food and drink are shared and consumed. (2) The food and drink are usually more abundant and/or of better quality than at an ordinary meal, and foodstuffs that are rarely available often become part of the festal repast. (3) The feast is longer than everyday meals, sometimes lasting a number of days and involving a sequence of meals. (4) The number of participants typically transcends the number of people in an individual household; that is, a feast may involve several households or lineages, a larger group (such as a clan) connected by kinship or proximity, or even an entire community.

The positive aspects of these features, and of the entire festival context, help to create an emotional dimension that affects the participants in multiple ways and in turn enhances the effectiveness of a feast's various functions. Several factors would have been present in ancient Israelite society and would have contributed to the affective power of the feasting experience. They include:

1. The emotional dimension of feasting is aroused by the heightened expectation, the overall enjoyment, and the sustained camaraderie of feasts. These qualities serve to move feasting out of the realm of the ordinary and into the realm of the extraordinary. Festivals offer a dramatic change from the tedium of daily life; and the opportunity to interact with a wider group of people than those in one's household and immediate environs is a welcome and highly anticipated departure from the rather circumscribed world of everyday activities. Given what is known about the agrarian basis of life for virtually all Israelites, we can be fairly certain that their quotidian subsistence tasks brought them into contact with relatively

44. Yannis Hamilakis, "Time, Performance, and the Production of a Mnemonic Record: From Feasting to an Archaeology of Eating and Drinking," in Hitchcock et al., *Dais*, 17–18.

45. Although ad hoc festivals are not part of this discussion, many of the functions described here would pertain to them too.

46. See, e.g., the working definitions of feasts in the various papers in Dietler and Hayden, *Feasts*.

few people and that they would surely have been eager to partake of the stimulation and excitement of festal events.

2. The emotional intensity of feasts is augmented by their sheer entertainment value, for they typically manifest something of a carnival atmosphere. In addition to the meals themselves, festal rejoicing is often dramaturgically charged with music, dance, and other performative expressions. These contribute, just as do the special and abundant food and drink, to the affective aspect of festivals. Indeed, there is ample biblical evidence that music or dance or both were a component of Israelite feasts just as at the banquets of royalty and other elites.[47] Young women "dance in the dances" at the annual feast at Shiloh according to Judg 21:21. Psalm 68:24 (MT 25) mentions a "procession" (NRSV) of musicians and singers going to the temple, although the occasion is not specified.[48] But Ps 81:1–3 (MT 2–4) refers to vocal and instrumental music in connection with the new moon festival, Isa 29:30 alludes to the singing and instrumental music of a festival, and Amos 5:21–23 links songs and instrumental music with festivals and sacrifice. Also, in enjoining those feasting at the central shrine to rejoice, especially on the occasions of the three annual festivals, Deuteronomy (e.g., 12:7; 16:10–11, 13–15) uses the verb *śāmaḥ*, which is frequently linked with the excitement aroused by music and dance.[49] Note too that the priestly anointing of Solomon is followed by both music and feasting (1 Kgs 1:40–41). The feasts of gods, no doubt conceptualized in relation to royal banquets, were likewise accompanied by music and song.[50]

3. The emotional aspect of feasting would also have been intensified for ancient Israel's three seasonal festivals because they were events marking milestones in the agricultural calendar. That is, they were the culmination of a process of planting and nurturing crops and caring for animals, a process often fraught with tension because of climate variabil-

47. For examples of music and other entertainment at banquets, see 2 Sam 19:35 (MT 36); cf. Qoh 2:8. The same was true in the ancient Near East in general, for banquet scenes typically depict performers along with the presentation of foodstuffs; see Denise Schmandt-Besserant, "Feasting in the Ancient Near East," in Dietler and Hayden, *Feasts*, 392–96.

48. Hebrew *hălīkōt* seems to refer to the procession of God as well as to a parade of human performers; cf. Ps 24:7–10.

49. See Gottfried Vanoni, "*śāmaḥ; śāmēaḥ; śimḥāh*," *TDOT* 14:142–43.

50. As, e.g., in Canaanite mythology; see Michael David Coogan, ed. and trans., *Stories from Ancient Canaan* (Philadelphia: Westminster, 1978), 37, 89–90.

ity and concomitant concerns about crop yield.[51] Agricultural celebrations meant a welcome relief from agrarian anxiety and also, as will be indicated below, provided an opportunity for struggling households to acquire needed sustenance.[52]

4. Finally, the emotional intensity of festivals was surely augmented by the sacrificial regimen itself, which included the slaughter of animals and consumption of meat. Even without the evidence of biblical texts specifying bloody sacrifices, faunal remains found at shrines in Palestine and many other places in the Near East and Mediterranean basin indicate that animal slaughter and consumption took place at local and village shrines as well as at regional and national ones.[53] Indeed, animals were the quintessential sacrificial foodstuff, one that was probably absent from daily fare except perhaps in elite households.[54] The killing of animals for sacrifice (and the concomitant feasting) was a highly charged event, for it involved the expenditure of a valuable commodity and provided a welcome oppor-

---

51. See David Hopkins, *The Highlands of Canaan: Agricultural Life in the Early Iron Age* (SWBA 3; Sheffield: Almond, 1985), 215–16, 224. Peter Garnsey (*Food and Society in Classical Antiquity* [Key Themes in Ancient History; Cambridge: Cambridge University Press, 1999], 2, 30, 34–35) likewise points to the great variability of crop yields in the Mediterranean basin, with frequent bad harvests creating periodic food shortages and causing persistent undernourishment.

52. This may have been less so for Passover, however, which came at a time when supplies of foodstuffs would have been at their lowest; see Walter J. Houston, "Rejoicing before the Lord: The Function of the Festal Gathering in Deuteronomy," in *Feasts and Festivals* (ed. Christopher Tuckett; CBET 53; Leuven: Peeters, 2009), 4–6.

53. Schmitt, "Typology of Israelite Cult Places." The national shrine in Jerusalem, of course, does not survive in the archaeological record. However, a state shrine of the northern kingdom is arguably represented in the ruins at Tel Dan, which provides evidence of animal slaughter and ritual meals; see Avraham Biran, *Biblical Dan* (Jerusalem: Israel Exploration Society and Hebrew Union College–Jewish Institute of Religion, 1994), 159–234. In fact, one of the rooms in the Iron II cultic complex at that site, perhaps to be identified with biblical *liškâ* (see below, n. 96), was arguably dedicated to the festal meals of offerants rather than priestly officials; see Andrew R. Davis, "Elite and Non-Elite Religion at Iron Age Tel Dan" (paper presented at the SBL annual meeting, New Orleans, 22 November 2009).

54. Raising animals for meat is not an economical use of land and vegetation resources in Mediterranean areas, including the southern Levant. In antiquity cattle (oxen) were kept mainly as draft animals; and the more numerous sheep and goats were raised for their skins, wool, and to a certain extent the dairy products they provided. Animals were also an important resource in times of agricultural shortfalls; see Hopkins, *Highlands of Canaan*, 248.

tunity to partake of meat. The slaughtering process itself would have produced additional emotional intensity. In his discussion of animals, feasting, and sacrifice in the Aegean world, Yannis Hamilakis paints a vivid scenario of bloody sacrifice:

> The violence involved in the killing ... of animals for a feast, [and] the associated visual and auditory impact (the screams of animals in distress as they face their death, the streams of blood, the bright red colour of blood and meat), would have made such occasions distinctive and special, and certainly memorable. In the presence of a large number of feast participants, such events would have acquired unique theatricality.[55]

All told, Israelite festivals would have taken place in an atmosphere of heightened emotion that enhanced the experience of the participants and contributed to the effectiveness of the various functions of community festal events.

Feasts thus constitute the "ideal stage" for multiple and important processes, all vital to ancient Israel as a premodern agrarian society.[56] Anthropological research not only allows us identify the characteristics of Israelite feasts but also informs the following discussion of their specific functions.

Functions of Israelite Festivals[57]

Ethnographic studies have identified a variety of roles, generally interrelated, that feasting plays but have rarely investigated its specifically religious functions or meanings.[58] In contrast, the religious dimension of feasting has long been part of Hebrew Bible scholarship, notably in the discussion of the origin and meaning of sacrifices in ancient Israel.[59] Thus I will not consider the religious aspect of the festivals here except to note

---

55. Hamilakis, "Time, Performance," 8. The olfactory dimension in the cooking of meat should also be mentioned as contributing to the emotional intensity.

56. Dietler and Hayden, "Digesting the Feast," 4.

57. This discussion of function draws to some extent on my comments about feasting in "Feast Days and Food Ways."

58. A list of nine feasting functions is provided in Hayden, "Fabulous Feasts," 29–30. Some of them concern the manipulation of political and economic power and would pertain to special feasts called by local or royal authorities but not to regular religious ones.

59. A summary appears in Gary A. Anderson, "Sacrifice and Sacrificial Offer-

briefly some of the major and overlapping theories about the meaning of sacrifice: (1) the sharing of a meal with the deity; (2) part of an exchange system with the deity, who both receives and bestows the products of agricultural activity;[60] (3) expressions of gratitude to the deity for having bestowed sustenance. Whatever the specific meaning, the participants affirm and intensify their loyalty to the deity or deities to whom they bring offerings. Religious functions, however, are both embedded in and enhance all others, especially the social (and socioeconomic) and political (and politico-economic) ones considered here. Although these functions are intertwined to a great extent, they are discussed separately.

Social and Socioeconomic Functions

Closely related to the religious aspects of feasts are the social ones, some of which have an economic element. Ordinary meals are about human relationships as much as they are about food,[61] and this is true all the more so for special culinary events. Festivals are powerful instruments for creating and maintaining social cohesion in the participants' present.

One of the ways this happens is by linking them to their shared history. Taking part in a feast fosters and maintains a sense of identity with all those understood to have performed the same rituals and eaten the same foods in the community's past.[62] Moreover, the images of the distant past, whether actual or constructed or some combination thereof, serve to legitimate the present order.[63] At some uncertain point in Israel's history, the historicization of the three main agricultural festivals contributed to this connection with the past.[64] Formative aspects of Israel's *Heilsgeschichte*—the story of departure from Egypt, wilderness journey, and Sinai

ings in the Old Testament," *ABD* 5:871–73. See also Hendel, "Sacrifice as a Cultural System," 366–89.

60. The related concept of gift exchange among people at feasts is discussed below.

61. Patricia Harris, David, Lyon, and Sue McLaughlin, *The Meaning of Food* (Guilford, Conn.: Globe Pequot, 2005), 8.

62. See Paul Connerton, *How Societies Remember* (Cambridge: Cambridge University Press, 1989), 66.

63. Ibid., 3.

64. The Deuteronomic mandate for Passover includes remembrance of exodus (16:3, 6) as do the instructions in Exodus, probably E, for the Passover sacrifice (12:26; cf. the P instructions for unleavened bread, the paschal sacrifice, and other elements of the Passover meal in Exod 12:1–20); Booths is connected to the exodus in Leviticus

covenant—were mapped onto these festivals, which thereby became the occasions for recounting the master narrative of escape to freedom and for affirming its associated values. As a dramatic departure from the tedium of daily routines, Israelite feasts surely provided the occasion for story-tellers—perhaps priests, elders, or sages—to regale the participants with the rousing songs and tales that conveyed their mnemo-history, the substance of their collective cultural memory.[65] In a world without television, newspapers, or the Internet, feasts were the setting in which collective memories were transmitted, maintaining and solidifying group identity and values in the process.

Not only the recited festival narratives but also the foods themselves served as important vehicles in that process. As is the case in many cultures, food and memory are powerfully interrelated.[66] Food is a material substance that both embodies and structures our relationship with the past in socially meaningful ways.[67] The special foods of a feast—and here the meat, unleavened bread, and bitter herbs associated with the exodus are the best examples—provided direct sensory engagement with the mythic Ur-experience said to have produced the first Passover.[68] Festival foodstuffs serve as material mnemonics, connecting people to their remembered past and to one another. Food, memory, and religious ritual intersect, with "ritual as a key site where food and memory come together."[69] Cultural identity is thus powerfully reinforced in the sensory materiality, especially the food, of community feasts.[70] The recurrent shar-

---

(23:42–43); and Weeks seems to be connected to the exodus in Deut 26:1–10. In addition, observing the Sabbath is linked with exodus remembrance in Deut 5:15.

65. Those "performances" may have been precursors of the public reading of texts at the three main festivals in later periods; see Arie van der Kooij, "The Public Reading of Scriptures at Feasts," in Tuckett, *Feasts and Festivals*, 27–44.

66. Feeley-Harnick, "Religion and Food," 567.

67. Deborah Lipton, "Food, Memory and Meaning: The Symbolic and Social Nature of Food Events," *Sociology Review* n.s. 42 (1994): 668. Lipton's research focuses on developed societies but is also relevant to developing or premodern ones.

68. See the detailed analysis, especially with respect to Deuteronomic materials, in MacDonald, *Not Bread Alone*, 70–99.

69. See David E. Sutton, *Remembrance of Repasts: An Anthropology of Food and Memory* (Oxford: Berg, 2001), 19.

70. See C. Nadia Seremetakis, "The Memory of the Senses: Pts. I and II," in *Perception and Memory as Material Culture in Modernity* (ed. C. Nadia Seremetakis; Boulder: Westview, 1994), 3.

ing of a special meal commemorating a significant past event joins people together into what is called a *communitas* (people who share an intense sense of commonality and a heightened feeling of togetherness).[71] Commensality itself thus "plays a central role in constructing and reinforcing social bonds," with the culinary event serving as a medium for integrating people into social units, whether based on real or constructed kinship.[72]

The forging and sustaining of social bonds would have been especially effective and important at ancient Israel's local or regional feasts, where people belonging to the same tribal subgroup or clan gathered for monthly new moon festivals as well as annual ones.[73] These suprahousehold bonds helped to legitimate, maintain, and strengthen the genealogical relationships, whether real or constructed, among these groups, which in turn promoted peaceful relationships among the groups gathered at a festival; the shared experience and especially the consumption of food together forestalls enmity and conflict. Just as important, these suprahousehold bonds were critical for community survival in the precarious subsistence economy of ancient Israel as is the case for all groups living in marginal environments.[74]

As Norman Gottwald noted long ago, one of the hallmarks of kinship bonds, whether real or fictive, is their role in effecting the mutual aid provided by members of related groups to each other.[75] Although he

---

71. Edith Turner, "Rites of Communitas," *Encyclopedia of Religious Rites, Rituals, and Festivals* (ed. Frank A. Salomone; Religion and Society 6; New York: Routledge, 2004), 97–101.

72. Katheryn C. Twiss, "Home Is Where the Hearth Is: Food and Identity in the Neolithic Levant," in Twiss, *Archaeology of Food and Identity,* 52. The dynamics of the commensal experience for binding together people with family or ethnic ties, or both, has also been noted in the study of the classical world; see Garnsey, *Food and Society,* 6–7, 128, 132–33.

73. Monthly festivals—as well as an annual *zebaḥ mišpāḥâ*—may also have served to preserve the solidarity with deceased ancestors that was essential for maintaining a household's patrimony; see Meyers, "Feast Days and Food Ways."

74. For an ethnographic example, see Carole M. Counihan, "Bread as World: Food Habits and Social Relations in Modernizing Sardinia," in *The Anthropology of Food and Body: Gender, Meaning and Power* (New York: Routledge, 1999), 37. For the classical world, see Garnsey, *Food and Society*, 41.

75. Norman K. Gottwald, *The Tribes of Yahweh: A Sociology of the Religion of Liberated Israel, 1250–1050 B.C.E.* (Maryknoll, N.Y.: Orbis, 1979), 253, 267, 316, 389, 464, 583, 613, 616. Gottwald emphasizes cooperative efforts in protection against enemies and measures to ensure the viability of tribal subunits as well as the economic func-

was describing ancient Israel's premonarchic period, his observations are pertinent to agrarian Israelite society throughout the Iron Age. Reciprocal help was essential in a society without government-sponsored agencies to deal with the problems—illness, death, food shortages, labor shortages—that inevitably arose in the rather precarious ecosystem of the Israelite highlands. Belonging to a group of connected households or a common clan entails a sense of mutual responsibility; it thus produces behaviors—contributing labor, food, or succor to group members in need—that would not otherwise be forthcoming.[76] The sense of a shared past and shared values fostered by the feasting experience helps create a culture of reciprocity, in which people feel obligated to help one another, thereby forming what has been called a "life-crisis support group."[77] Reciprocal relationships among social equals can significantly reduce the vulnerability of agrarians.[78] Festival commensality is thus essential for the material and social survival of a group.[79] Another highly significant mechanism for establishing and maintaining group bonds, of course, was marriage; and festal gatherings fostered this mechanism too. The gathering of related groups enhanced the ability of parents to find mates for their offspring and thus create new marital ties that would contribute to the likelihood of mutual aid in difficult times.[80] Despite its sordid context and the absence

---

tions of mutuality. See also Hopkins (*Highlands of Canaan*, 256), who calls social relations "the best insurance against environmental failure."

76. On the basis of ethnographic and archaeological data, I have argued elsewhere that these important connections were facilitated by the informal social networks established and sustained by women as a product of their intrinsic connections with their natal households and especially though their propensity to gather together to perform tedious household tasks. See Carol Meyers, "In the Household and Beyond: The Social World of Israelite Women," *ST* 63 (2009): 33.

77. Michael J. Clarke, "Akha Feasting: An Ethnoarchaeological Perspective," in Dietler and Hayden, *Feasts*, 163.

78. Peter Garnsey, *Famine and Food Supply in the Graeco-Roman World: Responses to Risk and Crisis* (Cambridge: Cambridge University Press, 1988), 55–58, 272. Commensal sharing was one of several strategies employed by peasants in marginal Mediterranean lands to deal with subsistence crises; see ibid., 43–68.

79. See Carole Counihan, "The Social and Cultural Uses of Food," in *The Cambridge World History of Food* (ed. Kenneth F. Kiple and Kriemhild Conée Ornel; 2 vols.; Cambridge: Cambridge University Press, 2000), 2:1514–15.

80. An ethnographic example comes from a rural Greek village with a ritual calendar that included twelve Great Feasts (*panēgýria*) as well as several minor ones. The *panēgýria* serve as "prime arenas for courtship, legitimate meeting places of young

of parental matchmaking, the narrative at the end of Judges about the procurement of wives for the Benjaminites at an annual festival may reflect that feasts were settings in which marital liaisons might be arranged.

The commensality of feasts has another, directly economic benefit for the participants in that people typically bring with them the foodstuffs produced in their specific eco-niches when they gather for festivals. Because of the extremely varied geo-climatic zones of ancient Palestine, crops that flourished in one area may have been in short supply in nearby or even adjacent areas. The survival of the small-scale dry farming typical of the Palestinian highlands was dependent to some degree on the exchange of commodities among householders, and festal occasions facilitated these exchanges. Sometimes called "gift exchange," intrahousehold sharing of agricultural products was an important structural component of agrarian life; it helped traditional farming populations achieve somewhat more nutritional balance in their less than ideal diets than would otherwise have been possible.[81] One of the leading theorists of gift exchange, Marcel Mauss, notes that festivals are the quintessential setting for these redistributive transactions.[82] His emphasis on exchanges sees them as a form of the mutuality just described—a mutuality that helps build and solidify relationships and thereby assures positive interactions among people by keeping them continually indebted to one another. However, the benefits for subsistence are surely part of the exchange of edible commodities. Mauss even suggests that a concern for others is part of the dynamics of gift exchange.[83] Others, however, doubt that exchanges

---

men and young women"; see Laurie Kain Hart, *Time, Religion, and Social Experience in Rural Greece* (Greek Studies: Interdisciplinary Approaches; Lanham, Md.: Rowman & Littlefield, 1992), 251.

81. Garnsey, *Food and Society*, 30–31. The so-called Mediterranean diet is overidealized, and the reality is that most peasants in ancient Israel would have suffered from periodic if not chronic dietary insufficiencies as well as inadequate amounts of vital nutrients. See ibid., 43–61; and MacDonald, *What Did the Ancient Israelites Eat*, 57–60, 91–93.

82. Marcel Mauss, *The Gift: The Form and Reason for Exchange in Archaic Societies* (1923–1924; trans. W. D. Halls; repr., New York: Norton, 2000), 79. Note too that the gift theory of E. B. Tylor (*Primitive Culture* [2 vols.; New York: Holt, 1871]), although much refined, still has value in the study of sacrifice.

83. Mauss, *Gift*, 15–18. Mauss's work on gift exchange is the theoretical basis for Menahem Herman's analysis of sacrifice, with the tithe representing a gift to the deity that will be reciprocated by divine gifts to the offerant; see his "Tithe as Gift: The Biblical Institution in Light of Mauss's 'Prestation Theory,'" *AJSR* 18 (1993): 51–73.

follow shared moral principles and believe that reciprocity is practiced only when it serves the self-interests of those involved.[84]

One final point about the special foods of a festival is their role in differentiation. For one thing, like the mundane foodways of a group, special foods contribute to the construction and maintenance of present group identity by differentiating the group from others. That is, the food practices of a feast, insofar as they diverge from those of other ethnicities, become cultural markers, signifying the boundaries between the collective self and the other.[85] Food is thus instrumental in strengthening group identity in relation to surrounding peoples.[86] This was undoubtedly the case by the postexilic period; but the role of foodways in Israelite identity formation may have already been present in earlier periods, as Hendel has suggested.[87] Another kind of differentiation is inherent in the bloody sacrifices themselves in that they mark out the hierarchy of the divine, human (priests and other participants), and animal spectrum.[88] The deity receives the choice parts, the priests then receive a portion (except for burnt offerings, in which the entire animal is immolated), the other offerants receive shares, and of course the animal itself as the substance of the entire process is the expendable end of the continuum.

Embedded in the social functions are what might be called psychological functions insofar as individuals were impacted by the social processes. The household was the basic unit of festival participation, and larger social or political units (village, clan, tribe, nation) were sometimes involved. Yet the festival experience contributed to the identity formation of the individual as well as one or more of the participating corporate entities. Feasting provides individuals with a sense of belonging to the commensal group—the household as well as the larger units observing the festival. This helps new members of a household (sojourners, servants, or women

84. Gerhard Lenski, *Power and Privilege: A Theory of Social Stratification* (Chapel Hill: University of North Carolina Press, 1984), 44.

85. Katheryn C. Twiss, "We Are What We Eat," in Twiss, *Archaeology of Food and Identity*, 2–3.

86. Lipton, "Food, Memory and Meaning," 680.

87. Hendel, "Table and Altar," 140–42. Although palaeozoological analysis and materialist considerations suggest that pig avoidance as an Israelite ethnic marker may be postexilic, categories of clean and unclean appear in J's flood story (Gen 7:2–3; 8:20) and suggest that they are preexilic.

88. Garnsey, *Food and Society*, 64–65. Cf. Hendel, "Table and Altar," 143–44.

marrying a family member) to actualize their new identity in an historical sense and, for new wives, in a genealogical one.

Another psychological benefit derives from the future orientation involved. Judging from ethnography and our own experience, festivals are highly anticipated events. As already noted, the expectation of special food, excitement, abundance, and entertainment not available on a daily basis provides a relief from the sometimes meager meals and humdrum character of ordinary life. Knowing that periodic feasts lasting up to a week or more are in the offing would have helped ordinary agrarian Israelites tolerate the difficulties of eking out a living in the often unforgiving highland environment. This future time orientation of feast days is called "prospective memory," and it would have brightened everyday life while also contributing to the power of the memories ritualized by feast days.[89]

In addition, regular feast days linked to the annual agricultural seasons and to the lunar and weekly cycles contribute to the overall integrity of a person's life experience.[90] Everyday life is structured by a series of events understood to be recurrences not only of historical experiences but also of natural processes, punctuating mundane existence with occasions partaking of the sacred.[91] Israelite feast days were events that marked the rhythms of nature and time as well as history and time. Thus the economic and social features of an individual's life were bound up in sequences that constituted an organic whole.

Political and Politico-economic Functions

Both regular and ad hoc feasts serve an explicitly political role, as anthropologists have shown. The ad hoc ones serving political functions appear in the Bible and deserve brief mention because the dynamics are similar to those of regular feasts. There are multiple biblical examples of feasting accompanying the establishment of a covenant. Jacob and his kin share a sacrificial meal after making a covenant with Laban (Gen 31:43–54); after the sacrifice (see v. 54), they "eat bread" (NRSV), which is probably a euphemism for having a meal as indicated by the NJPS translation, "partake of the meal." Moses and the leaders of the people (Aaron, Nadab, Abihu,

89. See Sutton, *Remembrance of Repasts*, 28–30.

90. See Laurie Hart, *Time, Religion, and Social Experience in Rural Greece* (Lanham, Md.: Rowman & Littlefield, 1992), 256.

91. Cf. Connerton, *How Societies Remember*, 65–66.

and seventy elders) mark the Sinai covenant with a sacrificial feast (Exod 24:9–11). In both instances, the commensal experience has transformative force, contributing as it does to the obligation of the parties to keep the agreement. Other specially called political feasts involve the assertion of power and the manipulation of economic resources, and again there are examples in biblical narrative.[92] A notable exemplar of an ad hoc political feast is found in the description, no doubt hyperbolic, of the extravagant and perhaps euergetistic sacrificial festival provided by Solomon at the inauguration of the temple (1 Kgs 8:62–66).[93] Such an event of royal patronage would have served not only to acknowledge divine presence and authority but also the power of the realm. It is no accident that after a week of rejoicing, the assembled masses are said to have blessed the king, not the LORD, as they departed the festivities (1 Kgs 8:66). The commensal hospitality inherent in the feasting of the dedicatory event helped to gain the support of the people and further legitimate Solomon's royal power. Regardless of this feast's historicity, the biblical account is an appropriate expression of the dynamics of inaugural feasts; and those dynamics, albeit on a less grandiose scale, were undoubtedly part of regular festivals too. That is, they acknowledge and strengthen the authority of the community leaders (elites)—priests, elders, clan officials, tribal heads, kings—who organize and implement them.

For both ad hoc and regular festivals, political functions are intertwined with economic ones in that they link the productivity of households with the economic resources of larger sociopolitical structures.[94] The offering of sacrifices at regular feasts entails the contribution of goods from the participants' households to the regional or national shrine; and significant portions of these offerings remain with the priestly and/or political elites who organize and carry out the festivities. Elites in this way augment their coffers or stores, which are the economic resources enabling

92. In his chapter on "Feasting Fit for a King: Food and the Rise of the Monarchy," MacDonald links feasting, and the concomitant distribution of food by a small elite, to the transition from tribal units to a monarchy; see *Not Bread Alone*, 134–65.

93. Cf. 1 Kgs 8:5, where a separate but similarly extravagant feast accompanies the bringing of the ark to Jerusalem (so Mordechai Cogan, *I Kings: A New Translation with Introduction and Commentary* (AB 10; New York: Doubleday, 2000), 288–89. Cogan points out (291, 293) that these dedicatory events were standard practice in the ancient Near East, but he does not comment on their politico-economic dynamics.

94. Dietler, "Food and Commensal Politics," 89.

them to maintain power.[95] Yet some of the contributed resources are, in a sense, returned to the participants as their share of the festal meal(s), as perhaps in 1 Sam 9:12–13.[96] Indeed, the general term for sacrifice, *zbḥ*, probably implies both slaughter and a meal, as does the similar term in Ugaritic,[97] and the term "sacrificial meal" would be appropriate.

Elites also contribute to feasts from their own royal lands and flocks or herds, typically providing some of the elaborate and bountiful food and drink constituting the feast, as Josiah does in the Passover account in 2 Chr 35:7, 13. This has been documented at Emar, where the king especially (but also others) provided certain provisions for week-long religious festivals.[98] Royal lands in ancient Israel perhaps produced surpluses for feasts as well as requisite supplies for the royal house and bureaucracy.[99] Such largesse garners the admiration and gratitude of the people, which in turn helps create the loyalty and fealty necessary for maintaining sovereignty. This aspect of commensal politics is called the "patron-role feast," for it "symbolically reiterate[s] and legitimize[s] institutional relations" of unequal power.[100] Indeed, anthropologists consider the munificence

---

95. The three-storied side chambers of the Jerusalem temple (1 Kgs 6:5–6), like those at the ʿAin Dara shrine and other ancient Near Eastern temples, should be understood as storage rooms not only for temple equipment (1 Kgs 7:52) but also for supplies and nonperishable offerings; see Cogan, *1 Kings*, 239.

96. After the sacrifices that followed the transfer of the ark to Jerusalem, David provides gifts of food to all women and men who were there (2 Sam 6:18–19). Note the equation of eating with offering sacrifices in 1 Sam 9:12–13; and see 1 Sam 9:22–24. The term *liškâ* seems to designate a room in a shrine or temple in which sacrificial meals were eaten; so P. Kyle McCarter Jr., *I Samuel: A New Translation with Introduction and Commentary* (AB 8; Garden City, N.Y.: Doubleday, 1980), 51, 180. McCarter also restores with LXX for 1 Sam 1:18, a reference to Hannah eating in a chamber of the Shiloh shrine. See also D. Kellerman, "*liškâ*," *TDOT* 8:35–36. The nature of the ceramic and animal remains at Iron I Shiloh suggests the redistributive functions of the site as a political and religious center; see Baruch Rosen, "Economy and Subsistence," in *Shiloh: The Archaeology of a Biblical Site* (ed. Israel Finkelstein; Monograph Series 10; Tel Aviv: Institute of Archaeology of Tel Aviv University, 1993), 366–70.

97. Jan Bergman, Helmer Ringgren, and Bernhard Lang, "*zābhach*," *TDOT* 4:10, 17.

98. Lev-Tov and McGeough, "Examing [*sic*] Feasting," 99.

99. References to royal estates and their productivity include 1 Sam 8:12 and 1 Chr 27:25–31.

100. Dietler, "Feasts and Commensal Politics," 96–97. In Hayden's typology, these events would be considered "political support" feasts and perhaps "tribute feasts," which were often held in conjunction with festivals for the polity's deities and were

of elites in returning or redistributing some of the foodstuffs brought to the festival the very "crux of commensal politics."[101] More generally, the positive emotions generated by a festival's carnival atmosphere and by the abundance of food and drink strengthen the psychological bond between the people and the authorities.[102] Festivals thus serve as tools for defining and sustaining political relations; to put it more bluntly, "food is a prime political tool," for it naturalizes sociopolitical asymmetries.[103]

Another political function is the role of community-wide feasts as a communications mechanism. Leaders and elders of subgroups typically use the occasion of being in the same location for up to seven days or more to gather or share information and discuss strategy for matters of common concern. A leader or official—village chief, clan officer, tribal head, or monarch—can disseminate policy and announce military or economic requirements to be imposed upon the group. Traditional feasting is thus an essential component in the functioning of a sociopolitical unit. One ethnographer has compared the political function of feasting to that of Congress or Parliament.[104]

Although most of the economic dynamics of a festival are tied up with the sacrifices and attendant celebratory feasting, there are subsidiary economic functions as well. Festivals serve as occasions for the selling or trading of goods such as ceramics, tools, durable foodstuffs, and other items to the throngs that gather to celebrate. Such practices go beyond the simple exchange of resources, mentioned above, that help agrarians in a difficult environment compensate for nutritional deficiencies. They provide access to commodities, many of them essential for agricultural work and the storage of products, that would not have been locally available.

Acknowledging the politico-economic functions of feasting seems particularly useful for understanding an important feature of Deuteron-

---

meant to amass resources (Hayden, "Fabulous Feasts," 38, 58). The distinction, however, between types of feasts is not perfect or permanent; cf. Dietler, "Theorizing the Feast," 94.

101. Dietler, "Theorizing the Feast," 91.

102. John F. Robertson, "Social Tensions in the Ancient Near East," in *A Companion to the Ancient Near East* (ed. Daniel C. Snell; Blackwell Companions to the Ancient World; Malden, Mass.: Blackwell, 2005), 206. Robertson is discussing the state-sponsored religious festivals of ancient Egypt and how they contributed to the esteem of the ruled for their rulers.

103. Dietler, "Rituals of Consumption," 87, 94.

104. Michael Clarke, cited in Brian Hayden, "Feasting Research."

omy and the Deuteronomic History, namely, the centralization of festal celebrations in Jerusalem, whenever and to whatever extent it occurred. Discovering archaeological correlates of the royal/priestly use of festivals in Jerusalem is virtually impossible because of the dearth of available materials. However, findings from analogous sites are surely relevant and indicate large-scale festal events at regional or national centers of power. That is, "centralization" is a feature of regional political entities, with feasting contributing to the sense of national identity or *communitas*.[105] For example, excavations at Late Bronze Age Hazor—a large regional center of considerable importance and rightly called "the head of all those kingdoms" in the biblical narrative (Josh 11:10; cf. 1 Kgs 9: 15)—have located the material correlates of feasting in a courtyard linking temple and palace, thus indicating the integrated religious and political functions of feasting.[106] Similarly, excavations at Iron I Shiloh, arguably Israel's earliest sacral and administrative center, have produced evidence of feasting and redistribution associated with public structures and, most likely, a sanctuary.[107] Such feasts serve to establish or reinforce the centralization of power.[108] To be sure, the centralization of the cult—the concentration of communal rejoicing and commensal activities in Jerusalem—is given a distinctly religious spin in the biblical account. However, it can surely be considered a strategy by the royal and/or priestly elites for amassing resources, creating loyalty to the royal house, and strengthening temple and throne, perhaps in the face of the external political threat from the Assyrians. Because large communal feasts can be transformative, inculcating new ideologies and establishing altered identities,[109] the emphasis on participation in feasts at a central location would have enhanced the policies of the Judean monarchy while at the same time signaling the special sanctity of the temple priesthood.[110] As already suggested, smaller

---

105. Houston, "Rejoicing before the Lord," 9–10.

106. Zuckerman, "Slaying Oxen and Killing Sheep."

107. Israel Finkelstein, "The History and Archaeology of Shiloh from the Middle Bronze Age I to Iron Age II," in Finkelstein, *Shiloh*, 384–88; see also MacDonald, *Not Bread Alone*, 151–53. As already noted (above, n. 53) evidence of feasting has been found at Tel Dan, a regional shrine of the northern kingdom.

108. Christine A. Haustorf and Mary Weisenthal, "Food: Where Opposites Meet," in Twiss, *Archaeology of Food and Identity*, 312.

109. Twiss, "Transformations," 418.

110. Noted by Hendel, "Table and Altar," 144.

scale versions of these dynamics can be posited for the leadership at community shrines throughout the biblical period.

To summarize briefly, understanding the regular Israelite festivals, which were surely part of ancient Israel's corporate experience in all periods, can be enhanced by drawing upon social-science research. Using the material and theoretical data provided by ethnographers and anthropological archaeologists is an important supplement, if not corrective, to the interpretive tradition in biblical studies, which has had an almost exclusively religious perspective. The biblical details about these festivals as well as their sacral context in the Hebrew Bible has clearly influenced and limited the explanatory possibilities. The recent burgeoning of anthropological research on the nature and function of feasts in traditional societies, along with the data that can be extracted from at least some of the reports of archaeological excavations at Iron Age sites, constitutes a valuable new resource for understanding the wider social (and socioeconomic) and political (and politico-economic) context in which Israelite religious festivals were embedded. Engaging those resources helps us transcend the vast gulf between our present and the biblical past. It allows us to see the specific ways in which Israelite religion is not a discrete feature of community life but rather is part of a complex mosaic of social and political forces, many of them with economic consequences. Some aspects of festival events were of social and economic benefit to the ordinary participants; others served the elites in political and economic ways. Presumably the lives of all participants were enriched by the excitement, camaraderie, and special or abundant foods that were the hallmarks of festal occasions as well as by the belief that their offerings and rejoicing, at God's command, would earn them divine favor. The specifically religious dimension of feasting—the sacrificial cult that has long been the focus of biblical scholarship—becomes more vivid and significant when seen within the larger context of community life.

Theorizing Violence in Biblical Ritual Contexts: The Case of Mourning Rites

Saul M. Olyan

In this paper I present some thoughts on how we might understand the place of violence in biblical ritual settings, specifically violence in relationship to mourning rites, a subject that I did not explore in my book *Biblical Mourning.*[1] I have become increasingly interested in what social anthropologists have had to say of late about violence as I have sought to understand the ritual dynamics of several biblical texts that describe violent acts in mourning contexts or violence in nonmourning ritual settings

1. *Biblical Mourning: Ritual and Social Dimensions* (Oxford: Oxford University Press, 2004). For a trenchant analysis of violence in the Hebrew Bible and its afterlife in ancient Jewish and Christian exegesis, as well as a balanced critique of scholarship on biblical and postbiblical violence, see John J. Collins, "The Zeal of Phinehas: The Bible and the Legitimation of Violence," *JBL* 122 (2003): 3–21. On the "ban" specifically, see Susan Niditch, *War in the Hebrew Bible: A Study in the Ethics of Violence* (New York: Oxford University Press, 1993). The Bible and violence is the general subject of Thomas Römer, "Violence de Dieu, violence des hommes: La question de la violence dans la Bible hébraïque," in *La Bible: 2000 ans de lectures* (ed. Jean-Claude Eslin and Catherine Cornu; Paris: Desclée de Brouwer, 2003), 470–79; and Pierre Gibert, *L'Espérance de Caïn: La violence dans la Bible* (Paris: Bayard, 2002). The essays collected in Yvonne Sherwood and Jonneke Bekkenkamp, eds., *Sanctified Aggression: Legacies of Biblical and Post-biblical Vocabularies of Violence* (JSOTSup 400; New York: T&T Clark, 2003), represent some of the directions taken in the last decade by nonhistorically oriented biblical scholars. A relationship between violence and monotheism is proposed by Regina M. Schwartz, *The Curse of Cain: The Violent Legacy of Monotheism* (Chicago: University of Chicago Press, 1997). For a treatment of violence and religion more generally, see, e.g., Leo D. Lefebure, *Revelation, the Religions, and Violence* (Maryknoll, N.Y.: Orbis, 2000); and David A. Bernat and Jonathan Klawans, eds., *Religion and Violence: The Biblical Heritage* (Recent Research in Biblical Studies 2; Sheffield: Sheffield Phoenix Press, 2007).

(e.g., contexts of legal conflict) apparently intended to result in the victim's transition to the ritual stance of penitential mourner. The texts of interest to me are 2 Sam 10:1–5; 2 Sam 16:5–13; Neh 13:25; and Isa 50:4–11. Before I discuss each of these passages, I shall say a few words about trends in recent theorizing of violence among social anthropologists, whose work I find potentially helpful given its sensitivity to sociohistorical and cultural context.[2] In my discussions of each biblical text, I include an assessment of anthropological theorizing in light of the biblical material under examination. Our reading of ancient literary representations of rites, as much as that of the ritual data of contemporary societies, has the potential to contribute to the ongoing interdisciplinary project of theorizing violence, including violence in ritual settings. It is to this interdisciplinary discussion that I hope to contribute.[3] Finally, I note that when I speak of mourning rites, I refer to a discrete set of behaviors that may be manifest in settings of petition and penitence, calamity, and disease, as well as in death contexts. These include weeping, tearing garments, fasting, strewing ashes or dust on the head, moving back and forth (*nwd*), sitting on the ground, depilation, shaving, and other hair manipulations, among other acts.[4]

Recent works on violence by social anthropologists typically begin with an acknowledgment of the influence of David Riches's classic paper, "The Phenomenon of Violence" (1986), and move on to assess it critically and elaborate upon it.[5] Following Riches, the majority see violence as a rational and meaningful rather than an irrational and meaningless form

---

2. By focusing on the theorizing of social anthropologists, I am not suggesting that they alone are sensitive to the sociohistorical and cultural dimensions of violence; it is simply that their theorizing happens to be of interest to me in this particular essay. For other approaches that consider seriously the role of culture and social context as well as biology, see my discussion in the latter part of n. 13.

3. Interdisciplinary theorizing of a number of topics of study (e.g., aging, deceit, gender, sexuality, borders) has become increasingly common. For an example from the study of borders, see Emmanuel Brunet-Jailly, "Theorizing Borders: An Interdisciplinary Perspective," *Geopolitics* 10 (2005): 633–49, esp. 642. My use of "project" is derived from Jonathan Z. Smith, "What a Difference a Difference Makes," in *"To See Ourselves as Others See Us": Christians, Jews, "Others" in Late Antiquity* (ed. Ernest S. Frerichs and Jacob Neusner; Chico, Calif.: Scholars Press, 1985), 46, 48.

4. See further Olyan, *Biblical Mourning*, 13–19, on the rites themselves. For the types of mourning mentioned, see 19–27 and chs. 1–3.

5. "The Phenomenon of Violence," in *The Anthropology of Violence* (ed. David Riches; Oxford: Blackwell, 1986), 1–27.

of behavior.[6] Like Riches, many also argue that violence is very often, if not always, instrumental, a strategically deployed, consciously adopted, goal-oriented social tool.[7] Embracing and elaborating upon Riches's work, scholars such as Jon Abbink have highlighted the profound communicative power of violent acts,[8] as well as their ability to transform society by reconstituting social relations.[9] Also frequently emphasized is the always contested legitimacy of violence, given the very different, and sometimes shifting, perspectives of perpetrator, victim, and witness;[10] the association of violent acts with humiliation of the victim;[11] and the historical and social contextualization of acts of violence.[12] Needless to say, this social-cultural focus contrasts sharply with some of the approaches of other disciplines (e.g., sociobiology) that tend to view violence as a biologically innate tendency and ignore or downplay its sociocultural dimensions.[13]

---

6. Ibid., 14. Among others, see Jon Abbink, "Restoring the Balance: Violence and Culture among the Suri of Southern Ethiopia," in *Meanings of Violence: A Cross Cultural Perspective* (ed. Jon Abbink and Göran Aijmer; Oxford: Berg, 2000), 78; Anton Blok, "The Enigma of Senseless Violence," in Abbink and Aijmer, *Meanings of Violence*, 23; Bettina E. Schmidt and Ingo W. Schröder, "Introduction: Violent Imaginaries and Violent Practices," in *Anthropology of Violence and Conflict* (ed. Bettina E. Schmidt and Ingo W. Schröder; London: Routledge, 2001), 18. Pamela J. Stewart and Andrew Strathern, *Violence: Theory and Ethnography* (London: Continuum, 2002), 6–8, 154–55, 159–60, acknowledge the meaningfulness of violence, though not necessarily its rationality.

7. Riches, "Phenomenon of Violence," viii, 5, 11–12, 25–26; Stewart and Strathern, *Violence: Theory and Ethnography*, 6–7.

8. Riches, "Phenomenon of Violence," 12; Abbink, "Preface," in Abbink and Aijmer, *Meanings of Violence*, xiii; idem, "Restoring the Balance," 78; Stewart and Strathern, *Violence: Theory and Ethnography*, 159.

9. Riches, "Phenomenon of Violence," 11; Abbink, "Preface," xii, xv.

10. Riches, "Phenomenon of Violence," 9, 11, 25–26; Abbink, "Preface," xi; Stewart and Strathern, *Violence: Theory and Ethnography*, 1, 3–4; Strathern and Stewart, "Anthropology of Violence and Conflict, Overview," in *Encyclopedia of Violence, Peace and Conflict* (online edition; Amsterdam: Academic Press, 2008).

11. Abbink, "Preface," xi; Aijmer, "Introduction: The Idiom of Violence in Imagery and Discourse," in Abbink and Aijmer, *Meanings of Violence*, 1.

12. For example, Stewart and Strathern, *Violence: Theory and Ethnography*, 1, 158; Strathern and Stewart, "Overview"; Schmidt and Schröder, *Anthroplogy of Violence and Conflict*, 19.

13. For sociobiology see, e.g., Anthony Walsh, "Sociobiology," in *Violence in America: An Encyclopedia* (ed. Ronald Gottesman and Richard Maxwell Brown; 3 vols.; New York: Scribner's, 1999), 3:177–82. A recent review of psychoanalytic

Among social anthropologists, as in other fields, less agreement is discernible when it comes to establishing a baseline definition of violence.[14] Some see hurtful, visible, physical acts as constitutive of violence,[15] while others have defended a broader understanding that would include the deployment of malevolent magic, sorcery, or any kind of threat, be it somatic or

---

approaches to violence may be found in Richard Mizen, "A Contribution towards an Analytic Theory of Violence," *Journal of Analytical Psychology* 48 (2003): 285–305, esp. 290–91. (My thanks to Frederik Schockaert for bringing this article to my attention.) For violence conceived as a universal human tendency allegedly sublimated through ritual, see, famously, René Girard, *Violence and the Sacred* (trans. Patrick Gregory; Baltimore: Johns Hopkins University Press, 1977) and *Things Hidden Since the Foundation of the World* (trans. Stephen Bann and Michael Metteer; Stanford, Calif.: Stanford University Press, 1987). Stewart and Strathern, *Violence: Theory and Ethnography*, 10, and Abbink, "Preface," xii, xiv–xv, critique the idea of violence as an innate tendency; but compare recently Strathern and Stewart, "Overview," who acknowledge a legitimate role for culture *and* biology in developing a theory of violence, as does Bruce M. Knauft, "Violence and Sociality in Human Evolution," *Current Anthropology* 32 (1991): 391–428. A balanced approach to the relationship of biology and culture has increasingly become the norm in a variety of fields (e.g., in cognitive anthropology, and cross-cultural and cognitive psychology). See, e.g., the recent work of Brian Malley and Nicola Knight, who theorize a possible relationship of "dynamic culture patterns" and cognition, and review scholarship in cognitive anthropology on the relationship of cognitive processes and culture ("Some Cognitive Origins of Cultural Order," *Journal of Cognition and Culture* 8 [2008]: 49–69). See also Richard E. Nisbett and Ara Norenzayan, who speak of the "mutual interdependence of culture and cognition," and "the complementarity of psychology and anthropology" ("Culture and Cognition," in *Stevens' Handbook of Experimental Psychology* [3rd ed.; online edition; New York: Wiley, 2002).

14. Seventeen years ago, Henrietta Moore noted that the concept of violence "still seems remarkably undertheorized" in the social sciences ("The Problem of Explaining Violence in the Social Sciences," in *Sex and Violence: Issues in Representation and Experience* [ed. Penelope Harvey and Peter Gow; London: Routledge, 1994], 138). See also the comments of Abbink, "Preface," xiv–xv. That debate continues to the present day in social anthropology is suggested by Strathern and Stewart, "Overview." For debate within international sociology regarding what constitutes violence, see, e.g., the essays in Trutz von Trotha, ed., *Soziologie der Gewalt* (Kölner Zeitschrift für Soziologie und Sozialpsychologie 37; Opladen: Westdeutscher, 1997). For psychoanalysis, see, e.g., Mizen, "Contribution," 285, 289, 293–94.

15. For example, Riches, "Phenomenon of Violence," 11; idem, "Aggression, War, Violence: Space/Time and Paradigm," *Man* 26 (1991): 295; Schmidt and Schröder, *Anthropology of Violence and Conflict*, 3.

nonphysical.[16] Finally, I note that little attention has been paid in the social anthropological literature under review to the role of violence in ritual settings, the primary focus of my interest.[17] Nor is it evident that there has been very much discussion of the role of violence in establishing political or social affiliation or disaffiliation,[18] or the part that acts of violence might play specifically in changing the victim's ritual status. Thus aspects of violence are evidently undertheorized in the discourse of contemporary social anthropology. Consideration of the biblical data will allow us to assess the utility of the theorizing of violence among social anthropologists for those of us who work on biblical texts, and, at the same time, allow us to focus on dimensions of violence neglected in social anthropological analysis in order to enrich the larger interdisciplinary discussion of violence.

The first text that I shall consider is 2 Sam 10:1–5. In this passage, David sends comforters (*mĕnaḥămîm*) to the Ammonite court after the death of his ally Nahash, the king of Ammon. His intent, according to 10:2, is to perpetuate his treaty with the Ammonites by demonstrating covenant loyalty (*ḥesed*) to the new king, Hanun, through the presence of an embassy of comforters during the period of mourning at the court. Verse 3 suggests indirectly that David also intends to honor the dead king through his actions. The Ammonites, seeking to terminate the treaty with Israel, accuse David of sending spies and humiliate his servants, the comforters, by seizing them, shaving off half their beards (MT), exposing their genitals, and expelling them (vv. 4–5). Coerced asymmetrical shaving of the beard and forced exposure of the genital area of the body are arguably acts of violence. They parody normal mourning rites such as hair and beard manipulation through shaving and depilation, and forms of nudity,

16. For example, Stewart and Strathern, *Violence: Theory and Ethnography*, 156; Strathern and Stewart, "Overview"; Abbink, "Restoring the Balance," 79. Riches speaks of sorcery that causes *physical* harm as violence ("Phenomenon of Violence," 8) but excludes acts that may cause only mental anguish (22).

17. See, however, Riches, "Phenomenon of Violence,"10, who comments briefly on what he calls "ritualized hurt"; Stewart and Strathern, *Violence: Theory and Ethnography*, 159 in passing; Strathern and Stewart, "Overview"; Alberto Bouroncle, "Ritual, Violence and Social Order: An Approach to Spanish Bullfighting," in Abbink and Aijmer, *Meanings of Violence*, 58; and especially the recent work of Thomas Hauschild, *Ritual und Gewalt: Ethnologische Studien an europäischen und mediterranen Gesellschaften* (Frankfurt: Suhrkamp, 2008).

18. Again, see however Riches, "Phenomenon of Violence," 14–15, who remarks on violence as an expression of political opposition or disaffiliation.

which in all cases are undertaken by the mourner himself or herself, not imposed by force by another person.[19] The seizing of the ambassadors and their forced expulsion can also be construed as acts of violence perpetrated against the emissaries themselves, and by extension against David, the ruler whom they serve.

What do these acts of violence accomplish other than the utter humiliation of the victims, mentioned explicitly in the text in verse 5?[20] First, I note that these actions effectively terminate the treaty that had existed between David and the Ammonites, the existence of which is indicated by David's desire to "do covenant loyalty" (*ḥesed*) with Hanun, the new Ammonite king.[21] Thus the violence perpetrated in this particular ritual setting—the royal court in mourning—functions to disaffiliate the Ammonites from David and vice versa, and this disaffiliation is signaled by the text's remark that the Ammonites had made themselves "odious" (*b'š*) to David through their actions (v. 6).[22] Second, these coercive acts change the ritual status of David's emissaries (and by extension, David himself), effectively turning an embassy of mourning allies (the comforters) and the ruler whom they represent into nonmourning enemies.[23] In addition to shaming the victims, it also seems quite clear that the violence of the Ammonites is strategically deployed, in this case to terminate a treaty; that it is highly communicative; and that it reworks the political and social landscape—all of which characterize violence as it is often theorized by social anthropologists. Its contested legitimacy can also be assumed, given David's negative reaction to the acts of Ammonite aggression. Thus many of the most frequently emphasized characteristics of violence according to recent social anthropological discussion are evidenced in this text, though other

19. For beard and/or hair manipulation undertaken by the mourner, see, e.g., Isa 15:2; Jer 16:6; 41:4; Ezra 9:3; for removal of shoes or articles of clothing by the mourner, see, e.g., Isa 20:2–4; Mic 1:8.

20. The comforters are described as *niklāmîm mĕʾōd* by the text.

21. Cf. the treaty of Hiram of Tyre and David, which Hiram seeks to perpetuate at Solomon's accession (1 Kgs 5:15).

22. The niphal of *b'š* in political settings such as 2 Sam 10:6 is probably an idiom for a treaty violation (see also 1 Sam 13:4; 2 Sam 16:21).

23. See Gary A. Anderson, *A Time to Mourn, a Time to Dance: The Expression of Grief and Joy in Israelite Religion* (University Park: Pennsylvania State University Press, 1991), 49–53, on mourning and rejoicing as ritual type/antitype. See also my own discussion in *Biblical Mourning*, 13–19. While allies and affiliates mourn at the time of calamity, petition, or death, enemies rejoice.

important features are also in evidence, features that are often neglected in anthropological theorizing (e.g., violence as a tool to disaffiliate socially and politically, or the role that violence might play in changing the ritual status of the victim [in this case, from mourner to nonmourner]).

My second text of interest is 2 Sam 16:5–13, which describes David's confrontation with Shimei of Benjamin, a kinsman of Saul, during the flight of David's court and his mercenaries from Jerusalem at the approach of the army of his rebellious son Absalom. David and those loyal to him have embraced mourning to mark the calamity of their flight, and very likely also in order to petition the deity for succor (see 16:12: "Perhaps Yhwh will see my affliction and respond positively"). David is described as weeping and walking barefoot, with his head covered (*wĕrōʾš lō ḥapûy*); his followers are portrayed similarly (15:23, 30).[24] When Shimei sees David at Bahurim, he curses him and stones him and his followers, accusing David of bloodguilt with respect to the house of Saul (16:5–8). In 16:13b Shimei is also said to throw dirt at them (*wĕʿippar beʿāpār*). Cursing should certainly be construed as a violent act in this cultural context, given the serious harm maledictions are intended to do to those who are execrated, and the power evidently invested by many ancients—if not most—in such imprecations.[25] Stoning David and his followers, though not a serious direct physical threat, is nonetheless to be understood as an act of violence. It appears to dramatize the form of execution Shimei believes that David deserves, and as such could incite others to pursue such a result given David's vulnerability as a fugitive.[26] There may also be a magical dimension to the stoning that is not entirely clear to us. For this one might compare other ritualized acts intended magically to elicit concrete results, as in 2 Kgs 13:14–19.[27] Finally, throwing dirt at David and his fellow fugitives dramatizes Shimei's refusal to mourn with David. Imitating the

24. For the probable meaning "covered" for the Qal passive participle *ḥāpûy*, see Olyan, *Biblical Mourning*, 92 n. 59. This meaning is suggested by forms of the niphal and piel, as well as forms in the cognate languages.

25. Many, though apparently not all: note the evidence of ancient tomb invasions, even in contexts where curses on tomb violators are evidenced. The thrust of these curses—if not the words themselves—was most likely understood by the intruders.

26. Arvid S. Kapelrud, "*sāqal*," *TDOT* 10:342, anticipates me with the suggestion that Shimei may be communicating symbolically that David deserves execution. I do note, however, that the verb *sāqal* is not otherwise used of the execution of murderers.

27. On this text and its magical dimensions, see Rüdiger Schmitt, *Magie im Alten Testament* (AOAT 313; Münster: Ugarit-Verlag, 2004), 275–79.

mourner, political allies normally toss dirt or ashes on *themselves* as a rite of affiliation in mourning contexts; they do not strew such material on the mourner! Like the Ammonite shaving of David's emissaries, Shimei's tossing of dirt on David and his entourage parodies normal mourning practice in an aggressive way. Thus all three of Shimei's acts—cursing, stoning, tossing dirt—are hostile, establishing or perpetuating in a very public way Shimei's disaffiliation from David and his followers. Rather than coercing a change in someone else's ritual status and sociopolitical affiliation as in 2 Sam 10:1–5, Shimei's acts of violence and hostility function to remove him from any kind of affiliation with David and his cause, dramatically establishing or perpetuating his ritual status as a nonmourner in a context in which he might be expected to mourn.

In both 2 Sam 10 and 16, violent acts are performed on other persons in mourning settings, and result in social and political disaffiliation, but there are significant differences between the two texts. In 10:1–5 the mourning of David's emissaries and their affiliation with Ammon is ended against their will by Ammonite acts of violence; in 16:5–13 willful violent acts realize and dramatize Shimei's own refusal to mourn, and in so doing affiliate with the mourner (that is, David). As with 2 Sam 10, violence is deployed strategically in 16:5–13, it is highly communicative, its legitimacy is contested (see v. 9), it is evidently intended to humiliate the victim, and it may reconstitute sociopolitical ties, making unambiguously clear Shimei's enemy status (or, it may perpetuate Shimei's already well-known position as David's adversary). The role of violence in realizing sociopolitical disaffiliation, a neglected dimension of violence as it has been theorized among social anthropologists, is also of central importance here, as it is in 10:1–5.

The third passage for analysis is Neh 13:25, which portrays Nehemiah "contending" (*ryb*) with intermarried Judean men, cursing them, striking some of them, pulling out their hair (*mrṭ*), and making them swear an oath of sorts by the deity in which they effectively renounce intermarriage.[28] The context is one of judicial (or pre-judicial) conflict, as the verbal root *ryb* and the actions of Nehemiah indicate.[29] Though

28. The wording of the required statement is odd for an oath, though the text clearly presents the statement as such, using the hiphil of *šbʿ*.

29. On the judicial, pre-judicial, and extrajudicial uses of *ryb*, see G. Liedke, "*ryb* to quarrel," *TLOT* 3:1232–37. Liedke considers Neh 13:25 an example of prejudicial conflict.

Nehemiah's violent acts have been characterized as "impulsive," "intemperate," "sudden," and "a matter of personality" by a number of biblical scholars, suggesting their irrationality, this does not strike me as the most cogent explanation for them.[30] Nehemiah is represented as politically astute and goal-oriented throughout the book's narrative, so why should he not be portrayed as such in 13:25? His acts appear to result in successful anti-intermarriage oath taking by his rivals; perhaps we are also to assume the expulsion of their alien wives and their children from the community, as in Ezra 10 and possibly Neh 13:30, a text that concerns cultic officials specifically.[31] In addition, it seems clear that a new political affiliation is forced upon Nehemiah's rivals by his violent acts. Once they take the oath, they have effectively embraced Nehemiah's negative position on intermarriage, abandoning their previous, positive stance.

But there is more. I believe that Nehemiah's violence is intended not only to coerce his opponents into taking an anti-intermarriage oath and by so doing reconstitute themselves as affiliates of Nehemiah rather than his rivals. It is also calculated to force the opponents into a ritual state of penitential mourning. This is evidenced by the pulling out of hair (*mrṭ*), a mourning act, and one prominently featured in the description of Ezra's penitential mourning in reaction to the report of the Judean intermarriages in Ezra 9:3, a text to which Neh 13:25 may have been intended to allude.[32] In Ezra 9:3 Ezra pulls out some of his own head and beard hair in

---

30. For example, H. G. M. Williamson, *Ezra, Nehemiah* (WBC 16; Nashville: Nelson, 1985), 398–99; Joseph Blenkinsopp, *Ezra-Nehemiah: A Commentary* (OTL; Philadelphia: Westminster, 1988), 364; idem, *Isaiah 40–55* (AB 19A; New York: Doubleday, 2000), 321. However, some who have commented on the passage have rejected this interpretation. See, e.g., Lisbeth S. Fried, "From Xeno-Philia to -Phobia—Jewish Encounters with the Other," in *A Time of Change: Judah and Its Neighbors in the Persian and Early Hellenistic Periods* (ed. Yigal Levin; Library of Second Temple Studies 65; London: T&T Clark, 2007), 194, who argues that Nehemiah's actions were not "impetuous" but that he was "applying normal Persian sanctions to violations of an edict." (On this idea, see my discussion in n. 33.) Wilhelm Rudolph views Nehemiah as restrained (and, by implication, calculated) in his reaction to the intermarriages, having allegedly learned from the failure of Ezra in this area (*Esra und Nehemia* [HAT 20; Tübingen: Mohr Siebeck, 1949], 209).

31. In Neh 13:30 Nehemiah states that he "purified them [the priests, or the priests and Levites] from all things alien," suggesting expulsion of foreign wives and possibly their children, or at least the dissolution of intermarriages.

32. The presence of such an allusion would suggest that the writer of Neh 13:25 knew Ezra 9:3, and composed Neh 13:25 with Ezra 9:3 in mind. There is no scholarly

response to the news of widespread Judean intermarriages; in Neh 13:25 Nehemiah pulls out the hair of his intermarried opponents.[33]

If my interpretation is correct, Neh 13:25 constitutes a third text in which violent acts are tied to mourning rites. But in contrast to 2 Sam 10:1–5 and 16:5–13, the violence does not take place in a ritual setting already devoted to some kind of mourning, be it mourning the dead, penitential petition, or mourning after a calamity. In the case of Neh 13:25, a stance of penitential mourning on the part of the victims of the violence is apparently the *result* of the violent acts themselves. The imposition of a penitential ritual stance forces the victims of the violence not only to realize and communicate affiliation with Nehemiah's political position, but also to communicate regret for their past behavior—intermarriage—

---

consensus on the relationship of the Nehemiah and Ezra "memoirs," the hypothetical sources from which Neh 13:25 and Ezra 9:3 are drawn, or even the relative chronology of the missions of Ezra and Nehemiah, assuming there were such missions (see, e.g., the review by Williamson, *Ezra, Nehemiah*, xxxix–xliv). But it is certainly possible that Ezra preceded Nehemiah, as many scholars believe (e.g., ibid., xxxvi), and that Ezra's "memoir" was known to the author of Neh 13:25. The alternative view, that Ezra 9:3 is dependent on the Nehemiah "memoir," is defended by Antonius H. J. Gunneweg, *Esra* (KAT 19; Gütersloh: Gerd Mohn, 1985), 162–63, among others. On the difficulty of determining dependency, see the discussion of Jacob L. Wright, *Rebuilding Identity: The Nehemiah-Memoir and Its Earliest Readers* (BZAW 348; Berlin: de Gruyter, 2004), 244–57, esp. 250.

33. The text might also allude to a pair of Persian sanctions (beating, forced depilation) as some scholars have argued, if indeed such punishments were known to the writer of the Nehemiah "memoir" and his intended audience. But such an allusion strikes me as secondary at best, given the prominent role of the pulling out of hair (*mrṭ*) in Ezra's penitential mourning and its symbolic association with opposition to intermarriage in Ezra 9:3. Furthermore, the same combination of violent acts (beating, depilation [*mrṭ*]) are known from Isa 50:6, likely a late exilic composition, suggesting that they might not necessarily have a Persian background. (The dating of the component parts of Isa 40–55 is debated, though see the comments of Blenkinsopp, *Isaiah 40–55*, 78–80, on 50:4–9 preceding the addition in 50:10–11 as well as the Trito-Isaiah-like passages in 50:1–3 and 51:1–6.) For the view that Neh 13:25 reflects Persian punishments for violators of an edict, see Michael Heltzer, "The Flogging and Plucking of Beards in the Achaemenid Empire and the Chronology of *Nehemia*," *Archaeologische Mitteilungen aus Iran* 28 (1995–96): 305–7, who cites a parallel from the Murashu archive; and following Heltzer, Fried, "Jewish Encounters," 194. Heltzer anticipates me in noting the parallel with Isa 50:6, though he considers the text a Persian period composition. My thanks to Brian Rainey for the Heltzer and Fried references.

which is characterized as a sin by the text (vv. 26–27). In all three passages that I have discussed, violent acts are performed by an agent on other persons in ritual settings, whether contexts of mourning (2 Sam 10:1–5; 16:5–13) or legal conflict (Neh 13:25). In the latter case, mourning of the victims apparently follows upon the violent acts. In two texts sociopolitical disaffiliation of victimizer and victim is the result, either voluntary (2 Sam 16) or coerced (2 Sam 10); in the third passage, forced sociopolitical *affiliation* of the victim with the victimizer is brought about through the violent acts of the victimizer. In all three texts, violence is strategically deployed to achieve an end; it is communicative; its legitimacy is either clearly or very likely contested; it is probably intended to shame the victim; and it may reshape the political landscape, or does so. In short, several aspects of violence as it is frequently characterized by social anthropologists are evidenced in Neh 13:25, as they are in 2 Sam 10:1–5 and 16:5–13. In addition, other aspects of violence that have often been neglected by social anthropologists, such as its role in generating sociopolitical affiliation, are also in evidence in Neh 13:25.

Isaiah 50:4–11 is the final text that I shall consider. I believe that the victimizers in this text, not unlike Neh 13:25, seek to force their opponent—the so-called servant—into a penitential mourning posture. They do this by pulling out his beard hair, one among several acts of physical aggression that they perform on him ("I turned my back to strikers," // "my cheek to those who pull out hair"). Their motive for performing violent acts in this text is not entirely clear, though mention of the speaker's "tongue of those who are taught" and his word (in v. 4), as well as allusions to the work of earlier prophets (vv. 5 and 7), suggest that his message might well have been objectionable to his rivals.[34] Though some commentators have interpreted the violence meted out to the speaker as "random and casual," not unlike views of Nehemiah's violence often seen in scholarship, this seems implausible, given what we have seen previously.[35] It is more likely that the speaker's opponents sought purposefully to silence him through a series of violent and humiliating acts (v. 6), including the attempted imposition of a penitential ritual stance on him which would signal both regret for his previous words, and a change of sociopolitical affiliation. The speaker is, however, defiant in his telling of the episode.

34. For example, Ezek 2:8; 3:8–9.

35. For example, Blenkinsopp, *Isaiah 40–55*, 319, 321.

On account of Yhwh's help, he will not be shamed (v. 7); rather, he will be vindicated in any legal proceeding that should transpire (vv. 8–9).

If I am correct in my reading of the ritual dynamics of this text, it resembles Neh 13:25 in several respects. First, the violence of the victimizer is intended to produce a ritual stance of penitential mourning in the victim, which represents a change of ritual status. Second, the sociopolitical affiliation of the victim with the victimizer rather than their disaffiliation is the intended result of the violence, as is an expression of shame and regret by the victim for previously held views. As with the three texts that I discussed earlier, the violent acts appear also to be goal-oriented, communicative, of contested legitimacy, intended to humiliate the victim, and may be, or clearly are, sociopolitically transformative in intent.

What can we conclude from this brief study? First, it is clear that the four biblical passages under consideration support a number of the conclusions characteristic of the cross-cultural theorizing of violence in recent social anthropological discussion. Features of violence such as its strategic, goal-oriented nature, its communicative power, its contested legitimacy, its power to shame, and its ability to reconstitute social relations are all evidenced in the four biblical texts that I have examined. It seems highly unlikely that the violent acts manifested in these texts represent irrational, impulsive, and meaningless behavior, though biblical scholars have frequently made this claim about some of the texts in question (e.g., Neh 13:25; Isa 50:4–11). That I have embraced a moderately maximalist understanding of violence, as have some social anthropologists, should be clear from my treatment of Shimei's cursing, stoning, and dirt throwing. It is simply too limiting not to do so given the common understanding of such acts of hostility in their sociohistorical context. Though these acts might appear harmless to us, they were not necessarily so perceived in their ancient context. Finally, my reading of the four biblical texts suggests that aspects of violence are clearly undertheorized in recent social anthropological discussion. Violence in ritual settings deserves more cross-cultural analysis than it has received of late. The role of violent acts in generating changes in ritual status (e.g., from mourner to nonmourner, and vice versa), and in constituting sociopolitical affiliation or disaffiliation, central themes of this essay, are especially in need of more attention from scholars. It is my hope that my reading of this biblical data and my assessment of the theorizing of social anthropologists will contribute something to the larger, interdisciplinary project of theorizing violence, particularly violence in ritual settings.

Theories Regarding Witchcraft Accusations and the Hebrew Bible

Rüdiger Schmitt

Witchcraft in Anthropological Theory

In his famous study *Witchcraft, Oracles, and Magic among the Azande*, first published in 1937, Edward E. Evans-Pritchard noticed that witchcraft accusations were raised against persons who did not conform or align with the values and the demands of society. In the case of the Azande, witchcraft accusations were not used in situations of struggle for social status: neither wealth nor poverty played a role in such accusations. Instead, they were used to stigmatize individuals of the same status group who were not behaving according to the codes and values of society, for example, women who were engaged in a lesbian relationship.[1] Witchcraft accusations thus arise in cases of social tension in everyday life, among people of the same social status in close contact, for example, neighbors or relatives.[2] Taking up Evans-Pritchard's analysis, Mary Douglas differentiates between two main types of witchcraft accusations with different social functions: Type (a) "The witch as an outsider," who can be a "far-away" witch (a[i]), or a witch who has been expelled (a[ii]). Both subtypes function to redefine group boundaries in order to strengthen internal coherence and solidarity. Type (b), "The witch as an internal enemy," can serve several functions: (b[i]) "The witch as member of a rival faction" creates demarcations and strengthens solidarity against competing groups and parties of the same society, aligns faction hierarchy, or splits community; (b[ii]) "The witch as a dangerous deviant" creates demarcations that isolate deviants in the

1. See Edward E. Evans-Pritchard, *Witchcraft, Oracles, and Magic among the Azande* (Oxford: Clarendon, 1937), 99, 322.

2. See ibid., 95.

name of community values; and (b[iii]) "The witch as an internal enemy with outside liaisons" promotes factional rivalry, splits community and stigmatizes a competing party in struggles over social hierarchies.[3] Thus, on the individual level, the witchcraft-complex helps groups cope with experiences of crisis and contingency, and defines individual social roles. On the social level, witchcraft accusations define social roles and hierarchies and stabilize societies by excluding dissident individuals or groups.[4]

Though Douglas's theory seems to be convincing in addressing basic functions of the witchcraft complex, it should be noticed that Douglas's analysis claims to be describing universal phenomena, and therefore must be applied carefully. Both Evans-Pritchard's and Douglas's approaches were based on fieldwork in segmentary societies that cannot be easily transferred and applied to other cultures, for instance, the high cultures of the ancient Near East. Thus the anthropological approach of Douglas is a valuable tool but tends not to be context-sensitive nor does it acknowledge that the roles of magic and witchcraft in different religious symbol systems may differ.

More recent anthropological studies have emphasized that functions of witchcraft beliefs and witchcraft accusations differ from society to society and are specific only to particular social situations. Thus they have to be understood in their specific context. Witchcraft phenomena therefore should best be understood as a matter of social diagnostic rather than belief, as argued by Henrietta Moore and Todd Sanders.[5]

In situations of dynamic social change, such as contemporary South Africa, jealousy becomes an important factor influencing witchcraft beliefs and accusations, providing people the justification to make witchcraft accusations and bringing alleged witches back to an acceptable, equal social status. Such accusations also occur between people in close contact, who compete with each other for scarce goods,[6] for example, against

---

3. See Mary Douglas, "Introduction: Thirty Years after *Witchcraft, Oracles and Magic*," in *Witchcraft: Confessions and Accusations* (ed. Mary Douglas; ASA Monographs 9; London: Tavistock, 1970), xxvi–vii.

4. See ibid., xxiv–xxvii.

5. Henrietta L. Moore and Todd Sanders, "Magical Interpretations and Material Realities: An Introduction," in *Magical Interpretations, Material Realities: Modernity, Witchcraft and the Occult in Postcolonial Africa* (ed. Henrietta L. Moore and Todd Sanders; London: Routledge, 2001), 4.

6. Riekje Pelgrim, *Witchcraft and Policing* (African Studies Centre Research Report 72, 2003; Leiden: African Studies Centre, 2003), 131–32.

businessmen and politicians in the urban centers who have become wealthy.[7] As Peter Geschiere puts it, witchcraft "is certainly related to the accumulation of power but can also serve to undermine it."[8] Though anthropological research has understood witchcraft beliefs and accusations as functioning to maintain the stability of a small-scale society, it is obvious that witchcraft accusations—in particular in South Africa—can also be dysfunctional for the society as a whole, since people, often children, have been severely assaulted and sometimes brutally murdered, and displaced "witches" have found themselves starving in witch villages, with no social network to support them.[9] The roots of the increase in witchcraft accusations in late apartheid and post-apartheid South Africa are to be found in the collaboration of local, traditional authorities with the apartheid regime, rebelling youth accusing the generation of their parents of being opportunistic with respect to the regime, as well as an increase in millenarian expectations closely linked to a renaissance of African culture. Thus witchcraft accusations became an element of the emancipation movement, often directed against "renegades."[10] Also HIV/AIDS has become part of the witchcraft discourse in many African societies, and witchcraft is often seen as the real reason for HIV infections.[11] However, contemporary witchcraft, in particular in Africa, is not a sign of backwardness according to most recent anthropological research, but is instead a thoroughly modern manifestation of coping with uncertainties and contingencies of modern life,[12] though it contributes to social dysfunction.

---

7. See Johannes Harnischfeger, "Witchcraft and the State in South Africa," *Anthropos* 95 (2000): 99–112; 103 with regard to witch hunts in Cameroon.

8. Peter Geschiere, *The Modernity of Witchcraft: Politics and the Occult in Postcolonial Africa* (Charlottesville: University Press of Virginia, 1997), 16.

9. Pelgrim, *Witchcraft*, 129.

10. See Harnischfeger, *Witchcraft*, 103–6.

11. See Moore and Sanders, "Magical Interpretations," 17; Gerrie ter Har, "Introduction: The Evil Called Witchcraft," in *Imagining Evil: Witchcraft Beliefs and Accusations in Contemporary Africa* (ed. Gerrie ter Har; Trenton: Africa World Press, 2007), 1–30; Elias K. Bongmba, "Witchcraft and the Christian Church: Ethical Implications," in ter Har, *Imagining Evil*, 123; Gomang S. Ntloedibe-Kuswani, "Witchcraft as a Challenge to Batswana Ideas of Community and Relationships," in ter Har, *Imagining Evil*, 221.

12. Moore and Sanders, "Magical Interpretations," 3, 10–13.

Witchcraft in the Social History of Europe

The phenomena of witch hunts and witch trials in the late medieval and early modern periods have been a topic of extensive research for more than a hundred years, beginning with the *Geschichte der Hexenprozesse* (History of Witchcraft Trials) by Wilhelm Gottlieb Soldan, published initially in 1843 and expanded by Heinrich Heppe in 1880.[13] Nineteenth and early-twentieth-century research on witchcraft—mostly done by liberal Protestants such as Heppe—put great emphasis on the theological reasons for witch hunts and the theological background of witchcraft beliefs. According to this line of research it was Catholic dogmatism and backwardness that established the ideological groundwork for witch-hunting. According to Soldan, witchcraft was nothing but an invention by monks and inquisitors to suppress uneducated folk.[14] Though the underlying symbol system of theology and Christian popular religion in medieval and early modern Europe are important factors, recent research on witchcraft accusations in the early modern period in Europe, inspired by the discourse in social anthropology, has focused in particular on the social functions of such accusations and witchcraft trials. Nevertheless, there is still an ongoing controversy among scholars about the social functions of witchcraft accusations and the reasons for the great waves of witch hunts in sixteenth- and seventeenth-century Europe and America. Scholars have considered confessional tensions, social tensions, increase of superstition, war, poverty caused by war and destruction, plagues, a minor ice age,[15] *longue-durée* mystical and magical beliefs, the incorporation of witchcraft beliefs in contemporary medicine,[16] gender issues such as Christian misogyny and male attempts to maintain superiority over women, an oversupply of

13. Wilhelm Gottlieb Soldan and Heinrich Heppe, *Geschichte der Hexenprozesse* (3rd ed.; 2 vols.; Stuttgart: Cotta, 1911). For the history of research, see Andreas Blauert, "Die Erforschung der Anfänge der europäischen Hexenverfolgungen," in *Ketzer, Zauberer, Hexen: Die Anfänge der europäischen Hexenverfolgungen* (ed. Andreas Blauert; Frankfurt am Main: Suhrkamp, 1990), 11–42; and Malcolm Gaskill, "The Pursuit of Reality: Recent Research into the History of Witchcraft," *Historical Journal* 51 (2008): 1069–88.

14. Soldan and Heppe, *Geschichte der Hexenprozesse*, 1–3.

15. Wolfgang Behringer, "Weather, Hunger and Fear: Origins of the European Witch-Hunts in Climate, Society and Mentality," in *The Witchcraft Reader* (ed. Darren Oldridge; London: Routledge, 2002), 69–86.

16. Darren Oldridge, "General Introduction," in Oldridge, *Witchcraft Reader*,

unmarried women as a disruptive element,[17] and so on, as reasons for a charged-up fear of witchcraft that led to waves of witch hunts. No matter what the explanation offered, individual jealousy is always involved. On the other hand, scholarship has rejected the idea that the practice of witchcraft or more or less secret healing practices among women led to witch hunts, and it has cast doubt on the existence of witch sects or witch cults,[18] although there is some controversy regarding the role of beliefs and practices in popular religion in medieval and early modern times.[19] Yet no grand unified field theory of witchcraft has emerged, as Malcolm Gaskill remarks in a recent article on the history of research,[20] or as David D. Hall stated in his book on the New England witch hunts: "Mystery remains, and will never vanish altogether."[21] Nevertheless, modern research on medieval and early modern witch hunts and witchcraft beliefs has shown that this is a multifaceted phenomenon that involves economic, legal, social, religious/theological, and psychological factors, as well as developments in the history of mentalities.[22]

Patterns of Witchcraft and Witchcraft Accusations in the Hebrew Bible and the Ancient Near East

Though understandings of witchcraft in anthropology and in medieval and early modern history provide us with possible social functions of witchcraft beliefs and accusations, these must be tested on the evidence of our sources. One major problem Hebrew Bible scholars have to face when dealing with witchcraft and magic is that the sources are scarce, random, and often polemical. In contrast to modern witchcraft phenom-

---

15; Robin Briggs, "The Experience of Bewitchment," in Oldridge, *Witchcraft Reader*, 60–62.

17. H. C. Erik Midelfort, *Witch Hunting in Southwest Germany 1562–1684: The Social and Intellectual Foundations* (Stanford: Stanford University Press, 1972), 195–96.

18. See Blauert, "Erforschung," 29–30; Dagmar Unverhau, "Frauenbewegung und historische Hexenverfolgung," in *Ketzer, Zauberer, Hexen*, 266–75; Oldridge, "Introduction," 17–18.

19. See Gaskill, "Pursuit of Reality," 1080, 1083–85 (on Emma Wilby's *Cunning Folk and Familiar Spirits*).

20. Gaskill, "Pursuit of Reality," 1075.

21. David D. Hall, *Witch-Hunting in Seventeenth-Century New England: A Documentary History 1638–1693* (2nd ed.; Boston: Northeastern University Press, 1999).

22. Cf. Gaskill, "Pursuit of Reality."

ena, we cannot observe the functions of witchcraft accusations in antiquity directly. Any kind of "thick description" that is possible in dealing with early modern witchcraft trials on the basis of an abundance of documents and related evidence is thwarted by the patchy character of our sources. We may use analogies to fill in gaps of evidence, but analogies should not be drawn from too far afield. Early modern and contemporary understandings of witchcraft drawn from particular, historically situated social and religious frameworks cannot simply be applied to ancient Near Eastern societies but have to be evaluated critically. Even using analogies from Late Bronze Age Syria, in particular Ugarit, and first-millennium Mesopotamia, where sources are more abundant, has to be done carefully for several reasons. First, though we may observe similarities in symbol systems, Mesopotamian society in particular is much more complex than that of ancient Israel. Second, the Mesopotamian witchcraft complex belongs to a learned, scholarly tradition in cuneiform literature that reaches back to the third millennium B.C.E. Although critical evaluation is necessary, social theory on witchcraft in general has nonetheless proven its value for historical studies. Moreover, structural and linguistic analogies between ancient Near Eastern magic and witchcraft beliefs are obvious and have proven their relevance for the analysis of ancient Israelite religion.[23]

The Hebrew verb usually translated "to perform magic/witchcraft" is *kāšap*.[24] Like its Mesopotamian and Ugaritic cognates, Hebrew *kāšap* denotes solely ritual practices that are prohibited in the Priestly and Deuteronomistic law codes.[25] It is also used to stigmatize certain persons such as the evil queen Jezebel as a "witch" (2 Kgs 9:22), or to brand alien religions and their practice as "witchcraft."[26] As in Mesopotamia, *kāšap* and its synonyms and cognates denote ritual practices that are considered illegitimate magic. In the Hebrew Bible we also find ritual practitioners and practices that are considered legitimate, such as the healing rituals performed

---

23. See Rüdiger Schmitt, *Magie im Alten Testament* (AOAT 313; Münster: Ugarit-Verlag, 2004), 67–106.

24. Exod 7:11; 22:17 (Eng. 18); Deut 18:10; 2 Kgs 9:22; 2 Chr 33:6; Isa 47:9, 12, Jer 27:9; Mic 5:11 (Eng. 12); Nah 3:4 (2 times); Mal 3:5; Dan 2:2. For the biblical terminology, see Schmitt, *Magie im Alten Testament*, 107–22.

25. Exod 22:17 (Eng. 18); Deut 18:10.

26. Isa 47:9, 12; Nah 3:4.

by the "men of God" Elijah and Elisha,[27] as well as those performed by the prophet Isaiah.[28] Nevertheless, Biblical and Post-Biblical Hebrew have no term for legitimate magical ritual actions analogous to Akkadian *āšipūtu.*

The relationship of witchcraft and gender has been an important issue in theorizing witchcraft both in anthropology and in history. In the Hebrew Bible, witchcraft and witchcraft accusations are often—but not exclusively—related to the female gender. Although the Hebrew verb *kāšap,* "to perform witchcraft," can be applied to both genders (males in Deut 18:10; Jer 27:9; females in 2 Kgs 9:22; Isa 47:1–15; Nah 3:4), the law against witchcraft in the book of the covenant, Exod 22:17 (Eng. 18) (*mĕkaššĕpâ lōʾ tĕḥayyeh,* "You shall not permit a witch to live"), is exclusively directed against female witches; in contrast, the Septuagint has here φαρμακούς, inclusive of both genders.

The use of *kāšap/mĕkaššĕpâ* to denounce a woman is also found in 2 Kgs 9:22, where Jehu refers to the "sorceries" of Queen Jezebel. (It is noteworthy that this is the only occurrence of a witchcraft accusation in the Deuteronomistic History.) The accusation of witchcraft is here paired with *zĕnûnîm,* "harlotries." We find the same stereotype associated with the "great whore" Babylon in Isa 47:1–15 and in a similar polemic against Nineveh in Nah 3, were the female personification of Nineveh is accused of being a "harlot" (*zônâ*) and a "mistress of witchcraft" (*baʿalat kĕšāpîm*). However, authors of the prophetic texts mentioned here are using a witchcraft stereotype to denounce foreign religions (in the case of Jezebel, that of the Phoenicians), not "real" witches, or witchcraft as a phenomenon in their own society.

The stereotype of the female witch can also be observed in Mesopotamia, where the witch, the *kaššāptu*, appears as the most important agent of harmful magic in antiwitchcraft rituals. Often the *kaššāptu* is addressed in ritual texts as a foreigner, an inhabitant of the peripheral mountain regions of Mesopotamia, an Elamite, Gutean, Sutean, Lullubean, or Hanigalbatean woman. A *kaššāptu* could be also a person with a defiling profession, such as a prostitute, or a woman whose profession is related to secret or dangerous procedures, for example, a female smith. Thus female outsiders are thought to be responsible for witchcraft. Therefore, "evil" witchcraft can be located outside one's own society, transferred to other places, which effec-

---

27. 1 Kgs 17–18; 2 Kgs 2:19–22, 23–24; 4:1–7, 8–37, 38–41, 42–44; 5:1–27; 6:1–7. See Schmitt, *Magie im Alten Testament*, 209–302.

28. 2 Kgs 20:1–11 = Isa 38:1–8, 21. See Schmitt, *Magie im Alten Testament*, 230–37.

tively avoids tensions in one's society. As Daniel Schwemer asserts in his recent book on Mesopotamian witchcraft, because combating witchcraft in Mesopotamia is primarily performed in antiwitchcraft rituals against an anonymous agent, actual witch hunts, and the social tensions resulting in witch hunts, are thereby avoided. However, the Mesopotamian witchcraft complex is not only confined to outsiders and women. A second important pattern is also that of close relatives, neighbors and friends, female and male, who are considered agents of witchcraft. Thus, though Mesopotamian witchcraft accusations can sometimes be an indicator of social tensions in close relationships, individual persons are usually not singled out as witches in the antiwitchcraft ritual, and witches remain anonymous, a pattern that functions to protect the family and social relationships.[29]

In Asia Minor it is often the so-called old/wise women (^{SAL}ŠU.GI or *ḫaššawa*)—despite being a legitimate ritual specialist—who can be accused of performing witchcraft, making her a somewhat ambiguous figure. Witchcraft cases are well known from the Hittite court.[30] In one case the queen mother Tawananna is accused of having bewitched King Murshili; and in the famous Telepinu Decree (*CTH* 19), we find the order to exile members of the royal family who are thought to be conspicuous performers of witchcraft. Also, a ritual performed by the *ḫaššawa* Tunnawya for a king and a queen is directed against a witchcraft plot at the Hittite royal court.[31]

Jewish writings of the Hellenistic and Roman periods are continuous with the broader ancient Near Eastern witchcraft complex and its pattern of witchcraft related to women. In 1 Enoch 6–7 the fallen angels are not only having sexual intercourse with human daughters, but they are also teaching them witchcraft. Even worse, in T. Reu. 5:5–6 women use witchcraft to seduce the angels, thus causing the heavenly rebellion and the final fall of the angels. Therefore, women are to be blamed for any evil in the

29. Daniel Schwemer, *Abwehrzauber und Behexung: Studien zum Schadenzauberglauben im alten Mesopotamien* (Wiesbaden: Harrassowitz, 2007), 146–48.

30. See Volkert Haas, "Verfluchungen am hethitischen Hof und ihre rituelle Beseitigung," in *Kult, Konflikt und Versöhnung: Beiträge zur kultischen Sühne in religiösen, sozialen und politischen Auseinandersetzungen des antiken Mittelmeerraumes* (ed. Rainer Albertz; AOAT 285; Münster: Ugarit-Verlag, 2001), 53–71; Schmitt, *Magie im Alten Testament*, 88–90.

31. Manfred Hutter, *Behexung, Entsühnung und Heilung: Das Ritual der Tunnawya für ein Königspaar aus mittelhethitischer Zeit* (OBO 82; Fribourg: Universitätsverlag, 1988), 113–20.

world according to this text. The same negative perception of women is found in the talmudic literature: b. Sanh. 67a treats the question why Exod 22:17 (Eng. 18) exclusively refers to female witches. The answer is that most women are witches. According to b. Pesaḥ. 110a, seeing two women sitting together at the road is enough to assume that they are performing witchcraft, and m. ʾAbot 2:7 states: "A lot of women—a lot of witchcraft" (*mrbh nšym mrbh kšpym*). In light of this, it is quite stunning that the female "witch" does not play an important role in the large corpus of late antique Jewish magical literature.

The use of *kāšap* in 2 Kgs 9:22 as well as in the prophetic polemics in Nah 3 and Isa 47 and their history of reception in postbiblical writings evince the existence of a certain gender-specific stereotype in biblical and postbiblical literature combining "witchcraft" with "harlotry."[32] These highly stereotyped references to female witchcraft in religious literature may also reflect stereotypes present in Second Temple period society. However, we have to be cautious about assuming that a stereotype in religious literature reflects a social reality. The polemics against Jezebel, Babylon, and Nineveh are directed against foreign religions in a more general sense, but do not refer to specific witchcraft phenomena. It is worthy of note that Wisdom literature, in particular Sirach, with all its misogynistic stereotypes, never refers to women as witches.

That witchcraft as a ritual practice meant seriously to harm a person is perceived as a capital crime is something that biblical law has in common with Mesopotamian laws. Middle Assyrian law A §47 reads:

> *šum-ma lu-ú* LÚ *lu-ú* MÍ *kiš-pe ú-up-pi-šu-ma i-na qa-ti-šu-nu iṣ-ṣa-ab-tu ub-ta-e-ru-šu-nu uk-ta-i-nu-šu-nu mu-up-pi-ša-na ša kiš-pe i-duk-ku*
>
> If a man or a woman performs witchcraft (*kišpum*) and is caught in the act, and if the fact is proven and if they are convicted, then the performer of witchcraft (*kišpum*) shall be put to death.[33]

---

32. See Schmitt, *Magie im Alten Testament*, 374–76.

33. Text from Rykle Borger, *Assyrisch-Babylonische Lesestücke* (2 vols.; AnOr 54; Rome: Pontificium Institutum Biblicum, 1963), 2:53. All translations in this essay are my own unless otherwise noted.

Biblical laws against witchcraft seen together with witchcraft polemics in the prophetic books are strong evidence for the existence of a witchcraft-related complex of beliefs in Second Temple society. It also seems clear that the law in Exod 22:17 (Eng. 18) cannot be understood without regard to the underlying stereotypes of witchcraft. Thus biblical law brings us a little bit closer to the social reality. We can conclude that there was a belief in witchcraft, and that the biblical legislators saw a need for such legislation. However, what the texts are not telling us is whether there ever was witchcraft as a manifest social problem, or if the witchcraft complex is only a social chimera. Thus we are faced with the same problem as scholars of medieval and early modern history: There was a belief in witchcraft, there were laws against witchcraft, but was there ever actual witchcraft?

Sigmund Mowinckel argued that the *pōʿălê ʾāwen*, the "evildoers" mentioned in the Psalms, have to be interpreted as witches and sorcerers seeking the suffering of people and causing illness, as in Ps 6:9–11 (Eng. 8–10).[34] The problem, however, is that the term *pōʿălê ʾāwen* is never associated with *kāšap* or its synonyms and cognates. There may be a hint of witchcraft in Ps 140:12 (Eng. 11), which mentions the *ʾîš lāšôn*, the "man of the tongue" who plans evil things, but this remains only a possibility. The descriptions of suffering in the individual psalms of lament are much too general and formulaic to be related exclusively to witchcraft.

The evidence of material culture, in particular the great number of amulets such as the Udjat-Eye, which may be understood as a counterforce to the evil eye, and other apotropaic amulets such as representations of Bes, from Iron Age II to the Persian period, evince the need for magical protection and a widespread fear of witchcraft and demonic attacks. However, these objects once again bear witness to popular belief rather than the social reality of witchcraft attacks.

Ezekiel 13:17–21 and the Social Reality of Witchcraft and Witchcraft Accusations

In the Hebrew Bible we find only one text that deals with actual witchcraft, Ezek 13:17–21:

34. Sigmund Mowinckel, *The Psalms in Israel's Worship* (trans. D. R. Ap-Thomas; 2 vols.; New York: Abingdon, 1962), 2:1–16.

> 17. And you, son of man, set your face against the daughters of your people, who prophesy out of their heart, and prophesy against them. 18. And say: Thus speaks Yhwh: Woe to the women who are tying knots on all wrists, and make veils for the heads of persons of every height, to hunt down human lives. Will you hunt down lives among my people, and maintain your own lives? 19. You have profaned me among my people for handfuls of barley and for pieces of bread, for putting to death persons who should not die and keeping alive persons who should not live, by your lies to my people, who listen to lies. 20. Therefore thus says Yhwh: I am against your knots with which you hunt down lives like birds, and I will tear them from your arms, and let the lives go free that you captured like birds. 21. And I will tear down your veils, and I shall save my people from your hands, so that they shall no longer be prey in your hands. And you shall know that I am Yhwh.

Ezekiel 13:17–21 accuses the "daughters of Israel" of having misused the name of Yhwh by performing magic through tying knots and other ritual manipulations such as making veils, which also seems to be a kind of magical binding known from Mesopotamian texts, intended either to kill a ritual enemy or to preserve the life of a ritual client. In addition, they have received payment for their deeds. The name of Yhwh is profaned (in v. 19) because these magical deeds were performed in the name of Yhwh to mobilize him against a ritual enemy with the goal of killing him or doing him serious harm. The text also condemns healing rituals in cases where it is not the will of Yhwh to let the client live. Yet the text presupposes that Yhwh could be mobilized by ritual activity to heal someone who is supposed to die. As I have already explained in my book on magic, Ezek 13 is a text about ritual authority, and we have to keep in mind that the prophet is a priest according to Ezek 1:3, and therefore he belongs to the group of official ritual specialists who are claiming a ritual monopoly for themselves.[35] Thus the actual practices performed by the "daughters of Israel" are illegitimate, otherwise referred to as *kĕšāpîm,* "witchcraft."

Because Ezek 13 deals with the problem of ritual authority, we have no reason to consider the text to be a mere theoretical or theological account of the sovereignty of Yhwh, who will not let himself be involved in unauthorized ritual practice. Rather, it is an account of ritual practices performed by freelance women healers in the exilic period. Ezekiel 13 thus

35. For a more detailed analysis, see Schmitt, *Magie im Alten Testament*, 283–87, 360–62.

reveals a disconnect between the priestly authority and its claim for ritual monopoly, which certainly suffered a crisis in the situation of the exile with the occurrence of freelance ritual specialists. However, we do not know if the ritual activities of those female ritual specialists were really meant to cause the death of people, or if this is a mere polemic. It is noteworthy that Ezekiel himself is reported to have performed an execration ritual against Jerusalem in 4:1–3, which is not regarded as witchcraft by the text, although the ritual could easily be interpreted as such. What Ezek 13 shows is that we have, at least in the exilic period, some evidence of the existence of female ritual specialists whose ritual authority was denied by religious officials.[36]

In Douglas's terms, Ezek 13 is evidence for type (b), "The witch as an internal enemy," subtype (b[i]), "The witch as member of a rival faction," as well as subtype (b[ii]), "The witch as a dangerous deviant," which creates demarcations against deviants in the name of community values, in this case the ritual authority of the traditional religious elites, the priests. In this example, therefore, social or anthropological theory can meaningfully be applied to biblical texts.

Some scholars, in particular Marie-Theres Wacker, have tried to relate the anthropological phenomenon of shamanism to Ezek 13.[37] Wacker has proposed a shamanistic belief system popular among Judahite folk, independent from official Yahwism and competing with it, in which female shamans play an important role in ritual healing. The problems with this interpretation are obvious. First, it is not possible to apply the religious phenotype of "shaman" as defined by anthropology (shamanic call, ghost possession, trance, visual ecstasy, as well as a certain pariah role)[38] to ancient Israel. It seems that we do not have shamanistic phenomena in the ancient Near East at all, where different phenotypes of religious specialists are dominant. The term *shaman* does not adequately characterize the "men of God" either, as proposed by some scholars. Recourse to shamanism seems to have become somehow endemic among scholars, but we have to be more careful in applying this term. Also, it is evident that

---

36. See Schmitt, *Magie im Alten Testament*, 360–62.

37. See Marie-Theres Wacker, "Schamaninnen in der Welt des Alten Testaments? Ein kulturvergleichendes Experiment," *Schlangenbrut* 57 (1997): 17–21; Erhard S. Gerstenberger, *Theologien im Alten Testament* (Stuttgart: Kohlhammer, 2001), 40, 154.

38. Cf. Klaus E. Müller, *Schamanismus: Heiler, Geister, Rituale* (Munich: Beck, 1997), 29–34.

the ritual practice of the freelance healers in Ezek 13 is perceived as being basically Yahwistic, though illegitimate. We may have forms of popular belief and ritual practice apart from the official cult, but these are better understood as manifestations of internal religious pluralism.

Conclusion

Witchcraft accusations in the Hebrew Bible are in most cases a literary phenomenon, in particular in prophetic writings such as Isa 47:1–15; Nah 3:4; and, of course, 2 Kgs 9:22, which denounce foreign religions as "witchcraft." Nevertheless, the prophetic accounts as well as the law against witchcraft in Exod 22:17 (Eng. 18) manifest a common Semitic "witchcraft complex" that denounces in particular women as prone to witchcraft. This witchcraft complex is rooted in the common marginalization of women in the patriarchal societies of the ancient Near East, a phenomenon that also has been observed by anthropologists and historians of the Middle Ages and the early modern period. Laws against witchcraft such as that in Exod 22:17 (Eng. 18) have a stabilizing function, projecting possible dangers for the individual, the family, and the society onto potential witches. Distress is explained by accusing a witch without blaming the victim for committing sins as the reason for suffering. More generally, the witchcraft complex explains the unexplainable. We know both from textual and archaeological sources that witchcraft beliefs were certainly part of the symbol system. But, in contrast to Mesopotamia and Asia Minor, we do not have antiwitchcraft rituals or documented cases of witchcraft, such as the Hittite Tawannana plot, which help us to determine the variety of social contexts in which witchcraft accusations may occur.

Nevertheless, Ezek 13 gives us some idea about the social setting of witchcraft accusations. First, there were freelance female ritual specialists performing healing rituals. Perhaps they also performed actual witchcraft, such as generating love charms and casting evil spells, but this must remain a speculation because of the polemical character of our sources. Second, witchcraft accusations arise in situations in which groups are competing over ritual authority and social authority. In the case of Ezek 13, we have on the one hand the exiled religious authorities, who are anxious to maintain their religious authority, and on the other hand the freelance healers, who are denounced as witches and denied their ritual authority. In the postexilic period, legislation against witchcraft and a variety of other ritual and mantic practices were used to reestablish priestly authority.

Social theory of witchcraft suggests that there are many possible reasons and social settings for witchcraft accusations. Clearly, it can be meaningfully applied to biblical traditions. Nevertheless, theory has to be critically reexamined in light of the evidence of the sources, which are not always as communicative as we might wish them to be.

Ritual Theory, Ritual Texts, and the Priestly-Holiness Writings of the Pentateuch

David P. Wright

Biblical studies thrives on the application of models and methods developed outside the discipline, especially those from the social sciences. This is particularly true in the study of ritual. The application of socio-theoretical approaches and perspectives has enhanced our understanding of this phenomenon or feature in biblical texts and will no doubt continue to do so.[1] Nevertheless, certain problems stand in the way of a straightforward application of socio-theoretical approaches to biblical texts that manifest ritual concerns and especially the *cultic* ritual material in the Priestly-Holiness corpus (PH) of the Pentateuch, the body of biblical literature

1. The literature is too vast to summarize here given the scope of biblical literature and the breadth of ritual phenomena (see the next note). Some recent books on biblical ritual, mainly cultic ritual and more specifically sacrifice, that have featured socio-theoretical perspectives to a greater or lesser extent include Roy Gane, *Cult and Character: Purification Offerings, Day of Atonement, and Theodicy* (Winona Lake, Ind.: Eisenbrauns, 2005); William Gilders, *Blood Ritual in the Hebrew Bible: Meaning and Power* (Baltimore: Johns Hopkins University Press, 2004); Ithamar Gruenwald, *Rituals and Ritual Theory in Ancient Israel* (Brill Reference Library of Judaism 10; Leiden: Brill, 2003); Jonathan Klawans, *Purity, Sacrifice and the Temple: Symbolism and Supersessionism in the Study of Ancient Judaism* (Oxford: Oxford University Press, 2006); Gerald Klingbeil, *Bridging the Gap: Ritual and Ritual Texts in the Bible* (BBRSup 1; Winona Lake, Ind.: Eisenbrauns, 2007); Jay Sklar, *Sin, Impurity, Sacrifice, Atonement: The Priestly Conceptions* (Hebrew Bible Monographs 2; Sheffield: Sheffield Phoenix Press, 2005). For an example of applying ritual and social theory beyond the sacrificial cult, see Nathaniel B. Levtow, *Images of Others: Iconic Politics in Ancient Israel* (Biblical and Judaic Studies from the University of California, San Diego, 11; Winona Lake, Ind.: Eisenbrauns, 2008). These works provide bibliography to earlier studies. See also other literature cited in this essay.

to which scholars gravitate for the study of biblical ritual.[2] In this essay I specifically explore the difficulty of applying theoretical approaches and perspectives to *texts*. I first look at a basic phenomenological dilemma, that our object of study is texts, not actual ritual practices. I then move to examine how the genre of PH may impede the application of theoretical approaches. Finally, I consider how analysis can deal with the multiple voices within PH itself.[3]

---

2. "PH" here refers to what scholars label as the P source or stratum of the Pentateuch. The composite appellation makes explicit the major distinctive strata within this collective corpus, a priestly base with augmentation by the holiness school (see later in this essay). While the PH corpus is paradigmatic for the study of ritual in the Bible and ancient Israel, ritual features pervade all genres of biblical literature, if a broad definition of ritual is allowed (see n. 9). For such a definition, which includes religious and secular ritual and allows for degrees of ritualization, see David Wright, "The Study of Ritual in the Hebrew Bible," in *Jewish Studies in the 21st Century* (ed. Frederick E. Greenspahn; New York: New York University Press, 2008), 120–38, esp. 120–22; idem, "Deciphering a Definition: The Syntagmatic Structural Analysis of Ritual in the Hebrew Bible," *JHS* 7 (http://www.arts.ualberta.ca/JHS/Articles/article_89.pdf); idem, *Ritual in Narrative: The Dynamics of Feasting, Mourning, and Retaliation Rites in the Ugaritic Tale of Aqhat* (Winona Lake, Ind.: Eisenbrauns, 2001), 8–13. The broad definition is based on Catherine Bell, *Ritual Theory, Ritual Practice* (New York: Oxford University Press, 1992); see her convenient description of ritualization on p. 74; see also n. 20 below). It should be kept in mind that cultic ritual (as found in PH) is a subcategory of ritual. The cult includes practices and phenomena associated with temples or sanctuaries, such as sacrifice, holiness, purity, priesthood, and festivals. A student interested in ritual in the Bible broadly should look beyond the cult and beyond PH.

3. My preoccupation with the issues in this paper began in the early 1990s when I reviewed Rolf Knierim, *Text and Concept in Leviticus 1:1–9* (FAT 2; Tübingen: Mohr Siebeck, 1992; the review is in *JBL* 113 [1994]: 123–24). He questioned the validity of applying ritual theory (particularly that of Victor Turner) to the biblical text. For example, he noted (19): "Turner's interpretations are the result of field studies of actually observed ritual performances. His text describes and interprets those performances. But while a prescriptive text about a ritual [i.e., like a PH text] will probably also reveal its hermeneutical system to a certain extent, it must not *e silentio* be presumed to be descriptive of actual performance, not only because there is—as in our biblical texts—no evidence for it but also because even such description represents an interpretive distancing vis-à-vis the performance." He says further (19–20): "the prescription of a ritual in a text is not identical with the description of an observed ritual, let alone with a performed ritual itself."

Texts as the Object of Ritual Analysis

I start with a philosophical-phenomenological difficulty, that the data source that biblical scholars use is a *text*. The theoretical problem here can be partly perceived by recognizing the equivocal use of the term *ritual* in relation to this source. It is common to call any description or prescription of a performance, such as the Day of Atonement legislation in Lev 16, a "ritual." But it is clear that the written text is not a ritual *as a performance*. It is a written artifact that describes or, more particularly, prescribes a performance. Such a text contrasts with what most social scientists work with when they do ritual analysis. Generally or ideally they look at the performances of live subjects. It is true that they necessarily *write up* their data along the way, and we their audience ultimately *read* their analyses. But this textualization is secondary.[4]

Calling a text that describes or prescribes ritual performance a "ritual" is akin to calling a piece of paper with staves, black dots, and tails "music," or a booklet with character names and what they are to say along with stage instruction a "play," or a verbal description of events of an earlier age a "history."[5] More accurately music and plays are what is performed before audiences, and history is the actual events that transpired in time. Written music, scripts, and histories are thus phenomenologically different from the actual performances or events. Our use of the terms for the notated versions is the result of the tropological operation of language, applying a term to something that is associated with it.[6]

---

4. While ethnographers and sociologists study directly the activity of groups, they at times extend their analysis to data as found in texts, and this includes the Bible. One thinks of Mary Douglas's *Purity and Danger: An Analysis of the Concepts of Pollution and Taboo* (London: Routledge, 1966), and Edmund Leach's analysis of Lev 8–9 in his *Culture and Communication: The Logic by which Symbols Are Connected, an Introduction to the Use of Structuralist Analysis in Social Anthropology* (Themes in the Social Sciences; Cambridge: Cambridge University Press, 1976), 81–93.

5. To some degree "history" stands apart from "play" and "music" in that one does not perform history from the written product—it is not a script or set of directions. But written "history" relates to written ritual insofar as the latter is a description of ritual as opposed to a prescription.

6. "Ritual" as a text operates as a metonym of "ritual" as performance. With this said, I am not trying to make a historical-linguistic statement about the development of the meaning of the term *ritual*.

The gap between written formulation and actual event can be seen in the creativity necessary for actualizing performance, to the extent that a text is viewed as prescriptive. Written music and a play's script, which are essentially of this genre, tell how a performance should proceed in some way. But they hardly provide enough information for full performance, especially in exceedingly truncated forms such as a jazz head chart, which generally gives only the melody and chord changes. Players, actors, conductors, and directors add interpretation and detail to create the actual performance, and this may involve intentional modifications or unintended infelicities. Similarly, written history is selective and constructed, so much so that theorists have likened it to the writing of fiction.[7] Similar considerations apply to written ritual, especially in PH and other biblical prescriptions. These texts, even the most detailed of them, do not contain enough information for a reconstruction of performances.[8]

Accordingly, the distance of text, phenomenologically and practically, from actual performance is almost enough to thwart sociological analysis. Keeping this in mind, I suggest that as study brings theory to bear on texts it be forthright about how a textual database limits and skews analysis. Often the application of theory, because of its imperfect fit to the data source, must be tentative and be applied only incompletely and heuristically, to *suggest* how the text and its described phenomena may be understood. Sometimes the application of these methods to text will necessarily turn toward or blend with literary analysis. Along these lines, study can look for intersections between theory and what is otherwise garnered through the study of a text's structure, *Leitwörter*, gaps, tensions, contrasts, skewing of conventional ideas, plot development, description of characters, use of dialogue versus description, word choice, and so forth.

---

7. See Hayden White, *Tropics of Discourse: Essays in Cultural Criticism* (Baltimore: Johns Hopkins University Press, 1978); idem, *Metahistory: The Historical Imagination in Nineteenth-Century Europe* (Baltimore: Johns Hopkins University Press, 1973).

8. The lack of detail that we find in PH may relate to the nature of its genre; i.e., as idealized prescription set in the past, it did not seek to fill in all particulars (see below). Nonetheless, prescriptions for actual ritual performances (e.g., Hittite, Akkadian, or Ugaritic ritual texts) often assume and depend on the background knowledge of performers. They prescribe only enough detail to activate this background knowledge. But this is exactly the problem with *real* prescriptive texts. The more they seek to prescribe actual practice, the less detail they may contain, rendering them almost impenetrable in terms of sociological analysis.

The loose fit between theory and what a text happens to tell us also means that only part of a theoretical approach or construct might be applicable. For example, it is possible to study the phenomenon or idea of ritually induced liminality as a feature or motif isolated from the more complex ritual phenomenon of *rites de passage*. This extracted motif may then be studied in different sorts of ritual texts in the Bible, even those that do not strictly feature transition rites, such as the sacrifice of Cain and Abel in Gen 4, the festivals of Deut 16, individual laments in the Psalms, or the descriptions of socially integrating and ostracizing behaviors in Job 29–30.[9] This allows for the application of theoretical perspectives to diverse biblical texts even though we lack a sufficient database or complete descriptions for certain ritual types.[10] In these cases, extracting or modulating aspects of theoretical approaches and application to biblical ritual texts becomes more the study of a literary motif in the text than of real world social phenomena. The application of theory in this way requires and allows for a certain amount of intellectual play to see how theory might be applied to text.[11] In any case, as noted before, the approach is heuristic and speculative, seeking elucidation rather than definitive sociological analysis.

Genre and the Priestly-Holiness Writings

A further complicating factor in using biblical texts for ritual analysis is the diverse range of genres in which ritual phenomena are featured and

9. The last example is an indication of the breadth of activity that may be analyzed as ritual. See n. 2 above. The ritual features in Job 29–30 include Job's sitting with people around him, their acting in a deferential manner by keeping silent or praising him (29:2, 5, 7–11, 13, 21, 25), and the reversal of Job's status to the bottom of the social order, pursued, and not allowed to sit among the people he once counseled (30:1, 10, 12).

10. While we have some notable examples of transition rites, such as the priestly consecration in Lev 8–9, the Bible generally describes only in passing ritual activities performed at the primary events in life. For example, nowhere in the Bible is a marriage described in enough detail for sociological analysis, even in the rather elaborate but folkloric stories about Jacob's marriages in Gen 29.

11. In my course on ritual I have students write four short papers, each of which involves taking a particular theory or theoretical motif found in Bell's two books (*Ritual Theory*, cited in n. 2 above, and her *Ritual: Perspectives and Dimensions* [New York: Oxford University Press, 1997]) and applying it to a biblical or Near Eastern text. This exercise seeks to cultivate analytic dexterity.

the different ideologies associated with these genres. As noted already, while modern sociological and anthropological analysis at times involves textualization of data, it tries to represent data accurately and objectively for the purpose of analysis.[12] The Bible's various genres by and large pursue goals that color or skew the portrayal of reality. Just as historians have difficulty in reconstructing biblical and Israelite history on the basis of so-called historiographic texts in the Bible, so those who study ritual should expect difficulty in applying social theory to or constructing it from ritual texts in the Bible.[13] Historians have learned to read between textual lines for their reconstructions; so too analysts must read ritual texts with critical sophistication. This complicates a social-theoretical analysis of those texts, which additionally has to concern itself with manifest and latent meanings of ritual performances apart from the obstacles of genre.[14]

As for the Priestly-Holiness writings in particular, the corpus has generally been understood to encode actual cultic practice at some particular point in Israelite or Jewish history or directly prescribe practice that is to be performed. This may misapprehend the genre. There are a number of indications that the portrayals of ritual in PH are academic abstractions or idealizations that significantly transcend practice.

The clearest mark of the artificial nature of PH's representation of ritual is the work's formulation as a piece of pseudepigraphy or perhaps, better, *pseudoarchaeography*.[15] Written much later than the events described,

---

12. I immediately stipulate here that even the most objective sociological data are colored, if only unintentionally, by the perspectives and choices that come into play in creating instruments of data gathering and otherwise describing data for analysis.

13. For biblical historiography, see Marc Brettler, *The Creation of History in Ancient Israel* (London: Routledge, 1995), and the discussion and references there.

14. Manifest, explicit, or surface meaning is that which performers (or writers) give to ritual action; latent, implicit, or submerged meaning is that determined through scholarly analysis. See David Wright, *The Disposal of Impurity: Elimination Rites in the Bible and in Hittite and Mesopotamian Literature* (SBLDS 101; Atlanta: Scholars Press, 1987), 3; Mary Douglas, *Implicit Meanings* (London: Routledge, 1975).

15. *Pseudepigraphy* or *pseudonomy* are not the best descriptions for PH because the text does not directly represent Moses as the writer and speaker of the whole. The speakers are an omniscient and anonymous narrator and incidentally the deity. The material represented as divine speech may be labeled *theonymy*. See Bernard M. Levinson, *Deuteronomy and the Hermeneutics of Legal Innovation* (Oxford: Oxford University Press, 1998), 34 n. 22 and pp. 47–48; idem, "The Hermeneutics of Innovation: The Impact of Centralization upon the Structure, Sequence, and Reformulation of Legal Material in Deuteronomy" (Ph.D. diss., Brandeis University, 1991), 157–61;

PH constructed an embroidered history by hermeneutically transforming sources, creatively filling in gaps, and inventing events and details. In doing this, the writers no doubt built on the customs prevailing at the time of their writing. But any such encoding of practice required adaptation to the simpler social world of the conceited past. In other words, the ritual performances are not directly those of seventh-, sixth-, or fifth-century Judah or Yehud (on the date of PH, see below). Yet the representation of ritual in PH likely goes beyond such a simple compositional operation of adapting the present to the past. Writing about the past would have been an adroit strategy for reforming ritual practice. The description of archetypical practice set down through divine revelation at the beginning of the nation's history could be used to contest contemporary customs that the writers perceived to be imperfect and compromised. This literary tactic, of course, had a shortcoming: the prescriptions given to the people in the wilderness could not simply be put into practice in the time and context of the writers. They would need to be adapted to the current social and institutional conditions of the time. This no doubt would have been a task that the PH writers and their heirs would have gladly taken on.[16]

The extent of pseudoarchaeographic contextualization of ritual in PH can be partly gauged by going through any given text and highlighting the elements that situate ritual performance in the wilderness context. These include architectural features of the sanctuary (its rooms, court, furniture) as well as the cast of ancient players (Aaron, his sons, or the

---

David Wright, *Inventing God's Law: How the Covenant Code of the Bible Used and Revised the Laws of Hammurabi* (Oxford: Oxford University Press, 2009), 472 n. 7, 292, 350.

16. In any case the prescriptions lack the details necessary for performance (see the first section of this paper). Some scholars have argued that the lack of prescription (or description) of a particular practice means that it was not performed, e.g., the recitation of prayer in sacrifice (Israel Knohl, *The Sanctuary of Silence: The Priestly Torah and the Holiness School* [Minneapolis: Fortress, 1995], 148–52), or that a lack of explanation in the prescriptions means that the rituals do not carry substantial symbolic meaning (see, e.g., William Gilders, "Blood as Purificant in Priestly Torah: What Do We Know and How Do We Know It?" in *Perspectives on Purity and Purification in the Bible* [ed. Baruch Schwartz et al.; New York: T&T Clark, 2008], 77–83; idem, *Blood Ritual*. Gilders's orientation stands in distinction to that of, for example, Klawans, *Purity, Sacrifice and the Temple*). See n. 37 below. (For *analogical* meaning in ritual, see David Wright, "Blown Away Like a Bramble: The Dynamics of Analogy in Psalm 58," *RB* 102 [1996]: 213–36, and the earlier papers cited there on p. 214 n. 1.)

general offices of priest as the main player in the sacrificial, purity, and festival rules without mention of a more complex and developed temple hierarchy).[17] These features pervade the prescriptions and descriptions and cannot be removed or translated into later analogues to render what might be confidently imagined as real ritual performances of the times of the writers. In fact, these elements are indications that the prescriptions have been expressly written for the narrative. In other words, they may not be based, for example, on preexisting individual temple instruction documents (*tôrôt*) that prescribed or described actual practice.[18]

In addition to these general historiographic and contextual considerations, several specific ritual and related legal passages in PH lay out highly idealized, utopian, and impractical practices. These include, for example, H's seventh-year and Jubilee laws in Lev 25 and the Levitical city and homicide-asylum laws of Num 35. That these laws are rather theoretical is underscored by the fact that they *rewrite* earlier seventh-year, debt-slave, and homicide legislation from the Covenant Code and Deuteronomy. As such they are academic scribal productions.[19] As H reconceived these laws, it filtered them through its interests in sabbatical observance and maintenance of the purity of the land. This gave H's versions of these laws a more pronounced ritualized character than the counterparts in its sources.[20] The seventh-year and Jubilee laws were formulated into a

17. On the materials about the Levites as an addition by H, see later in this essay.

18. The study of the Ugaritic corpus, for example, shows that description of ritual in narrative deviates substantially from ritual of actual performance (see Wright, *Ritual in Narrative*, 223–29). A narrative context allows authors to modify practice and custom to serve the larger goals of story. Ritual description in PH may therefore be markedly different from actual practice owing to the requirements of telling a story.

19. See Wright, "'She Shall Not Go Free as Male Slaves Do': Developing Views About Slavery and Gender in the Laws of the Hebrew Bible," in *Beyond Slavery: Overcoming Its Religious and Sexual Legacies* (ed. Bernadette Brooten and Jill Hazelton; Basingstoke: Palgrave Macmillan, 2010), 125–42; Bernard Levinson, "The Manumission of Hermeneutics: The Slave Laws of the Pentateuch as a Challenge to Contemporary Pentateuchal Theory," in *Congress Volume Leiden 2004* (ed. André Lemaire; VTSup 109; Leiden: Brill, 2006), 281–324; Jeffrey Stackert, *Rewriting the Torah* (FAT 52; Tübingen: Mohr Siebeck, 2007), 282–302.

20. The various source laws in the Covenant Code and Deuteronomy do have ritualized features. For example, the seven-year pattern of debt and slave release reflects a sacral rhythm (see Wright *Inventing*, 127–28). The adjudication of homicide in the Covenant Code takes place at a sanctuary (Wright, *Inventing*, 158). But H imbues the various laws with a national-geographical theology. Therefore, Bell's theoretical per-

system of embedded or concentric cycles of seventh-period rest (seventh day, seventh year, seven groups of seven years), based on a cosmic pattern of divine rest set down in the preface to PH (Gen 1:1–2:4a). The homicide-asylum law, more than its sources, worked out a system of how the killing of humans polluted the land. This was implicitly connected to history's primordium (cf. Gen 9:3–6 and bloodshed as the reason for the flood indicated by P's keyword *ḥāmās*, 6:11, 13; see also Lev 17) as well as to the national cultus, whose high priest provided a mechanism for expiation through his death. Both laws are ultimately concerned with the people living in the land. Ignoring these rules becomes the basis, implicitly if not explicitly, for expulsion from it (Lev 26:34–35, 43; Num 35:33–34; and see Lev 18:24–30; 20:22–24).

Idealization also appears in the sacrificial laws, which primarily belong to P with some updating by H.[21] These laws appear to have expanded and systematized a simpler sacrificial system that obtained toward the end of the First Temple period.[22] If basic prescriptions in P were created not

---

spective, which sees degrees of ritualization along a spectrum of related action rather than a simple dichotomy between ritual and nonritual action (see n. 2), helps to clarify how H has intensified the ritual aspects of the laws that it took over. The death of the high priest in Num 35 as a mechanism of atonement shows just how far H is willing to go in its ritualization of previous legal practice. For Deuteronomy's ritualization of homicide law in other respects, see Deut 21 (and David Wright, "Deuteronomy 21:1–9 as a Rite of Elimination," *CBQ* 49 [1987]: 387–403). For H's interest in Sabbath issues, see Knohl, *Sanctuary*, 8–45.

21. For example, H is responsible for the *ḥaṭṭāʾt* prescriptions in Num 15:17–31 (see Knohl, *Sanctuary*, 53, 105), which expands P's basic legislation in Lev 4 and 16.

22. A number of scholars have come to a similar conclusion. For a recent discussion, see James Watts, *Ritual and Rhetoric in Leviticus: From Sacrifice to Scripture* (Cambridge: Cambridge University Press, 2007), 66–67. Watts argues that the rhetoric of P's sacrificial laws is such as to mark the *ḥaṭṭāʾt* as a particular innovation. For other works on the history of sacrifice, see Rolf Rendtorff, *Studien zur Geschichte des Opfers im alten Israel* (WMANT 24; Neukirchen-Vluyn: Neukirchener, 1967); Baruch A. Levine, *In the Presence of the Lord* (SJLA 5; Leiden: Brill, 1974); Bernd Janowski, *Sühne als Heilsgeschehen: Studien zur Sühnetheologie der Priesterschrift und der Wurzel KPR im alten Orient und im Alten Testament* (WMANT 55; Neukirchen-Vluyn: Neukirchener, 1982); Gary Anderson, *Sacrifices and Offerings in Ancient Israel: Studies in their Social and Political Importance* (HSM 41; Atlanta: Scholars Press, 1987); Wolfgang Zwickel, *Räucherkult und Räuchergeräte: Exegetische und archäologische Studien zu Räucheropfer im Alten Testament* (OBO 97; Fribourg: Universitätsverlag; Göttingen: Vandenhoeck & Ruprecht, 1990); Ina Willi-Plein, *Opfer und Kult im alttestamentliche Israel: Textbefragungen und Zwischenergebnisse* (Stuttgarter Bibelstudien 153;

long after Deuteronomy's basic laws, as I will later suggest, it is therefore remarkable that P's sacrificial laws are significantly different from those in Deuteronomy. P gives extensive prescriptions about two sacrifices not mentioned at all in Deuteronomy: the *ḥaṭṭāʾt* ("sin" or "purgation" offering) and the *ʾāšām* ("guilt" or "reparation" offering). The omission of these in Deuteronomy does not seem to be merely a matter of divergent interests or emphases. Deuteronomy in various other passages is interested in sin, purification, purity in sacrificial practice, and even *kippûr*. It is also interested in sacrifices that individuals bring to the central sanctuary. P's *ḥaṭṭāʾt* would be a preeminent example of such. We would expect a mention of this sacrifice if it were a standard performance.[23]

What P has apparently done in developing its system is to have blended various rites of purification in which animals and their blood were used for purification with an earlier more limited system of sacrifice consisting mainly of the *zebaḥ* (P's *zebaḥ šĕlāmîm*) and *ʿōlâ*. This created the *ḥaṭṭāʾt* proper, as prescribed in Lev 4 and 16, where an animal is slaughtered as a sacrifice and its blood is daubed or sprinkled to purify various sancta. P's assimilation of other animal-blood purification rites, however, was only partial. The rites of the red cow in Num 19 and the dispatch of the (live) scapegoat on the Day of Atonement are both labeled with the term *ḥaṭṭāʾt* (Num 19:9; Lev 16:5), but they are not performed like the "standard" slaughtered version.[24] A blood purification rite that P brought into

Stuttgart: Katholisches Bibelwerk, 1993); Ulrike Dahm, *Opferkult und Priestertum in Alt-Israel: Ein kultur- und religionswissenschaftlicher Beitrag* (BZAW 327; Berlin: de Gruyter, 2003). For a collection of essays with helpful bibliography, see Adrian Schenker, ed., *Studien zu Opfer und Kult im Alten Testament (mit einer Bibliographie 1969–1991 zum Opfer in der Bibel)* (Tübingen: Mohr Siebeck, 1992). See also the works mentioned in n. 1 above.

23. Deuteronomy would further be interested in the *ḥaṭṭāʾt* as found in P because it purifies the sanctuary, and the sanctuary is at the heart of Deuteronomy's laws. Deuteronomy is elsewhere interested in the issue of *kippûr* (Deut 21:8), though in a nonsacrificial context. Hosea 4:8 sounds like Lev 10:17 and may attest to a sacrifice with proto-*ḥaṭṭāʾt* characteristics. But the Hosea verse is cryptic and may not refer to the *ḥaṭṭāʾt* as it is found in PH. Moreover, the Hosea passage refers to a northern (not Jerusalemite) practice. The alternative to this reconstruction would be to argue that the *ḥaṭṭāʾt* was in place in the Jerusalem temple in the seventh century, and that Deuteronomy expunged it. In that case, Deuteronomy represents a radical reformulation of sacrificial custom.

24. The Day of Atonement rite blends two distinct aspects of *ḥaṭṭāʾt* performances: animals sacrificed for purification blood and an animal on which sins are placed and

its system of purification but not into the *ḥaṭṭāʾt* system was the bird used for purifying from the impurity of *ṣāraʿat* (Lev 14:4–7, 49–53; interestingly this achieves *kippûr* outside the context of sacrifice according to 14:53).[25] In short, P may not be giving us a transcript of practices of the First Temple period, but instituting substantial innovations.[26]

In addition to content, legal abstraction is visible in the literary *structure* of the legislation in PH. While the corpus includes laws that are, relatively speaking, briefly formulated (such as in the miscellany of Lev 19), it more often presents detailed legislation on a particular topic, which lists a series of subcases arising from variables. The corpus formulates such groups of laws in a coherent fashion, such as cases of descending or ascending weightiness (as in the *ḥaṭṭāʾt* legislation of Lev 4 or the Jubilee legislation of Lev 25) or chiastic formulation (as in the sexual impurities laws of Lev 15). This detail and rationality reflect a preoccupation with legislation that appears to go beyond reproducing everyday practice. It may arise from an abstract process of thinking about and intellectualizing matters of law and ritual, and systematically working out implications and the expansion toward a fuller system.[27]

A final and important matter to consider is how PH operates as ideological literature—how it responds to events and ideas—in its local social and international context. This certainly is not easy to describe because of the difficulty in dating the corpus and its individual components. Different datings will lead to different assessments in this regard. For me, the network of innerbiblical textual relationships (including those of Ezekiel, Deuteronomy, the Covenant Code, and pentateuchal narratives) indicates

---

which is dispatched alive. The former facilitated the assimilation of the scapegoat to the *ḥaṭṭāʾt* system, to provide phenomenological symmetry in the people's offering, including the reference to *kippûr* in 14:53.

25. The introduction to the pericope on the leprous house (Lev 14:33–53) manifests H phraseology (cf. Knohl, *Sanctuary*, 95 n. 119). This raises suspicion that the whole pericope is an H composition.

26. Idealization is evident in other P prescriptions. For example, while the symptomatology of *ṣāraʿat* appears to be based in some pathological reality, some of the features of the disease(s) appear to be abstractions, particularly a conflation of symptoms from different discrete conditions. See David Wright and Richard Jones, "Leprosy," *ABD* 4:277–82.

27. For the issue of system in the legislation of PH, see David P. Wright, Baruch Schwartz, Jeffrey Stackert, and Naphtali S. Meshel, "Introduction," in Schwartz et al., *Perspectives on Purity*, 1–5.

PH began to be formulated during Neo-Babylonian domination of Judah, at the very end of the seventh century on into the exile of the sixth century, with continued expansion into the exilic and postexilic periods. Thus the beginnings of the PH corpus—and I am trying to be quite open-ended here—may respond to Neo-Babylonian oppression generally and not specifically the loss of temple and kingship, though the catastrophe of 586 B.C.E. must have been a significant catalyst in the development of the corpus.[28]

In this context PH can be viewed as articulating a theology of divine presence in the cult and specifically prescribing the mechanics as to how to maintain that divine presence.[29] Babylonian practices and ideas may have been influential.[30] P's picture of history that moves from creation to the establishment of the cult (the P material from Gen 1 to Lev 16) fits the pattern and rationale of creation in Mesopotamian texts such as *Enuma Elish* and *Atrahasis*.[31] The system of *kippûr* in the cult has similarities with Babylonian *kuppuru* rites.[32] "Freedom" (*dĕrôr*) granted in the Jubilee Year echoes the freedom (*andurāru*) instituted by Mesopotamian kings. That PH would take motifs from the imperial culture and use them to its own ends is consistent with what we find in earlier biblical legal texts. Deuteronomy transforms Assyrian treaty to create obligations of loyalty to Yhwh

---

28. For a discussion of the chronology, see the appendix at the end of this essay.

29. Benjamin Sommer, *The Bodies of God and the World of Ancient Israel* (Cambridge: Cambridge University Press, 2009), discusses how three different theologies competed with one another around 600 B.C.E. (Deuteronomic name theology, Zion-Sabaoth theology, and Priestly theology of divine presence). I would stress the international factor in the development of these theologies. They did not simply grow up in a closed world of local competition, but each is an ideological reaction whose goal was the security of the Judean state in the face of imperial pressure.

30. Postcolonial perspectives can be used with caution to elucidate the development of pentateuchal and other biblical literature under the influence of foreign hegemony in the Assyrian and Babylonian periods. See William Morrow, "Resistance and Hybridity in Late Bronze Age Canaan," *RB* 115 (2008): 321–39; idem, "'To Set the Name' in the Deuteronomic Centralization Formula," *JSS* 55 (2010): 365–83. On Babylonian influence, see Kenton Sparks, "*Enūma Elish* and Priestly Mimesis: Elite Emulation in Nascent Judaism," *JBL* 126 (2007): 625–48.

31. See Wright, *Inventing*, 358–59, 509 n. 31.

32. See Wright, *Disposal*, 291–99; and for a recent discussion of *kippûr* in the Bible, see Jay Sklar, "Sin and Impurity: Atoned or Purified? Yes!" in Schwartz et al., *Perspectives*, 18–31 (see also his *Sin, Impurity, Sacrifice, Atonement*). *Kippûr* in PH is not simply a borrowing from Mesopotamian practice, but its semantic complexity may indicate a convergence of meanings from a native lexeme impacted by foreign idiom.

and to partly construct curses for violation (Deut 13 and 28).[33] The Covenant Code, according to my analysis, used the Laws of Hammurabi as a source and model for its laws with the notable replacement of the Israelite deity for the Mesopotamian lawgiver.[34]

The larger point that I seek to make here is that the sociocultural world in which PH was created, whatever that may have been, has to be considered as a factor in its formulation. The corpus has been written in dialogue with that environment and in reaction to it. As such it is probably not merely descriptive but prescriptive in the larger ideological sense in that it seeks to shape opinion and motivate response. As a programmatic text, therefore, whatever material it took up from authentic custom it repackaged and expanded in the service of present exigencies.

The foregoing considerations demonstrate in various ways how distant PH's ritual descriptions are from actual practice. Theoretical approaches brought in from anthropology and sociology must be adjusted accordingly to account for this particular and even peculiar object of study. I mention a few possible directions for research here. One modification is to adapt approaches to literary analysis, already recommended earlier. In terms of the issues raised in the present section of the paper, one may go beyond the study of individual pericopae and examine *ritual in the narrative context of PH*.[35] This would examine the dynamic relationship of the various pericopae to one another, how they operate in the formulation of the plot development, and how one passage affects the meaning and interpretation of another. A specific point of analysis could be to examine the interplay and concatenation of prescriptions and descriptions of felicitous ritual—cases where ritual is portrayed as proceeding properly—versus cases of infelicitous ritual.[36] The latter include stories about the unauthorized fire offered by Aaron's sons (Lev 10), blasphemy (Lev 24), gathering wood on the Sabbath (Num 15), and Korah's incense offering (Num 16–17). One could scrutinize how ritual is portrayed across the whole of PH, from creation that anticipates the Sabbath (which becomes a focus of H in particular), through the primeval and patriarchal history

---

33. See Wright, *Inventing*, 103–4, 397 n. 116 (with bibliography).

34. Wright, *Inventing*, 287–300, 346–52.

35. See Wright, *Ritual in Narrative*, esp. the summary in 223–29.

36. See Ronald Grimes, "Infelicitous Performances and Ritual Criticism," in *Ritual Criticism: Case Studies in Its Practice, Essays on Its Theory* (Columbia: University of South Carolina Press, 1990), 191–209; Wright, *Ritual in Narrative*, 98–138.

where only noncultic ritual prevails (the prohibition against blood ingestion and command to circumcise), to the eventual inauguration of cultic worship under Moses, the fulfillment of creation. This would throw light on the meaning of any given ritual phenomenon by contextualizing it in the whole. For example, the meaning of sacrifice, even its core symbolic import, may be visible only by considering when and how it appears in PH's larger story of human history.[37]

Another approach would be to look at PH in terms of models and theories of *ritual change*.[38] The foregoing discussion has given examples of such in PH's rewriting of laws on debt release and homicide and its expansion of the scope of sacrificial practice. Sociological and anthropological study demonstrates that ritual adapts to fit the needs and the world of its practitioners. This is especially to be expected when it is recognized that ritual is a means of forming relationships between groups and individuals.[39] As those relationships and conditions evolve, so does ritual. Even though a ritual performance may be studied synchronically, a clearer view of its rationale and logic may be gained by studying the diachronic dimension, much as when studying the historical development of a language. Models of ritual change from sociology and anthropology can help to constructively complicate a more straightforward historical analysis of the practices and institutions described in these texts. They can advantageously draw attention to how events, such as domination by foreign powers, the loss of temple and kingship, and battles between local groups seeking power, led to modifications in ritual practice.

---

37. This would provide added dimension to the current debate about whether ritual has meaning, symbolic or otherwise (see n. 16; note the resistance to finding meaning in ritual by Fritz Staal, *Rules without Meaning: Ritual, Mantras and the Human Sciences* [New York: Lang, 1989], 115–40; idem, "The Meaninglessness of Ritual," *Numen* 26 [1975]: 2–22; see also Gane, *Cult and Character*, 4–6). If ritual has meaning in its narrative, then it is governed by methods of literary study as much as by methods of strict sociological or ritual theory. Of course, one could say that ritual has meaning in its narrative, but lacks meaning when it is actually performed, a compromise that would interestingly complicate the reading of ritual in PH.

38. See Bell, *Ritual: Perspectives and Dimensions*, 210–52, a chapter entitled "Ritual Change" (also see pp. 172, 263–64). See also Clifford Geertz, "Ritual and Social Change: A Javanese Example," in *The Interpretation of Cultures* (New York: Basic Books, 1973), 142–69.

39. This is a fundamental feature of ritual in Bell's theoretical model (*Ritual Theory, Ritual Practice*).

Still another approach, which combines literary and diachronic outlooks, is to study *ritual literature as ritual*. For example, the priestly consecration rite in Lev 8–9 can be examined as a rite of transition in terms of how social hierarchy and relationships are reflected, how binary schemes are deployed, how bodies experience ritual, the employment of action versus speech, practice theory, semiotic analysis, the use and meaning of cultural symbols, the linking together of ritual elements to form a "syntactic" whole, and the degree of ritualization of such elements. These modes of inquiry can be complemented by what the legislation seeks to achieve in its generative historical context. The rite from this perspective does not just speak about the installation of individual priests in antiquity, but seeks to elevate the whole category of priesthood to a new status in society in the age when the text was written.[40] The synchronic individual-social function of the rite as a rite is thus nested in the operation of a larger contextual diachronic national-political function of the narrative context. Though this priestly consecration never occurred in actual history, as far as critical scholarship is concerned, the story presented as real history imbues the recipient groups with all of the powers and privileges as if the rite was actually performed. It creates and defines power relationships between groups and individuals. Thus the report of a ritual performed can be as effective as actually performing or witnessing the ritual, even if the report is a fiction. This is the particular sociological impact of ritual description or prescription in pseudepigraphic literature broadly.

Redactional Strata in the Priestly-Holiness Writings

While in the foregoing discussion at times I pointed out differences between P and H, I proceeded in large part in view of PH as a whole over against other books and corpora in the Bible. The application of social-theoretical approaches to PH, however, must on a more detailed level take

40. I stress that this is not necessarily a reflection of a postexilic institutional reality (see the appendix, point 9, below). The priestly power play as reflected in PH is relative to the institutions of the period in which P and H were created, even in an age with a puppet king under Neo-Babylonian power or soon thereafter, even as there might have been hope for a reestablished Davidic dynasty. Sight should never be lost of the pseudoarchaeographic context for PH, where a king did not exist and primary leadership would naturally have fallen to priests, servitors in the cultus that symbolized and concretized the nation's relationship to its deity.

into consideration the differences between P and H as well as subdivisions of these literary strata, as a particular critical analysis may suggest. Even though H is an addition to a basic P narrative, includes legislation about sacrifice and purity, and is sympathetic to that source, it develops it in new directions and introduces new concerns.[41] While it is possible for certain analytic purposes to approach the text as a conceptual unity, to rigidly hold to a holistic approach ignores a chief feature of the text and may even skew analysis. The text contains multiple voices that must be considered. Successive contributors to the corpus probably did not simply assent to everything in their sources, but sought to revise them, either by expansion or rewriting. This would have been a reason why later writers would have taken up the pen in the first place.

For example, an analysis of the Day of Atonement ritual must distinguish between the rite as prescribed in P in Lev 16:1–28 and the addendum of H in 16:29–34, as well as recognize the additions made by H to the Day of Atonement regulations in a basic P calendar in Lev 23:26–32.[42] As Knohl has shown, H has taken an ad hoc sanctuary purification rite and merged it with an annual fast observance on the tenth day of the seventh month to produce the Day of Atonement performance as we know it in the final form of the text. The blending of these two performances thus gave each a new meaning. The sanctuary purification, which sought quite mechanically through priestly performance to remove the impurity of a variety of sins and impure situations, was now accompanied by ritual behavior on the part of the nation as a whole that sought to obtain the notice and sympathetic response of the deity.[43] The purification of the

---

41. One of the difficulties in examining H over against P is that H will often speak of matters untouched by P. The temptation is to argue that an idea or ritual performance in H, unmentioned in P, is novel. Knohl's analysis of the distinctiveness of H's theology over against P has been criticized along these lines. On the fallacy of a negative proof (or argument from silence), see David Hackett Fischer, *Historians' Fallacies: Toward a Logic of Historical Thought* (New York: Harper, 1970), 47–48. He notes that "a simple statement that 'there is no evidence of *X*' means precisely what it says—no evidence." Then he adds: "The only correct empirical procedure is to find affirmative evidence of not-*X*—*which is often difficult, but never in my experience impossible*" (emphasis added). See n. 43 below.

42. See Knohl, *Sanctuary*, 13–14, 27–34. He sees three strata in Lev 23:26–32: P in vv. 26–28aα*, early HS in vv. 28aβ–31, and later HS in v. 32.

43. For contextualization of H's prescription of abstention on the Day of Atonement as a feature of petitionary mourning, see Saul M. Olyan, *Biblical Mourning: Ritual*

sanctuary with *ḥaṭṭāʾt* blood and the dispatch of sins to the wilderness were matched by a performance that signaled and sought to generate a penitential spirit in community at large. The shift in the rite's demographic dimensionality from P to H is clearly an adaptation ripe for detailed socio-theoretical evaluation.

Another case of difference between P and H is in their cultic cadres. The Levites as auxiliary cultic functionaries, whose duties include guarding the sanctuary and transporting it when dismantled, is the major concern and contribution of H to the PH corpus.[44] The Levites appear in this capacity only in Numbers and, quite remarkably, outside P's primary cultic legislation in Exodus and Leviticus.[45] Because the procedures for the consecration of the priests and dedication of the Levites, in Lev 8 and Num 8, respectively, display some similar features, the latter may have been created in part to resonate with the former.[46] At the same time there are nota-

---

and Social Dimensions (Oxford: Oxford University Press, 2004), 65–68. He notes that the motivation for such rites is "to convince Yhwh to reverse his negative judgment against them [i.e., the people] and restore their fortunes" (65). One of the difficulties with H's prescription is that it does not say explicitly whether self-denial is observed at home or at the sanctuary. (Joel 1:14, which Olyan discusses, places fasting at the sanctuary.) This is one of the points of silence in H (see n. 41) that may be of significance. Indirect *positive* evidence that the people are at home includes the requirement to practice self-denial overnight (Lev 23:32) and to avoid work "in all your settlements" (v. 31) which is comparable to the requirement of Sabbath rest, presumably observed at home (v. 3; note also that H uses the special term for sabbatical rest, *šabbātôn*, for the Sabbath and the Day of Atonement, vv. 3, 24, 32).

44. On the Levitical texts in Numbers belonging possibly to a late stratum in H, see n. 28 above. For some recent studies about the Levites and the priesthood, see Dahm, *Opferkult*; Deborah Rooke, *Zadok's Heirs: The Role and Development of the High Priesthood in Ancient Israel* (Oxford Theological Monographs; Oxford: Oxford University Press, 2000); Risto Nurmela, *The Levites: Their Emergence as a Second-Class Priesthood* (South Florida Studies in the History of Judaism 193; Atlanta: Scholars Press, 1998); Richard Nelson, *Raising Up a Faithful Priest* (Louisville: Westminster John Knox, 1993).

45. The Levites appear specifically in Numbers in the census of ch. 1 in the appendix there (vv. 47–54), the camp layout in ch. 2, the Levitical census in ch. 3, the Levitical duties in ch. 4, the setting apart of the Levites in ch. 8, the march of the camp in ch. 10, the rebellion of Korah and Levites and its aftermath in chs. 16–17, and Levitical dues in ch. 18. Within P, the Levites offer ad hoc cultic aid in Lev 10:4 (see n. 49 below), and in H^1 (see the appendix, below) Levitical cities appear in Lev 25:32–33.

46. Both groups are "taken" (*lāqaḥ*; Lev 8:2; Num 8:6); both are "brought near" the sanctuary or specifically its door (*hiqrîb*; Lev 8:6, 13, Aaron and sons distinguished;

ble differences in the two rites, which divulge their distinct goals.[47] The main difference is in the resulting status of the two groups. The priests are consecrated, made holy. This is achieved by a combination of rites, including investiture in priestly robes, anointing with oil, and application of consecration offering blood to their bodies. The Levites, by contrast, are not described as being sanctified. Even though the Levites are a replacement for the firstborn of the Israelites, whom God, as the text says, *consecrated* to himself upon the exodus, and even though their dedication rite is the metaphorical extension of sacrificial procedure, they are never called holy in H (or PH).[48]

Num 8:9); the congregation (*'ēdâ*) is gathered (*hiqhîl*) to witness or participate (Lev 8:3–4; Num 8:9–10); both groups are purified, though in different ways (laver washing versus sprinkling, shaving, laundering; Lev 8:6; Num 8:6–7); both undergo a procedure through which they are ritually set apart (Lev 8:5–9, 12, 22–25, 30: investiture, application of oil, application of oil and blood to extremities; Num 8:10, 11, 15: being offered metaphorically with sacrificial gestures; see n. 48); both rites include elevation (*tĕnûpâ*) performances (though performed on different ritual patients); sacrifices are offered on both occasions (Lev 8:2, 13–17, 18–21, 22–29: a *ḥaṭṭā't*, *'ôlâ*, and *millû'îm*; Num 8:8, 12: an *'ôlâ* and *ḥaṭṭā't*).

47. The Levites' dedication is much less complex than the priestly consecration in respect to the sacrifices offered and the rites performed to achieve dedication. Part of the complexity in the priestly consecration is the separate treatment of Aaron versus his sons. In other words, the priestly rite gives attention to priestly hierarchy, whereas the Levites' rite does not distinguish, for example, between the Levitical ancestral houses (see the implicit hierarchy in Num 3–4). The priestly rite also continues for a week, and the dedication rite is apparently repeated every day over the course of this week (Lev 8:34). It actually concludes with the eighth-day ceremony described in Lev 9. This includes the people's participation in the sacrificial activity and culminates in their being blessed and the issue of divine fire that consumes the sacrifices.

48. The Levites receive hand placement like sacrifices, and they are elevated like sacrificial materials. The rite performed on them, however, only "separates" them (*hibdîl;* Num 8:14) and they are "given," and even labeled as *nĕtûnîm* "those dedicated/given" (8:16, 19). They are further characterized as subservient to Aaron and his sons in their being stood before Aaron and his sons (8:13), by their being given by God to Aaron and his sons to do their labor (8:19), and by Aaron himself performing an elevation rite on them (8:11, 21; I am leaving aside here the possibility that the description of Aaron's elevation rite and associated verses are an addition). The Levites' subordination to the priests is otherwise found in the wilderness camp arrangement and in the duties of the Levites to guard the outer borders of the sanctuary, while the priests officiate inside the sanctuary precincts.

While various anthropological and sociological perspectives can be used to elucidate the inner logic of the priestly consecration and Levitical dedication as self-contained entities, the ideological and historical dimension must also be considered. The book of Ezekiel attests to a power struggle between Levites in general and the specific priestly class, the Zadokites (Ezek 44:9–17). Only the latter were to function as priests, while the Levites were to become subordinate servants. The rites for the two classes in P augmented with H recast this distinction as being set down at the nation's birth. The procedures are described as events that occurred in the past. What for Ezekiel was a matter of ad hoc ritual change due to recent circumstances was re-presented as a distinction based on foundational revelation of ritual procedure.[49] Again, this is an example of ritual literature as ritual operating in a context of ritual change.

Conclusion

In this essay I have not charted a definitive path for the application of socio-theoretical approaches and perspectives to the Priestly-Holiness writings or to other ritual texts in the Bible. Rather, I have highlighted the imperfect fit that exists between theory and the biblical text and have therefore suggested that a certain amount of creativity and artistry is required to bring the two together. Indeed, as an art the theoretical study of ritual texts will naturally be combined with techniques of literary analysis rather than proceed on strict socio-analytical lines. At the same time, an analysis should also consider a text's genre and history, including its relationship to other texts and the relationship of its internal strata. While these matters may be disputed by scholars, staking out a position or at least identifying possible positions in an analysis provides a real-world

49. It is not that P did not imagine a functional distinction between priests and Levites. That the Levites broadly are not a sanctified class is implied by the general silence of P about their status over against that of the priests. P also provides positive evidence of the distinction of the classes when it calls on Aaron's cousins—i.e., Levites—to remove the corpses of Aaron's sons on the culminating day of priestly consecration (Lev 10:4). They are chosen for the task because they have no cultic obligations as priests and may therefore become impure from handling corpses. The silence of H about any special Levitical obligations of purity, as it gives for priests in Lev 21–22, reinforces the picture of the nonholy status of the Levites. In addition, H's narrative about Korah and the Levite rebellion emphasizes the holiness of priests and the lack of that status for Levites (Num 16–17; see Knohl, *Sanctuary*, 73–85).

anchor, especially through points of contrast, to the study of the otherwise self-contained and ideal world presented by the text. All in all, what is recommended here is the pursuit of complex analysis where a variety of approaches are brought to bear simultaneously and where the approaches mutually inform one another.

Appendix: The Dating of PH

This is hardly the place to fully justify this chronology. In brief, however, the following considerations are starting points for me:

1. H supplements and expands—hence is *later than*—a foundational P text consisting of narrative with embedded legislation (Knohl, *Sanctuary*; Jacob Milgrom, *Leviticus 17–22* [AB 3A; New York: Doubleday, 2000], 1319–67; Stackert, *Rewriting*; Christophe Nihan, *From Priestly Torah to Pentateuch* [FAT 2/25; Tübingen: Mohr Siebeck, 2007]).

2. P together with essentially all of H constituted an independent source prior to incorporation into the Pentateuch, which means that P and/or H are not tied to the later date of the Pentateuch's creation in the Persian period (see Baruch Schwartz, "The Priestly Account of the Theophany and Lawgiving at Sinai," in *Texts, Temples, and Traditions: A Tribute to Menahem Haran* [ed. Michael Fox et al.; Winona Lake, Ind.: Eisenbrauns, 1996], 103–34; Ernest Nicholson, *The Pentateuch in the Twentieth Century: The Legacy of Julius Wellhausen* [Oxford: Clarendon, 1998], 196–221; Jeffrey Stackert, "Review of Nihan, *From Priestly Torah*," *RBL* [September 2008]).

3. The general historical horizon of the redacted book of Ezekiel appears to be the second half of the sixth century during the era of return and rebuilding of the temple, and several core passages in the book (apart from chs. 40–48, which are clearly late in the book's redactional history) reflect knowledge not only of Holiness Code texts as many have recognized (see the convenient list and discussion in Walther Zimmerli, *Ezekiel 1* [trans. Ronald E. Clements; Hermeneia; Philadelphia: Fortress, 1979], 48–52), but also some P texts and ideas, including narrative elements (e.g., Ezek 14:13 reflects the *ʾāšām* legislation of Lev 5:21; Ezek 18:4 and 20 reflect P's use of the noun *nepeš* with the verb *ʿśh* in Lev 4:2; 5:1, 17, 21; cf. 4:27; 5:15; Ezek 18:11 reflects P's use of the verb *ʿśh* plus the preposition *min* with reference to sin in Lev 4:2; cf. 4:22 and vv. 13, 27; 5:17, 22; the term "crimes" [*pěšāʿîm*] in Ezek 14:11; 18:22, 28, 30, 31; 21:29; 33:10, 12; 37:23, 24 [cf. 20:38] is a central term in P's Day of Atonement *ḥaṭṭāʾt* ritual

[Lev 16:16, 21]; the historical and highly idealized "narrative" in Ezek 20 reflects motifs of P in Exod 6). This evidence points to the existence of a version of PH by around the mid-sixth century. If the relevant passages in Ezekiel were created or largely revised in the second half of the sixth century, and not primarily the product of the persona Ezekiel in the first half of the century, then P may be dated to just after 586 and be a response to the events of that year, with H expansion beginning at the end of the exilic period. For attribution of Ezekiel's contents to scribes working in the middle and latter half of the sixth century, see Rainer Albertz, *Israel in Exile: The History and Literature of the Sixth Century b.c.e.* (SBLStBL 3; Atlanta: Society of Biblical Literature, 2003), 345–76. For Ezekiel's correlations with PH, see Risa Levitt Kohn, *A New Heart and a New Soul: Ezekiel, the Exile and the Torah* (JSOTSup 358; Sheffield: Sheffield Academic Press, 2002); Michael Lyons, *From Law to Prophecy: Ezekiel's Use of the Holiness Code* (LHBOTS 507; London: T&T Clark, 2009). Note the caution of David Carr, *The Formation of the Hebrew Bible* (Oxford: Oxford University Press, 2011), 301 n. 101.

4. H depends on the Covenant Code and hence postdates it (see point 7 and Wright, *Inventing*, 506–7 n. 19; Stackert, *Rewriting*).

5. H reflects dependence on the basic laws of Deuteronomy (datable to ± 620 B.C.E.) and hence postdates that corpus (see Stackert, *Rewriting*).

6. P's narrative appears to build on the *narratives* of E and J (though it uses these more as *templates* than sources that are revised; see Wright, *Inventing*, 358–59; see also points 7 and 8; very provisionally, see Sean McEvenue, *The Narrative Style of the Priestly Writer* [AnBib 50; Rome: Biblical Institute Press, 1971]); also Michaela Bauks, "La signification de l'espace et du temps dans 'l'Historiographie Sacerdotale,'" in *The Future of the Deuteronomistic History* (ed. T. Römer; BETL 147; Leuven: Leuven University Press, 2000), 30–31.

7. E (an independent documentary source) is the narrative in which the Covenant Code was written or at least expands a more limited narrative in which the code was situated (see Wright, *Inventing*, 332–45; Joel Baden, "Review of Wright, *Inventing God's Law*," *RBL* [July 2009]; I theoretically allow a broad window of 740–640 for the Covenant Code, but the date appears close to 700).

8. J (also an independent source) reacts to E's narrative, yet has to be prior to Deuteronomy's introductory materials (see Joel Baden, *J, E, and the Redaction of the Pentateuch* [FAT 68; Tübingen: Mohr Siebeck, 2009]) and prior to P's narrative (see point 6).

9. The sociological picture in PH (e.g., the ascendancy of priests), because of the document's pseudoarchaeographic contextualization, cannot be taken as decisive or straightforward evidence for the dating of PH, despite what I have said about PH's connection to its sociocultural world (see similar considerations with regard to the Covenant Code, Wright, *Inventing*, 97–98, 389 n. 36).

10. P's ritual prescriptions were created in connection with a larger narrative that gave them context.

Less clear to me at this point is how PH developed. I am working presently with a theoretical model of three main stages: (I) P, a narrative with embedded legislation, consisting of the material assigned in general analyses to P from Gen 1 through (approximately) Lev 16, including basic sacrificial, purity, and festival laws. This is a story of the nation's founding that begins with creation and runs through the erection of the sanctuary (see Wright, *Inventing*, 358–59, 509 n. 31; see also Nihan, *From Priestly Torah*). (II) An H legislative supplement (H^1) in Lev 17–26* (the "Holiness Code"). This provided a new conclusion to P, ending in blessings and curses (Lev 26). These chapters were roughly modeled on the pattern of Deut 12–28. (III) A further H supplement (H^2) of some narrative and legislative materials, mainly in Lev 24 and 27, and the material of Numbers normally assigned to P and/or H, especially the passages on the Levites (see Knohl, *Sanctuary*, 71–85). Isolated H^1 and H^2 additions may be identified in the sections prior to their main contributions, and some P materials are identifiable (having been relocated?) in the H^2 section. It is also possible that some narrative elements in Numbers belong to P. In this very provisional outline of three main stages of PH, the P materials (especially some law passages, not yet contextualized in narrative) could have begun to arise in the Neo-Babylonian period before 586, but jelled as a narrative with contextualized law soon after the catastrophe of that year; the H^1 materials arose later in the exile (the book of Ezekiel would have been at home in this "school"; H^1 could be partly responsible for "finishing" P; cf. Exod 12:1–20, which is largely H in character but necessary for the P narrative to make sense); the H^2 materials were added in the second half of the sixth century B.C.E. or later (note, e.g., that the explanation of the cultic subordination of the Levites in Numbers [H^2] appears to postdate that in Ezek 44, one of the latest chapters of the book of Ezekiel).

Contributors

Susan Ackerman is the Preston H. Kelsey Professor of Religion and Professor of Women's and Gender Studies at Dartmouth College. She is the author of *Under Every Green Tree: Popular Religion in Sixth-Century Judah* (HSM 46; Atlanta: Scholars Press, 1992); *Warrior, Dancer, Seductress, Queen: Women in Judges and Biblical Israel* (New York: Doubleday, 1998); and *When Heroes Love: The Ambiguity of Eros in the Stories of Gilgamesh and David* (New York: Columbia University Press, 2005).

Stephen L. Cook is the Catherine N. McBurney Professor of Old Testament Language and Literature at Virginia Theological Seminary. He is the author of multiple books and articles, including *Prophecy and Apocalypticism* (Minneapolis: Fortress, 1995); *The Social Roots of Biblical Yahwism* (SBLStBL 8; Atlanta: Society of Biblical Literature, 2004); and *2 Isaiah* (Harrisburg, Pa.: Morehouse, 2008). Most recently, he has coedited *Thus Says the Lord: Essays on the Former and Latter Prophets in Honor of Robert R. Wilson* (New York: T&T Clark, 2009).

Ronald Hendel is the Norma and Sam Dabby Professor of Hebrew Bible and Jewish Studies at the University of California, Berkeley. His most recent books are *The Book of Genesis: A Biography* (Princeton: Princeton University Press, 2012); and *Remembering Abraham: Culture, Memory, and History in the Hebrew Bible* (New York: Oxford University Press, 2005). He is editor-in-chief of the *Oxford Hebrew Bible*, a new critical edition of the biblical text.

T. M. Lemos is Assistant Professor of Hebrew Bible and Ancient Near Eastern Language and Literature at Huron University College at the University of Western Ontario. She is the author of *Marriage Gifts and Social Change in Ancient Palestine: 1200 BCE to 200 CE* (Cambridge: Cambridge

University Press, 2010). She has also contributed to the *Journal of Biblical Literature*, the *Journal of Religion*, and various edited volumes.

Nathaniel B. Levtow is Assistant Professor of Biblical Studies and Religion at the University of Montana in Missoula. He is the author of *Images of Others: Iconic Politics in Ancient Israel* (Winona Lake, Ind.: Eisenbrauns, 2008). He is currently writing a book about the violation and destruction of scrolls and inscriptions in the Hebrew Bible and the ancient Near East.

Carol Meyers holds the Mary Grace Wilson Professorship in the Department of Religion at Duke University. A specialist in biblical studies and also Syro-Palestinian archaeology, much of her research engages social-science methods and paradigms. The author, co-author, or co-editor of seventeen books, including excavation reports and commentaries on Haggai and Zechariah (with Eric Meyers) and on Exodus, her forthcoming book *Rediscovering Eve: Ancient Israelite Women in Context* (Oxford University Press) has an explicitly anthropological approach.

Saul M. Olyan is the Samuel Ungerleider Jr. Professor of Judaic Studies and Professor of Religious Studies at Brown University. He is the author of *Asherah and the Cult of Yahweh in Israel* (SBLMS 34; Atlanta: Scholars Press, 1988); *A Thousand Thousands Served Him: Exegesis and the Naming of Angels in Ancient Judaism* (TSAJ 36; Tübingen: Mohr Siebeck, 1993); *Rites and Rank: Hierarchy in Biblical Representations of Cult* (Princeton: Princeton University Press, 2000); *Biblical Mourning: Ritual and Social Dimensions* (Oxford: Oxford University Press, 2004); *Disability in the Hebrew Bible* (New York: Cambridge University Press, 2008); and *Social Inequality in the World of the Text: The Significance of Ritual and Social Distinctions in the Hebrew Bible* (Göttingen: Vandenhoeck & Ruprecht, 2011).

Rüdiger Schmitt is Professor of Old Testament at the University of Münster. He is the author of *Philistäische Terrakottafigurinen: Archäologische, ikonographische und religionsgeschichtliche Beobachtungen zu einer Sondergruppe palästinischer Kleinplastik der Eisenzeit* (Groningen: University of Groningen, 1994); *Bildhafte Herrschaftsrepräsentation im eisenzeitlichen Israel* (AOAT 283; Münster: Ugarit-Verlag, 2001); *Magie im Alten Testament* (Münster: Ugarit-Verlag, 2004); *Der "Heilige Krieg" im Pentateuch und im deuteronomistischen Geschichtswerk* (AOAT 381; Münster: Ugarit-

Verlag, 2011); and *Family and Household Religion in Ancient Israel* (with Rainer Albertz; Winona Lake, Ind.: Eisenbrauns, 2012).

Robert R. Wilson is the Hoober Professor of Religious Studies and Professor of Old Testament at Yale University. He is the author of *Genealogy and History in the Biblical World* (New Haven: Yale University Press, 1977); *Prophecy and Society in Ancient Israel* (Philadelphia: Fortress, 1980); *Sociological Approaches to the Old Testament* (Philadelphia: Fortress, 1984); and numerous articles on prophecy, historiography, and judicial practice in ancient Israel.

David P. Wright is Professor of Hebrew Bible and Ancient Near East at Brandeis University. He is author of *Inventing God's Law: How the Covenant Code of the Bible Used and Revised the Laws of Hammurabi* (Oxford: Oxford University Press, 2009); *Ritual in Narrative: The Dynamics of Feasting, Mourning, and Retaliation Rites in the Ugaritic Tale of Aqhat* (Winona Lake, Ind.: Eisenbrauns, 2001); and the *Disposal of Impurity: Elimination Rites in the Bible and in Hittite and Mesopotamian Literature* (SBLDS 101; Atlanta: Scholars Press, 1987).

www.ingramcontent.com/pod-product-compliance
Lightning Source LLC
LaVergne TN
LVHW091052080826
845145LV00002B/716

* 9 7 8 1 5 8 9 8 3 6 8 8 4 *